D1193843

THE VALADON DRAMA

The Valadon Drama

THE LIFE OF SUZANNE VALADON

by John Storm

ILLUSTRATED

E. P. DUTTON & CO., INC.

New York · 1959

Copyright, © 1958, by John Storm
All rights reserved. Printed in the U.S.A.

SECOND PRINTING FEBRUARY 1959

No part of this book may be reproduced
in any form without permission in writing
from the publisher, except by a reviewer
who wishes to quote brief passages in con-
nection with a review written for inclusion
in a magazine, newspaper or broadcast.

Library of Congress Catalog Card Number: 58-9605

For Margaret
with love

Contents

Illustrations

9

THE VALADON DRAMA

Preface

SUZANNE VALADON LIVED HER LIFE AMONG PEOPLE WITH whom communication was largely on a personal and vocal basis. She had no opportunity to express herself to them in writing, and as she was extremely wary of the written word, it is unlikely that she would have written had there been opportunity. She kept no journal or diary.

Suzanne Valadon acted and she talked. Almost all her life she lived in the heart of the Montmartre Butte, and for the greater part of that time one of the most dynamic movements in the history of art raged about her. Only during the first months of her life was she physically detached from that history. Alone, of all the artists who flocked to "the Sacred Hill" with their causes of Impressionism, Symbolism, Fauvism, Cubism, and other "schools," she belonged to the Montmartre scene quite literally from the cradle to the grave. It is interesting to note that on the Butte, which is strangely loath to commemorate the passing of its great personages with the blue and white plaques so often seen elsewhere in Paris, the *Montmartrois* themselves have installed a marble plaque on the Moulin Joyeux in rue du Mont-Cenis in her honor. No such marking records the passage of Lautrec, Degas, Cézanne, Monet, or Manet, nor Picasso, Braque, Modigliani, or Dufy.

"*Dans ce restaurant La Grande Artiste Suzanne Valadon*

a diné de 1919 à 1935 accompagnée souvent de son fils Maurice Utrillo."

But her life was in nowise spent solely among artists. Tradesmen, waiters, police, postmen, concierges, models, prostitutes, critics, writers, actors, musicians, sportsmen— the ragtag and bobtail of the quarter were among her friends and confidants. In many respects they were also her audience, for there was always something of a theatrical air in both her private and her public performances. It is largely from their recollections of her that I have drawn her story.

Suzanne Valadon loved to talk; and in her later years particularly, she was eager to speak to almost anyone who would listen to her. In her studio, in her kitchen, in any of the dozens of cafés and restaurants about the Place du Tertre, she would regale her listeners with theories about her work and art in general, about her domestic difficulties and personal problems, and, above all, with memories of her past.

How truthful was she? How accurate were her listeners' and observers' accounts? Frankly it is hard to say. In the main, I am sure, most of the people I have interviewed have sought scrupulously to contribute only pertinent and honest material. For her own part, there can be no doubt that much of what she told people of herself was fanciful. But if her imaginings and untruths fail to throw a dependable light on biographical incidents, they do sharpen the sense of her personality, which was, after all, a more direct source of her art. I feel that whatever inaccuracies there may be in the fabric of her story today, there are bound to be a great many more as time goes on. Memories do not sharpen with time. Many of the people who knew her well are now dead. Is it not better, then, to capture what is left, imperfect though it may be, than to wait until Time has erased all?

During the past forty years the importance of Suzanne Valadon's work has met with gradually increasing recognition. Savage and extremely personal, unconnected with any "school" of the past or present, her work was submerged for a long time beneath the surging tides which began with the birth of Impressionism. Today we realize that it stood alone as a statement of the independence of a creative intelligence, of uncompromising belief in draftsmanship in an era in which drawing was no longer considered overly important. It is primitive, strong, and frank, abounding in health and vigorous color; and it owes its power solely to the nervous energy and personality of a woman who came to grips with deeply tragic experiences of life. An insight into that life is important to an understanding of the work of one who is considered by many to be "France's greatest woman artist."

Of more than a hundred people I have talked with I am deeply indebted especially to Mme. Georges Kars, Paul Pétridès, Edmond Heuzé, Mme. and Louis Chervin, Mme. Agnès Humbert, Jean Vertex, Henri Level, Demetrios Galanis, André Pillet, Georges Bernheim, Mme. Félice Colas, Mme. Yvonne Vigneron, Raymond Bordage, Gazi-I.G., Georges Delize, Mme. Gustave Coquiot, and Robert Attilo, who, besides helping me gather anecdotal material, were at pains to have me understand Suzanne Valadon's personality. It is with their composite judgment that I have selected the substance of the book. In making decisions in respect to all interviews I have been guided less by the characters of the other witnesses than by the character of the remarkable subject they have limned for me. At times, as is inevitable in the circumstances, I have written imaginatively of what must have occurred.

For permission to reproduce the illustrations in the book and for access to the various collections of Suzanne Valadon's work, I am grateful to the Musée de l'Art Moderne in Paris, the Ny Carlsberg Glyptothek in Copenhagen, the Arts Council and the Lefevre Gallery in London, the Archives Na-

tionales, the Art Institute of Chicago, Edmond Heuzé, Paul
Pétridès, André Bernier, Gazi-I.G., Mme. Georges Kars,
Mme. Yvonne Vigneron, and Mr. and Mrs. J. Garfunkel.
And finally, I should like to express my debt to my wife,
without whose support, criticism, and constant help the book
could not have been written.

J.S.

I Mother and Daughter

It was not until she was an old woman that Madeleine Valadon talked much about herself. It pleased her then to relate that as a young girl she had been married to a citizen of Limoges named Courlaud, by whom, as she put it, she had had "several children." When she was twenty-one, Courlaud died very suddenly in the city jail before charges against him had been entered on the books of the constabulary. Madeleine claimed she could not remember exactly what the charges had been. She thought he had been arrested for political reasons or on suspicion of forgery.

Following Courlaud's death Madeleine resumed her maiden name and returned to her native village of Bessines, a few miles from the outskirts of Limoges, where she went to work as a seamstress in the household of a prosperous family named Guimbaud. Bessines was inhabited, for the most part, by workers from the Limoges porcelain factories. At the end of their day's work, if not ensconced behind the flaked façades of their cubic houses, they busied themselves in raising pigs, goats, and poultry in their back yards, or in tending the multitudinous garden plots which ringed the little community. The atmosphere of Bessines was rural rather than suburban.

To the east of the village a screen of gray oaks across the crest of a gentle slope hinted at the proximity of a forest which, in reality, was not there. To the south, in the small

17

rectangular patches of wheat and oats for which the countryside was famous, stood the bulbous white windmills, their
huge black sails squeaking in the breeze as they ground the
flour. Around the village square the slate mansard roofs of
half a dozen large rectangular houses, including that of the
Guimbauds, bespoke the prosperity to which the free citizens
of the village aspired.

Madeleine's people had been factory workers. She had
been taught to read and write by the village priest; and once
she was thought to have mastered these essentials, she was
dispatched to a convent in Limoges for more practical education in needlework. She proved an apt pupil, and the course
toward which she was directed showed shrewdness. As
things turned out, once Madeleine was widowed she was
proficient enough as a needlewoman to be able to look out
for herself.

In the Guimbaud household she was soon established in
black bombazine suits with lace collars and cuffs of her own
tatting. In no wise a handsome woman, she was thin-lipped
and angular; her hair was drawn sharply across her ears and
tied in a bun at the back of her neck. Nevertheless, she
brought to the Guimbaud household a cool authority and
dignity not easily come by among provincial domestics.
Visitors to the house often mistook Madeleine for an impoverished relative of the family—an impression the Guimbauds seem to have encouraged. Madeleine's position in their
home might be interpreted as a mark of their charity.

Indeed, Madeleine Valadon lived in the Guimbaud home in
rather more splendor than was customarily accorded a servant. She had two rooms to herself—a bedroom and a sitting
room under the mansard roof—and a free-and-easy run of
the house. For more than thirteen years she maintained a
kind of placid tyranny over the rest of the Guimbauds' staff,
issuing orders from her bedroom citadel and letting it be
known where dust lurked as she passed through the rooms

and hallways. To the little sitting room adjoining her bedroom she bade the ladies of the household come for their
fittings, for here, with the dusty view of the Limoges spires
from her window, she spent most of her day at her needlework. It was generally conceded that the Guimbaud ladies
were fortunate to have her as a seamstress; their clothes were
the most *Parisienne* of all the families' about the countryside.

Madeleine ate her meals with the Guimbauds, was consulted in all matters of household crises, and went for rides in
the family *calèche*. In the village, she remained stolidly silent
on all the Guimbaud family affairs, business problems, and
intrigues, thereby strengthening the belief that she was a
member of the family rather than an employee.

Although Madeleine's taciturnity was generally attributed
to loyalty, it might more accurately have been attributed to
apathy. Apart from her needlework, Madeleine had little
interest in anything. Her marriage to Courlaud had been
miserable, and she continued to bear its misery with her. She
had no friends, nor did she make any effort toward acquiring
any. Her children made their home with her family only a
few hundred yards away at the other end of the village, but
only rarely did she summon enough interest to visit them.
So it was certainly a great surprise to the Guimbaud family
as well as to the rest of the population of Bessines when
Madeleine Valadon suddenly became pregnant.

By her own account, she had been "seduced in a very cold
part of January" by a Bessines miller. Retelling this story in
her later years, Madeleine would often conclude it by declar-
ing that the man was subsequently crushed to death in an
accident in retribution for the sin he had committed against
her person. But her accounts varied widely, and sometimes
the miller was not a miller at all but a construction engineer
who met his just deserts by falling off a bridge and drowning
in a swift river.

Whatever Madeleine Valadon's reputation had been at the

time she startled Bessines with the news of her pregnancy, she realized that once the child was delivered she would no longer be able to remain in the village. As the widow of a felon and mother of a bastard she would be hard pressed to cope with the disapprobation which would be heaped upon her. Nevertheless the Guimbauds, perhaps out of uncommon affection for her, perhaps in an effort to display their philanthropy, prevailed upon her to remain in their house until after her confinement. And so it happened that it was in the Guimbaud home on September 23, 1865,* that Madeleine bore the child who a few days later was to be baptized in the village church as Marie-Clémentine Valadon. When that child was nineteen her friend Toulouse-Lautrec urged her to change her name to "Suzanne." And it is as Suzanne Valadon that her story is here recounted.

A neighbor, Matthieu Masbeix, and one of the baby's half-sisters, Marie-Céline Courlaud, were the godparents. It was a christening without the usual Limousin festivities. A few months later Madeleine and her baby left Bessines for Paris. Madeleine never returned to the village. Nor did she ever again communicate with anyone there—not with her family, nor with the Guimbauds nor with any of the "several children" whom she left behind in the house where she was born, including Marie-Céline.

When Madeleine Valadon arrived in Paris early in 1866 she was terrified. The long merciless walls of buildings, the noise, the bustle of the crowds, the whirring of traffic gave the impression of stepping into the middle of a nightmare. For hours she wandered aimless and panic-stricken amid the hubbub, the baby in a basket on her arm—or so she said in later years. Then finally she saw the windmills on the crest of the hill

* The official record reads ". . . née en 1865, le 23 Septembre à 6 heures du matin. . . ." In spite of the record, Suzanne insisted she was born in 1867, and her wishes in this matter have been respected by most of her biographers, as well as by the Musée de l'Art Moderne, where the Valadon-Utrillo Room bears the date of 1867.

overlooking the city to the north, and the sight of the battered sails twisting lazily in the clear air had a sedative effect upon her. The Limousin countryside! How welcome! How comforting! Only a few hours before, she had fled it in rage and shame. Now what relief it brought! Wearily she climbed the hill. And so she came to Montmartre, to her hardly more than a little country village perched high above and seemingly indifferent to the terrorizing turmoil of the big city.

Along the narrow grassy streets she passed the blotchy white houses coated with gypsum quarried on the hill and already known all over the world as "plaster of Paris." She gazed up at the eaves of blue slate roofs and at the long jalousied windows with their caged finches and canaries, their potted geraniums and philodendrons, their fluttering lace curtains and tricolors. And seeing this ordered and comfortable domesticity, she could feel the stirrings of—was it ambition? Did she really want for herself these pleasant accoutrements of living? She did not quite know. But here, in this faraway place, she, Madeleine Valadon, might some day come by goose-down featherbeds and silk cushions like those now being aired on the little iron balconies overhanging the streets. She might have crisp lace curtains, good napery, and handsome dress fabrics, and perhaps even little porcelain figures like the ones in Mme. Guimbaud's drawing room . . . perhaps. . . .

In the village square (now the Place du Tertre) little iron chairs and tables stood about under the plane trees in whose shade old men played dominoes and *piquet* and old women tatted and dozed in the sun. Madeleine saw herself at peace in such old age as theirs.

One of the old women pointed out to her, across the road from the red-brick *mairie*, the ancient church of St. Pierre, older than the cathedral of Notre Dame de Paris. It had been desecrated by the atheist revolutionists in 1793, the old woman told her in shocked tones, and a signal station had been erected above its apse in 1795. In another year or so it would be rededicated by the archbishop to the glory of God. Madeleine made a mental note that she would worship there. But as it turned out, she did very little worshipping. In the course of her life she was to go to St. Pierre's only when she felt in need of material assistance. The Church held small comfort for her.

Unnoticed by Madeleine, the ramshackle stables, the tin-topped laundry sheds, the shops, bars and cabarets hugging the crazy hump of the hill bespoke the coming of less rustic days. But for the present there were still flower gardens and vineyards, small orchards of espaliered fruit trees, even small meadows with cows; and here and there springs of clear well water bubbling from the clayey soil. Occasionally, among the plane trees, a catalpa or tree of heaven, rooted in the pavement, leaned crazily out over the road like a permanent drunk. There was plenty of washing on the lines. Goats, chickens, and geese chased along the streets, fat cats dozed on walls and the tops of fences, and a host of pigeons nested under the eaves or waddled along the roof tops. And if the permanency of this pleasant atmosphere was in any way threatened, Madeleine Valadon believed strongly enough in the eternity of a French village to be sublimely oblivious of the fact.

Had Madeleine had an inkling of the history of this place, she might have been more realistically prepared for what was in store for her. The hill was supposed to have derived its name, "Mount of Martyrs," from the fact that it was the scene of the execution of St. Denis, the first bishop of Paris, and of his lieutenants, St. Rustique and St. Éleuthère. They had come to Gaul as refugees from the persecutions of the Emperor Decius (A.D. 201-251) and were put to death in the cause of the Redeemer. St. Denis is said to have carried his severed head from the place of his martyrdom at the top of the hill to the spot in the rue de l'Abreuvoir where a pitying woman took it from him and allowed him to lie down in eternal tranquillity. Immediately a spring arose at the spot where this deed of compassion took place. There it was to refresh wayfarers for centuries until in 1855 the hill was incorporated into the city and the Ministry of Works saw fit to divert the miraculous water underground to clear the road for vehicular traffic.

In the ninth century the industrious monks of St. Martin-des-Champs commemorated the martyrdom of the three saints by erecting a monastery on the site of their execution. A group of Benedictine nuns took over the monastery building in the following century, and it was here, in the "Holy Martyr's Chapel" of the Benedictine sisters, that Ignatius Loyola and his six followers assumed the vows by which they founded the Jesuit Order.

For five hundred years the life of the hill was dominated by the piety of these good women. It was the misfortune of the Benedictines that ultimately, in their long tenure, the convent amassed great wealth and the sisters became corrupted by their prosperity. By the middle of the fifteenth century stories about the corruption and lechery of the convent became bywords throughout France. The convent was the butt of hundreds of obscene jokes, and concurrently with the deterioration of morals in the holy place there began to appear on the hill an agglomeration of gaming houses, cabarets, pothouses, brothels, dens, and dives—all of which paid tribute for their existence to the reverend sisters of the Benedictine convent. The situation was such that many a devout priest who mounted the hill on a pilgrimage to "the Martyr's Chapel" claimed he had done so only after having crossed the River Styx.

In the shadow of the once noted convent, drinking, gambling, and prostitution had become the business of "the Holy Hill." Not without a show of grim humor the pestholes devoted to these amusements sported such sanctimonious names as "the Image of St. Anne," "the Image of St. Louis," "the Cross of Lorraine," or "The Arms of Madame the Abbess"; or frankly advertised their fleshly wares as "the Island of Love," "the Suckling Calf," or "Women's Ways." In the beginning these places offered the pleasure-bent Parisians, especially members of the court, a measure of salty entertainment. However, before long, crime throve so much among them that eventually the customers dared not come to the hill for fear of assault and possible loss of life. The flow of gold stopped, and vice as a business collapsed.

After the Revolution the impoverished village, its monastery now destroyed, its ancient church a grocery warehouse and signal station, assumed the aura of a remote chapter in romantic history. The Arms of Madame the Abbess became a tumble-down stable, the Island of Love the village laundry. Visitors from the city on Sunday afternoon excursions wandered along the crooked byways wrapped in somewhat the same pleasurable sentiments as those in which, on another Sunday afternoon, they would stroll the gray, ghostly streets of Versailles or Chantilly.

It was inevitable that artists would be struck by the picturesqueness of the village and its historical atmosphere. It was a place removed from the present, brushed by the shifting moods of sailing white clouds, its colors made vibrant by clear air washed in the basin of the Seine valley.

Georges Michel was the first to paint the village, in 1796— from the valley, in the gold and black of a setting sun—a Gothic pile fretted by minute windmills. Michel was the first artist to take refuge on the Butte, where he lived with his wife and the five children, all born before he was twenty, in a den formerly occupied by a band of thieves. Camille Corot and Théodore Géricault were among the early artists to become fascinated with the atmosphere and lore of the hill. Corot came thither to stay weeks at a time in one of the tiny inns; Géricault came on horseback with his paintbox and easel dangling from his pommel to spend his days painting. Others took up permanent residence. Georges Bruandet, who tossed his unfaithful mistress out the window, was one of the first of many free spirits to live in the rue Norvins. Louis Daguerre, the pioneer photographer, was an early inhabitant. In a small cottage in what was later to become the rue St. Denis, Hector Berlioz lived with the English girl whom he later married. Another musician, the Pole Frédéric Chopin, lived in the rue Tronchet and soon became a familiar figure about the little village square, with his tight-fitting clothes, his proud Bourbon nose and bloodless lips looking, as the painter Moscheles remarked, "like nothing so much as the music of Chopin." Franz Liszt, lean and tremulous, lived "among the laundresses." To a room over the greengrocer's the novelist Eugène Sue, already the author of the enormously popular *Mysteries of Paris*, retired after six years as a naval surgeon to begin his *Wandering Jew*. And for a time, in a sewer close to the Place Blanche, Gérard de Nerval, the poet, lived with his friends the tramps who were supposed to be the scourge of the nearby chicken yards. When de Nerval committed suicide on January 25, 1855, he hanged himself from what is believed to be the first street lamp erected on the Montmartre hill, in the rue de la Vielle-Lanterne.

As early as 1855, on the lower fringe of the hill facing the city, the new boulevards cutting from Chantilly and the eastern suburbs to Neuilly and the west had already begun once again to attract the night life of Paris, as well as much of its political and intellectual disputation. Always Paris had drawn its life breath and spirit from its cafés, its taprooms, its restaurants. The nineteenth century did not break this tradition. Around little wire tables on the sidewalks and in the cacophonous, mirrored back rooms of cafés, philosophers, politicians, labor leaders, artists, musicians, and writers found noisy forums for ideas which would bring about tomorrow's revolutions. Nowhere in the city was change incubating at a faster rate than at the base of the Montmartre hill, for the restoration of the Empire in 1852, with its suppression of the freedom of the press, its establishment of bourgeois bureaucracy and the police state, had kindled the fires of revolt among the Parisians—proletarians and intelligentsia alike.

Madeleine Valadon found a room for her child and herself not far from the smoldering fires of revolution. The Boulevard de Rochechouart, recently widened and lined with young plane trees, sliced across the base of the hill into the very heart of the revolutionary furnace. In a few hundred yards it penetrated the thick of the seething masses of humanity which were the Place Blanche, the Place Clichy and the Place Pigalle. Sometimes in the night the wind brought the sound of uproar into the tenement room. A volley of shots fired by student rioters would be heard. A chanting company of workingmen would pass below the window under the plane trees bearing banners: "Arise, Prisoners of Starvation," "We Have Been Naught, We Shall Be All," or "The Earth Shall Rise on New Foundations."

To Madeleine, bemused by thoughts of future lace curtains and porcelain figurines, the noise in the streets meant nothing. She had her own problems and was already considerably disenchanted by the turn things had taken for her. She had been compelled to accept certain facts of life for which she had made no preparation. One did not simply arrive in Paris and find a job as a seamstress in a pleasant household—not when one had an infant to take care of. Not even Mme. Guimbaud's glowing references were enough to prevail upon a Parisian family to take in a young woman with a child. Slowly the realization came over Madeleine that the dingy room she had rented might well be a permanent home. It was a painful admission to have to make.

It would have been fairly easy for Madeleine to find employment in a dressmaker's establishment or in one of the sweatshops in the quarter. She did try one or two such jobs, but to one who had never known anything but the easy freedom of small village life and a comfortable house to live in, the suffocating atmosphere and the close physical and mental relationship with other women was terrifying. Ultimately a measure of contentment came to her in being a scrubwoman, doing odd jobs in shops and offices, and entrusting the care of her small daughter to the wife of the concierge in the tenement.

So, she was scrubbing floors when the Emperor Napoleon III was pushed into his war with Germany. On the park benches in the Place du Tertre the old men playing *piquet* said it was the Empress' fault. It was the Empress who had forced the war. Granted the Emperor had made his own disastrous involvements in the past—in the Crimean War (1854-1856), in the Italian War (1859-1861), and in the fiasco of Maximilian's adventure in Mexico (1863-1867). The Empress was at the root of all evil. Madeleine went about her daily job tidying up the office of a young doctor named Georges Clemenceau; she could not have cared less about a war between nations. And when after two months, somewhere near the German frontier, the Emperor was defeated and taken prisoner at Sedan, and the Empress fled to England, the old men in the square said, "Didn't we tell you so? Now *her* skin is safe." Madeleine took her little daughter to the Convent of St. Vincent de Paul and registered her there as a day pupil with instructions that more emphasis be put on her reading and writing than on her needlework.

She could hardly be expected to cope with life as it erupted in the wake of the Franco-Prussian War. She had a deaf ear for the febrile confabs of her neighbors. She was not one to sit in the cafés and listen to political chatter. She scrubbed floors. It meant nothing to her that a "Government of National Defense" had voted to carry on the war after the Emperor's surrender. This was a decision strongly opposed by a group of reforming Communards who saw in the continuation of the war an attempt to extend "the bourgeois expression of public liberty" initiated by the monarchy. What was "liberty" anyway? Was it any more than being able to travel from Bessines to Montmartre, to make of one's life what one could? There were Communards in the tenement where she lived. The concierge loathed them and prayed early each morning for the safe return of the Emperor. Madeleine shied from associating with them, but only as she shied from associating with anyone.

The Communards were calling for dissolution of the Prefecture of Police and the City Guard at a time when it was obvious to Madeleine that if one worked steadily at an honest job one did not have to traffic with the police at all. The Communards were agitating for the constitution by election of the Parisian municipality or Commune. For the life of her, Madeleine could not see what possible bearing such a cause might have on the lives of simple working people.

But somehow, for reasons she could in no wise fathom, the prices of everything rose daily, and the supplies of food in the shops were very low. In September, 1871, the German army laid siege to a Paris whose supplies were already reduced to a quarter of normal. Madeleine could now understand enough of what was going on to be able to muster hatred for the invaders. The bestial Germans were responsible for all the troubles which now began to shower down upon her. It was a hatred she harbored for the rest of her life.

By January the German guns commenced the bombardment of the starving capital. Everywhere families burned their furniture in order to protect themselves from the bitter cold. The city's gas supply failed. Many people took refuge in the cavernous sewers by day and night. An artilleryman in the National Guard, an artist named Édouard Manet, whom

Madeleine might well have seen many times when she passed the Café Guerbois in the Grande Rue des Batignolles, wrote to his wife in the Pyrenees: "We are eating horse meat when we can get it. Cats, dogs and even rats are now sold in the shops." A few days later Manet reported that the population's appetite for horse flesh was so ravenous there were no longer any cabs or drays in the streets. The day after Christmas, Victor Hugo noted in his journal, "Yesterday I dined on rat."

Throughout these desperate times Madeleine could console herself in the knowledge that she had been able to provide something better than the common lot for her daughter. The child was in the hands of the sisters of St. Vincent de Paul. There, for the greater part of the day, the little one was safe. Miraculously, the sisters fed their charges on fresh eggs from their own poultry farm and on butter from their own churns. For her own part Madeleine could forage for the strange ingredients of her own eternal *ragout* and feel that her lot was perhaps a good bit better than that of many of her neighbors.

When the news swept the hill that the war was over, Madeleine expected the grocery shops to be full by the following morning and things to be normal once more. The past six months could be forgotten in a single night's sleep, so she reasoned. What had been horror suddenly seemed to be only foolishness. But things did not suddenly become "normal." The same people who had chattered about bourgeois suppression of public liberty, constitution by election, and dissolution of the Prefecture of Police, now ranted on about "the large indemnity we have to pay," the "ignominy of ceding Alsace and Lorraine to the Germans," "the dishonor of allowing the enemy to occupy Paris for forty-eight hours as a gesture of surrender." There was talk about the government's sending out feelers for a restoration of the monarchy.

Incredible as it appeared to Madeleine, people seemed to be

more aroused by talk of political matters than by thoughts of food. Suddenly the gaunt, sunken eyes of the hungry were afire with a passion for battle. In a desperate onslaught the Communards seized the Hôtel de Ville, and the Government of Paris gave warning that it meant to defend the city against the forces of the Government of National Defense, which had fled from the city to Versailles. Not far from Madeleine's tenement room in the Place Pigalle a Communard mob seized, tried, and summarily shot the two generals, Lecomte and Thomas, who had ventured into the city calling for surrender to the Versailles government's terms.

The Commune lasted only seven weeks. On the 21st of May the troops of the Versailles government, under General MacMahon, broke through the Communard cordon at Point-du-Jour and swept into the city. While part of their forces defended the crumbling barricades, the Communards set fire to the Hôtel de Ville, the Cours des Comtes, the Tuileries, the Louvre, and the Palais Royale. The homes of everyone suspected of loyalty to the Versailles government were bombed or burned. Libraries and museums were senselessly fired. Frantic revolutionaries wrought havoc upon churches and public buildings. Despairing of victory, the defenders now began to slaughter hostages. At La Santé prisoners were shot in their cells or mowed down by riflemen against the prison walls, their bodies left for the children of the neighborhood to mutilate. Elsewhere in the city as many as fifty hostages at a time were marched into the streets to be butchered with bayonets, rifles, or bludgeons by the blood-soaked "police." Bombs shattered shops and factories. The Archbishop of Paris and five of his diocesan clerics held in the prison of La Grande Roquette were shot by a communist firing squad.

Slowly, across the barricades the Army of Versailles fought its way to the heart of the city. It took a week to reach there; and 17,000 men, women, and children perished in the drive.

Ditches were filled with the stripped bodies of the dead. Human scavengers preyed over the streets like voracious kites.

In the name of law and order the Army of Versailles proved itself no less bloodthirsty than the Communards. "There is everywhere now," wrote Puvis de Chavannes to his friend Bally, "an immense poisoning of all morality, and I can't but be confounded when I think of the illusions of both sides and how they have hoped to cure *our* ills." To the politically ignorant Madeleine and thousands like her, what took place in the summer and autumn of 1871 was heinous beyond all philosophizing. Vengeance and hate swept aside everything men had striven for all their lives. Love, religion, friendship, social consciousness, decency, idealism tumbled as easily as heads had fallen into the baskets in 1793. Mankind was cut off from all the ethical and moral concepts which had been the mainstream of its progress since the time of Christ. Blistering hostility, suspicion, fear, and revenge flashed like hard coals of fire in the gaunt, sunken eyes of hungry people. Everyone was adrift and wracked by terror in a world without trust, affection, or kindness. Spies denounced Communards and Communard sympathizers—real or imagined. A few minutes of trial without legal defense and their fate was settled. In the Place Maubert street cleaners tumbled three hundred executed corpses into a common grave in a single day following the findings of one court. Lunatics, freed from asylums in order to make room for the ever-increasing swarms of prisoners, ran howling through the streets. Children disappeared from their homes, never to reappear. The sisters of St. Vincent de Paul barricaded themselves inside the convent and refused to open their gates to anyone, their day pupils included. "From that day the streets of Montmartre were home to me," Suzanne said many years later. "It was only in the streets that there was excitement and love and ideas— what other children found around their dining-room tables."

The last pitched battle of the struggle took place, fittingly enough, in Père Lachaise Cemetery, against the wall to be known thereafter as the "Wall of the Federals." It was the evening before Pentecost. And when the sun rose the following morning, the grim work of the White Terror began. Within the next three months 13,450 Parisian citizens were sentenced to prison, to exile, and to death. In nearly all cases their chief accusers were their neighbors.

"Paris had buried her dead," wrote Hector Berlioz. "The paving stones from the barricades are laid down in their places again. . . . What a sight! What hideous devastation! The Spirit of Liberty on the top of the column of the Bastille has a bullet through her body. The fallen trees, the mutilated houses, the squares, the streets, the quays seem still to be quivering from the hideous struggle . . . rats in the corners gnaw bleeding vertebrae . . . swarms of sparrows now fight for scraps of sustenance. . . ."

This, then, was the first playground of Suzanne Valadon. The years 1870-1872 had completely demoralized Madeleine. Whatever illusions of a future good life she had been able to hold onto since arriving from the Limousin she had lost under the impact of the war and the long months of civil strife. The behavior of her fellow men had sickened her spirit. She made a few perfunctory attempts to restore her perspective by involving herself in amatory affairs with neighborhood widowers, but each affair was brief and unrewarded. She finally resigned herself to the drudgery of cleaning floors, to callous knees and work-hardened hands, and the torment of rheumatism. And with her resignation to this drab lot she developed a sullen disposition and a feeling of apathy toward the tenement room as much as toward humanity. The room was seldom cleaned. The linen was dirty. The dress materials (she was never able to resist buying them) lay in dust-covered packets and boxes under the bed. The porcelain figures accumulated grime.

She drank. Alcohol was something to anesthetize her sense of frustration and failure as well as the growing bitterness she felt toward mankind. In her canvas bag she carried a bottle of brandy and a bottle of Montmartre red wine and on the job she consumed both steadily. No one could tell if she were drunk or not. Her movements had already become sluggish and faltering, and she was surly and taciturn. Her body was flabby, her shoulders painfully stooped. Aging with merciless speed, her teeth badly decayed, her gray eyes dull and watery, and an intricate mesh of grimy lines masking her leathery face, she shuffled listlessly between her tenement room and the appointed job. Shaken from her reverie by a friendly greeting, she appeared bewildered or hostile. People said that she "wasn't all there," that she was dim-witted, crazy. And when she was not at work she would sit by her second floor window sipping brandy from a coffee-stained cup, staring vacantly at the parade of imperfect humanity passing below in the Boulevard de Rochechouart, and giving the gossips something more to say about her.

Once the terror of the Commune was past, the sisters of the Convent of St. Vincent de Paul attempted once again to instill in Suzanne Valadon the fundamentals of reading and writing, to be rewarded only by the most prodigious record of truancy the school had had in its history. It was a hopeless task. The little girl had already found a wonderful world: she had become a creature of the twisted Montmartre streets.

Smaller than most children her age, agile and quick, with a wide-eyed willful little face and tousled cognac-colored hair, Suzanne darted about the hill with the zigzagging energy of a wasp. What struck people first about her was her eyes. They were very large, dark gray, stiffly lashed, and set wide apart under a pure broad forehead, and looked out with an expression of simple candor and singularly innocent sweetness. Only the mouth, too massive for her little face, a rigid line more likely to be sardonic than merry, gave a hint of anything but sportive childishness. Alone of all her features it bore a resemblance to her mother.

Now she went where she liked, did what she wanted, wore what clothes she pleased (what clothes she possessed), with but the haziest remembrance in her mind that once she had been the object of maternal affection, cared for as other children were cared for. If now by some mysterious change in circumstances she was rejected or neglected by the morose woman with whom her life was strangely coupled, she could not brood over it. She went her breathless way, roaming the streets by herself, playing games or performing acrobatic stunts with the boys of the hill (she preferred their company to that of girls), bantering with workingmen and tradespeople, consorting with the flotsam—the outlaws, apaches, or prostitutes, all of whom, she insisted in a high-pitched voice perpetually charged with excitement and wonder, made better soups and preached more edifying homilies than people who ran greengroceries and butcher shops.

In the world to which she had been turned loose and to which she clung with the passion she might have had for a favorite doll, reading and writing had no place. They required time, and time belonged to the teeming life about her. Furthermore, she had begun to draw pictures; and pictures were to her a far more effective means of communication than pages of cramped type face or wriggling penmanship. Indifference to reading and writing were to remain with her all her life, and as a grown woman, it bothered her not the slightest that her handwriting was that of an inept schoolgirl, or that she licked her lips when she read a newspaper to herself.

She disappeared from school at every opportunity. The Mother Superior attempted to bribe her into regular attendance with little gifts. Schoolmates were given special privileges for preventing her escapes from school. Madeleine administered beatings. But the little girl had fallen in love with a way of life, and there was no preventing her from enjoying it. What she had found for herself had already begun to charm hundreds of young people from all over the world. They came, the beauty seekers, the truth seekers, the world shapers, all to this curiously enchanting mecca high above the violet light of Paris, bringing their dreams with them. If at the age of nine Suzanne had not yet crystallized her dreams, rebellion was in her blood and she sensed that in some mysterious way her lot was with the newcomers. So when the sisters of St. Vincent de Paul finally acknowledged their defeat and suggested to Madeleine that it was pointless for them to attempt to continue the child's education, Suzanne felt that in the battle for her soul, the streets of Montmartre had won and would hold her always. Before she was ten she went to work.

Now, as her coevals remembered her, there was a certain ridiculous, breathless savagery in almost every mood she experienced. People on the streets often stopped to stare at her as she thought aloud or enacted fragments of her daydreams. Those who believed her mother was crazy muttered about the sins of the fathers. Barefoot a good part of the year, she paraded the streets, her hands clasped behind her back, a miniature human being, almost a midget, with long, deliberate masculine strides, her toes pointed in. It was her idea of how François Villon, the only figure in history who ever had any interest for her, walked. She called herself "Mademoiselle Villon," and assumed an air of boastful pride in the fragmentary state of her wardrobe and her personal uncleanliness. "Water is for washing pigs," she bawled at the schoolmate who took exception to her grime. Often she perched on walls or fences—"I am a monkey. I am a cat"—and caterwauled obscene argot ballads, loud and far off key. Physically fearless, she once swung for a quarter of an hour six stories above the street, clinging to the bottom of a French window and advising the paralyzed onlookers to stop shouting at her until the fire department came to her rescue. Singlehanded, she caught a runaway Percheron in the Place Blanche while men, women, and children ran for shelter.

Nervous, loquacious, given to gusts of hysterical gaiety and paroxysms of strident laughter, she could level her ready vulgar wit at playmates or elders with equally telling effect. "The little Valadon terror," she was dubbed, not unadmiringly, by those who knew her. Years later her very good friend Degas was to call her "terrible Maria." As a child she was extremely quick to explode in ungovernable rage, attacking her adversary with fingernails or with stones, crockery, or any other loose object within reach, accompanied by a staccato onslaught of gutter profanity. Once the storm passed, she made as dramatic a display of her remorse which, passionate and tear-sodden, blossomed almost instantaneously into transports of affection and even tremulous adoration, for there was in all her frenzy a poignant desire, above all else, to be loved.

Even in those early childhood days she knew, it seemed, that she was destined to be someone important in the world of grownup people. What it was to be she did not know: she had no clear objective ahead of her. In her daydreams she did not see herself as a future diamond-decked princess, a fur-draped gentlewoman, an elegant hostess, or a glamorous actress, as most little girls might see themselves. If she had dreams, they were of eating unlimited supplies of sausages and pastries, of enduring passionate friendships with disreputable tramps and criminals, of winning races, of performing miraculous feats of strength and daring, or of putting an end to one of her enemies with the flashing steel of a long blade. Her dreams gave her no clue as to where she might go in the world ahead. And yet she was always certain that when she was grown up she would be one of the rare ones— one of those whose lives were apart from the masses.

Her desire to ingratiate herself with others stemmed from this solid belief. Popularity was the only rung she recognized in the climb she knew some day she must make to the top of the ladder. Often this determination to win applause took a strangely pedantic or whimsical turn. She saw fit to advise her elders as to how they should take care of their health, their children, their in-laws, their finances—all with disarming seriousness.

When she was seven or eight years old, she said much later, she once stopped to watch Renoir working at his easel in the rue Lepic and advised him solemnly to keep on with his painting and not be discouraged; that he had a future in it. At times her longing for sympathetic attention was so great that she would follow funerals—tag along at the end of a cortege wending its way to one of the Montmartre cemeteries, shedding a steady stream of tears all the way to the edge of the grave. On one occasion this performance achieved unexpected results when at Père Lachaise a bereaved young widow comforted her at the conclusion of the obsequies, took her home, fed her, and gave her some money, all in the belief that the child was one of her dear departed's "little mistakes."

Only with her mother were her efforts to ingratiate herself wholly unfruitful. A barrier she could not break through stood between them. Dutifully she did the housework and the shopping. In a fever to win approbation she labored long hours perfecting her needlework and executing embroidery. She gathered flowers from neighborhood gardens and windowboxes (not always with respect for property rights) to brighten the drabness of their living quarters. None of these efforts seemed to arouse the reaction she hungered for, and ultimately she was to give them up as hopeless. Her early drawings—cats, flowers, dogs, and horses, drawn with pencil stubs on scraps of paper in a curiously unimaginative way and presented to Madeleine as gifts, were received with bovine disinterestedness. But when Madeleine found the child drawing nude figures, either as she knew her own body or as she imagined the body of the opposite sex, Madeleine roused herself from her torpor long enough to give the little one a sound beating. Suzanne's reaction was matter-of-fact. Henceforth she spent considerable time drawing her nude figures on the pavements of the Place Vintimille, where they were certain to attract attention. In the alleys of the Butte she cajoled her masculine playmates into taking off their clothes and posing for her.

The strange, elfin figure of Suzanne was eternally beyond Madeleine's comprehension. Beyond sympathy with the run of common human behavior, she was unable to cope with the dynamic energy and fantasies of the little one who was her charge. While she herself stood sodden and earth-bound, the child flitted in zigzag butterfly flights about the Butte. It was all Madeleine could do not to hate the creature. Happily, the apathy which enveloped her was a barrier to any passionate feelings. Nothing about her own life or sentiments could she express in fiery terms any longer. Weariness and lethargy permeated her entire being. She was totally unable to muster the intense emotions which might have created active battle or concord between mother and daughter. The child's sudden bursts of rage or her passionate show of remorse were equally unreal to Madeleine. Observed in a dull glass at long range, they were but one of the manifestations of dismal human behavior—little more. With something almost akin to terror she shied from physical contact with her small daughter. In their life together there were no embraces or kisses. The little gifts the child brought from time to time were received with surly indifference. When Madeleine addressed her daughter directly it was only to nag, to complain, to bicker. They ate their meals separately for the most part, or, if together, in silence. They never appeared together in public.

But Suzanne did not brood on the rejection. She went her breathless way—dancing in the streets, acting out her daydreams, following funerals. And as she grew older she roamed farther and stayed away longer from the series of tenement rooms they called their homes. People said that Suzanne was heartless, neglectful of her poor, hardworking mother, that she was "an unnatural daughter." It was a judgment they were obliged to reverse later.

There came a time when a daughter could be expected decently to desert her mother and make an independent life for herself. Amazingly, for "the little Valadon terror" this time never came. In spite of the fact that mother and daughter rarely spoke to each other, that they went nowhere together, that they shared no interest in each other's doings, that they snarled and bickered at one another continually, they remained in the same household for almost sixty years.

Not until Suzanne, harnessing her vitality and restlessness, begins to assert herself as a creative artist, does their real relationship come into focus. The unfaltering pencil, the savage charcoal line, the bold and certain brushstroke speak poetically for their meaning to each other. In hundreds of Suzanne's drawings, etchings, paintings, the square-hipped figure of Madeleine is present.

The woman (old always) is eternally at work, although it is no longer the painful drudgery of those first years on Montmartre. It is pottering, fribbling work. She combs a model's hair. She helps a figure disrobe. She cuts a child's toenails. She sews. She bears water or prepares a bath. Rarely is she the subject itself: usually she is background— the lifeless straight hair parted in the middle and pulled severely into a bun on the back of her head, the long terrier-like nose, the toothless munching mouth, the lacework of grime-filled wrinkles masking her face. She is never a lovable figure—an old family antique, unneeded, unlovely but cherished. For she speaks of a time of golden sentiment, of unfettered youth, of brave fantasies and unbounded energy; so that many years later, when caught up by the tragic circumstances of her own motherhood, Suzanne Valadon the artist could never look through her portfolios and, on seeing the hovering figure of her mother, not experience a lift of tender happiness in her heart.

II In Flight

PERHAPS SUZANNE OCCUPIED HERSELF, RATHER MORE THAN other children, drawing pictures. The few toys she had, she told friends in later years, were shabby, broken ones rescued from rubbish bins or found in the streets. She owned one doll in her life, and it lacked a leg and an arm. Pencil stubs and pieces of chalk or coal were more easily come by; nor was it especially painful to her to conclude that these could provide as much entertainment as dolls or toys. Her interest in drawing, however, was sporadic. For months she would do no drawing at all, only to start again with a frenzy which might last anywhere from half-an-hour to a couple of weeks. That was the way she went at everything—in furious spurts. Suddenly, in bold charcoal lines she would draw outsize cats and dogs and jungle beasts all over the tenement-room wallpaper, or make pencil drawings of flowers, nosegays, or bouquets on scraps of loose paper. In the Place de Vintimille the unemployed and even an occasional artist would watch with amusement as the excited, chattering youngster limned her nude figures of little boys and girls on the pavement.

Her art could hardly be said to be superior to other childish scribblings one might have found in thousands of nurseries or kitchens in the city or on miles of cement pavements. By her own account, her figures were crude and static. The dogs were always in the same stiff attitudes, the cats always had arched backs; the naked children all had the same face. There was no suggestion of the childish fantasy, the imagination, the naïve and primitive wit, which in our day have come to be the yardstick of a child's artistic propensities. No mental or emotional impact revealed itself in her drawings, no glimmer of invention or even of fancy marked them with a tinge of her temperament or personality. Faced with these stolid, ungracious figures, one could not have imagined that they were the work of this elfin, mercurial child. They revealed nothing more than a desire to contain within the perimeter of crude, heavy lines the shapes of objects which interested her at the moment. They were hardly the auspicious beginning of the career of a great artist.

Had she lived elsewhere than in Montmartre, this disposition to draw pictures might well have been dissipated in other directions at an early stage. But it was her good fortune to be growing up in a place and at a time when almost any artistic skill had extraordinary importance. Montmartre had become the center of the world's artistic life.

In some inexplicable way, migration to "the Sacred Hill," which had begun after the Revolution of 1793 with the coming of Michel, Géricault, Berlioz, Daguerre, de Nerval and others who found there a pleasant semirural tranquillity and charm, with the setting-in of the Third Republic now swelled to tremendous proportions. First from the Latin Quarter on the Left Bank, then from all over Europe, and finally even from America, artists, sculptors, writers, actors, musicians, and students swarmed to the hill—to the cafés, to the tenements as full of teeming life now as rabbit warrens, to the renovated stables, the defunct potteries, the garden tool sheds and unplastered lofts under the mansard roofs—the "studios" and "garrets" of future autobiographies. In their former habitat, George du Maurier had summed them up—"All laugh, and chaff and mischief, *blague et blaguet Parisien*— wits, butts, bullies; the idle . . . the good and the bad, the clean and the dirty (especially the latter)—all more or less animated by a certain *esprit de corps*." With them came night life—*cafés concerts, cabarets artistiques,* dance halls, music halls, their air of feverish, profligate jollity to dominate the life of the hill. These places would be immortalized by the lithographs of the little misshapen aristocrat Henri de Toulouse-Lautrec, or those of the lean, peppery Pierre Bonnard —the Moulin Rouge, the Mirliton, the Chat Noir, the Elysée-Montmartre, the Divan Japonais. And that last of the thirty windmills, spotted by Madeleine Valadon the day she arrived in the city, the "motif" for the artists—Michel, Théodore Rousseau, Corot, Daguerre, Vollon, Renoir, Van Gogh, Rusiñol—the Moulin de la Galette.

First converted to a *goguette,* or wine shop, which also specialized in serving its customers thin little pastry wafers or *galettes,* the Moulin eventually became a dance hall. Here in the rose- and vine-trellised pavilion under the shady trees, on Sunday afternoons and evenings, mothers and chaperones, drinking beer and watered wine and chattering like sparrows, kept their eyes on the young girls waltzing with scrubbed, pomaded young plumbers and draymen. Behind them in the garden the more irresponsible elements of the community squealed in garden swings and on the small carousel. Young republicans played skittles, gambled at the wheel of fortune, or took pot shots at clay statuettes of the politician Adolphe Thiers, Louis Philippe, or the Tsar of Russia. In the Avenue de Clichy laundresses, milliners, flower vendors and workingmen crowded noisily about Dutrou's bar. Students held wild drinking parties in the garden of Père Lathuile's restaurant or at the Franc-Buveur in the rue des Saules. Parisians and foreigners jostled shopmen and the indigent along the bar at Wepler's or Boivin's. Musicians, actors and circus performers lounged about Chez Olivier's fusty little room or the oilcloth-covered tables at Mme. Bataille's.

The Café de la Nouvelle-Athènes in the Place Pigalle, the

rendezvous of the artists who now called themselves "Impressionists," had succeeded the ormolu atmosphere of the Café Guerbois in the rue des Batignolles. Until the outbreak of the Franco-Prussian War, the Guerbois had been in the nature of an unofficial headquarters for the "new painting" and the "new painters." There, under the leadership of Édouard Manet, the writers Zacharie Astruc, Edmond Duranty, Théodore Duret, and Émile Zola joined forces almost daily with the artists Antoine Guillemet, Félix Bracquemond, and Frédéric Bazille. And often to their company on Friday evenings came Fantin-Latour, Edgar Degas, Pierre Auguste Renoir, Paul Cézanne, Constantin Guys, Alfred Sisley, Claude Monet, Camille Pissarro, and the photographer and balloon enthusiast Félix Nadar, whose studio in the Boulevard des Capucines was to become the setting for the historic First Group Exhibition in 1874—the culmination of the Impressionist movement.

At the Nouvelle-Athènes, after the war, the composition of the group changed considerably. Bazille had been killed at Beaune-la-Rolande. Monet and Sisley lived outside the city and rarely appeared. Writers like Villiers de l'Isle Adam and the Irishman George Moore were to be found there now along with other newcomers like Puvis de Chavannes, Alfred Stevens, and Degas' earnest young friend, the painter Zandomeneghi. Always, too, at a table by himself sat the rock-ribbed monarchist Marcellin Desboutins, in tatters and grime, gazing pensively at the floral ceiling decorations by Petit, who had given his adored Empress Eugénie water-color lessons.

Pausing before the Nouvelle-Athènes on one of her butterfly flights one evening, Suzanne, at the age of ten, stopped to stare into the bright gold-and-white interior. She long remembered one figure she saw there—or so, at any rate, she claimed many years later—a small round-shouldered man, fragile and sad-eyed, in pepper-and-salt tweeds, his throat swathed in woolen scarves. But for the pepper-and-salt tweeds this recollection of the Nouvelle-Athènes might be dismissed as one of her late-in-life fabrications. It is interesting to note, however, that the pepper-and-salt tweeds caught George Moore's eye as well, and he noted them in his *Confessions*, a volume Suzanne Valadon was most unlikely to have seen, much less heard of in the course of her life. The figure in the pepper-and-salt tweeds was Edgar Degas.

While the little village* spent its nights in boisterous revelry or in high-spirited discussions of the present and future of art, its days were preoccupied with work. Red-armed laundresses, midinettes, dressmakers, pushcart vendors, laborers, shop assistants, delivery boys, and farmers scurried about the tangled cobblestone streets, while the artists—the successful ones in tight-fitting frock coats and broad-brimmed black hats, the impoverished ones and students in working-men's corduroy trousers, smocks, and berets—toiled at their easels on the sidewalks and in the little squares.

It was one of the most important tenets of the "new art" that painting should no longer be confined to the artificial arrangements of a studio room, but should seek out its subjects and evolve its techniques in the life of the city. The rapid development of post-Revolutionary technology was quickening the city's pulse; and with its new dynamic motion, its new machinery and smoke, its fragments of life and fleeting moods, the city had become a kaleidoscope of new and exciting landscapes. There was in the air a nervous tension to capture the ephemeral impressions of this fast-moving and turbulent world. Even the countryside itself was to be seen now in new terms of changing light and shadows, of quivering variable colors. The moment, never to be repeated, was the goal of the Impressionist's art. To achieve it, the artist's observations had to be made on the instant, while he stood face to face with the volatile temper of nature. He

* It was actually incorporated into metropolitan Paris in 1855.

had to bring to his work the vibrations of light, and this he sought to do by dissolving the scintillating colors before him into "mists" or by breaking them into minute dabs and patches while simultaneously he abandoned much of his emphasis on contour, modeling or chiaroscuro. In order to do this and yet preserve the precarious balance between subject and surrounding atmosphere which he felt to be essential, he now had to forgo the meticulous "licking" of the academicians and attack his canvas with rapid, loose brushstrokes. Concentrating on this fluid play of light, he was often compelled to lose his outlines at the expense of speed. But whatever his particular problem might be, to secure and develop the "new vision" he had to work out of doors. And so he became an integral part of the working Montmartre scene.

The Impressionist movement culminated with a series of eight exhibitions stretching over a period of twelve years and beginning with the First Group Exhibition of April 15 to May 15, 1874, at Nadar's studio at No. 35 Boulevard des Capucines. Here, at one franc a head, Parisians flocked to look at the work of thirty painters—among them Pissarro, Renoir, Cézanne, Monet, Sisley, Degas, and Berthe Morisot— and to hear every boulevard wit fire some caustic jibe at the display of "dabs" or "blotches" on the walls.* Thus began the series which continued until the "Eighth Exhibition of Painting" (May 15 to June 15, 1886), from which most of the old Impressionists, in fact, abstained, leaving the exhibition to be dominated by the "Divisionist" work of Georges Seurat** and his followers and the dawn of yet another

---

* At the sight of one of Monet's canvases entitled "Impression: Rising Sun," the critic Louis Leroy is supposed to have exclaimed, "The whole show is an impression." This outburst naturally got a laugh, and the exhibitors were thus dubbed "Impressionists." In the April 25, 1879, issue of *Charivari*, Leroy first set the word "Impressionism" in print. The painters liked the term and soon adopted it as a group name.

** Notably by the exhibition of his "A Sunday Afternoon on the Island of La Grande Jatte."

movement. This last exhibition of the Impressionists was less a breakup than a regrouping of their inquiring spirit and analytical drive. The field now passed into the hands of younger men—Signac, Odilon Redon and Gauguin (only Pissarro remaining of the Impressionists). Manifestoes, treatises, clashes, and coalitions were to signal further grouping and regrouping for a period of thirty years, and from their vitality was to emerge the painting which today we so loosely call "modern." It was during these years that Suzanne Valadon became an artist.

If she was unaware of the artistic and philosophical arguments being forged about her, Suzanne could not be unconscious of the extraordinary personalities who invaded the hill following the Franco-Prussian War. The atmosphere in which she grew up fairly cracked with their will to assert themselves. The cafés, *bistros*, and *brasseries* reverberated with their arguments. In their unpredictable, often eccentric behavior, she sensed an affinity with her own restlessness, with her intense feelings. Somehow she belonged to them, hungered to share the comradeship of these strange, blustering, dedicated men, to join in their altercations, their spontaneous parties, their quivering excitement.

But to want to be a part of the artists' social and temperamental existence was one thing; to want to be an artist was quite another. Suzanne fostered no such ambition. It did not even occur to her that she might possibly become an artist. There existed in her childish mind no connection at all between the little drawings which she executed sporadically for her own amusement and the accomplishments of the young men whose easels bristled about the Montmartre hill. Once she left the Convent of St. Vincent de Paul she had to earn a living—an earnest business, and a far cry from the indolent occupation of standing around on street corners putting daubs of paint on canvas.

She was first apprenticed at nine to an *atelier de couture* in the Place de Clichy, where, in a murky, cluttered work-room a hundred times more oppressive than the classroom at St. Vincent's, she was supposed to lay the groundwork for the future life of a seamstress. As she remembered in later life, she loathed the place, with its great masses of flimsy dress materials, tinsel, and artificial flowers, and the cheap perfume of her co-workers. Madeleine had to take her to work every morning, and the forelady, not without a show of brutality, saw to it that she stayed on the job through the day. For although Suzanne accepted the necessity of having to work and was rather boastful of the fact that hers was grim employment, she was not above removing herself from the hated atmosphere when the fancy struck her. On the occasions when she was able to effect an escape (by climbing out a second storey window) she was beaten both at home and in the factory. But the freedom was worth the pain.

She worked in the sweatshop for over three years, until she was almost thirteen. Then, according to her own account, she escaped one day and stayed away from home until she was able to tell her mother that she had found a more remunerative job—"taking care of rich children in the Tuileries." It is difficult to imagine that this story tallies with the truth, or by what persuasion Madeleine was induced to accept it. One look at the scrubby urchin should have convinced her that rich people would be most unlikely to entrust the care of their children to her daughter.

In rapid succession Suzanne found employment as a waitress and dishwasher in a cheap working-class restaurant, as a pushcart vendor of vegetables at Les Halles des Batignolles, and as a groom in a livery stable. In this last job she is remembered by some of her living contemporaries, who many times stood before their parents' tobacco shop to watch her go up the rue Lamarck, a wild, tiny figure trotting between a pair of giant Percherons held by their halters, or bobbing along on a horse's bare back executing handstands, head-

stands, somersaults, and cartwheels. This extraordinary performance on the rue Lamarck was apparently what eventually
won her a job as an equestrienne in a circus troupe, a job
she was to look back upon with considerable sentimentality
for the rest of her life.

There seems to be a curious unanimity among those who
knew her that Suzanne was a member of the troupe of the
Cirque Molier. However, a very careful review of the circus
programmes between 1879 and 1881 fails to reveal among the
performers either her name or one which might be taken for
a stage name. Considering the nature and the objectives of
the Cirque Molier, this is not surprising. M. Ernest Molier
was a wealthy gentleman and an equine enthusiast who, convinced that it was very important somehow to prove that
"aristocrats could be as clever and amusing as plebeians,"
created a circus which gave two gala performances each year
—one for "the ladies of high society," as the *New York
Herald* put it, and the other for "their sisters of the 'half-
world.'" It was therefore a real matter of principle with
M. Molier and his audience that the entertainment be supplied
solely by members of the Parisian elite. It would have been
quite impossible for anyone from Suzanne's stratum of society
to be among these performers.

That she might have been employed by one of the four
permanent circuses established in Paris at the time—the Hip-
podrome, the Cirque Medrano, the Cirque Fernando (now
the Cirque d'Hiver) or the Nouveau Cirque—also seems most
unlikely. There was, as may well be imagined, extremely
keen competition among the four. Their scouts scoured
eastern Europe and the Orient to bring to their rings the most
exotic and sensational acts, and the standards of performance
demanded were extremely high. It is doubtful whether a
young girl with no training, who could perform only simple
acrobatics on the back of a horse, would have been taken on
as a member of one of these troupes. More probably

Suzanne's "circus career" was spent not in a circus but in one of the tent shows or carnivals at Neuilly or Le Trône, which were the showcases for performers aspiring to be taken up as acts by the managers of music halls, *cafés concerts*, cabarets, or the small traveling shows in the provinces.

The legend that Suzanne was associated with the Cirque Molier seems to have originated with Suzanne herself. It was her own little joke. In her last years she often spoke ironically of "the grandeur of my past." The hideous days of the Commune and the White terror were for her "our hunting days"; the tenement room was "Chateau Rochechouart." Her son Maurice was born in "La Grande Salle du Poteau" (the Great Hall du Poteau). In the same vein she remembered her father as "an aristocratic baron," and hinted that Madeleine was not really her mother but an old governess retained on a family pension; that the Empress Eugénie was her godmother; that as a debutante she was secretly betrothed to the Prince Imperial (who was dead at the time); that she had inspired M. Guerlain to create his famous scent Jicky in her honor—a host of similar fantasies. It was absurd, of course, that she, Suzanne Valadon, the untidy old wasp of the Butte, should have originated in or had anything to do with the effete world of Parisian high society. Such a paradox amused her hugely, and if someone believed it, it was all the funnier. Still, we must face the fact that the dream world she created for herself as a lonely child was something she never quite discarded as she grew older and that, indeed, toward the end of her life it re-established itself compellingly. If the Cirque Molier story was not her little joke, then she believed it herself just as she came half to believe anything about the past, not knowing (and not caring) where the facts and the fantasies had become confused. Truth or reality lay in the pictures she had produced. She was an artist. Truth was in her pictures. Where else it lay was unimportant.

Whatever her "circus career" was, it ended disastrously after about seven months. With characteristic daring she took it upon herself, during a performance, to substitute for the trapeze artist, who was indisposed. She had done a few turns on the trapeze, it is true, but she was hardly skillful enough to turn in a professional performance. During one of the turns she missed her timing and fell, and although the injuries she sustained were not severe enough to maim her seriously, she was forced to leave the circus.

It was a cruel blow. For here, for the first time, it seems, she had an expression of her temperament in her work. The excitement, the color, the atmosphere of the carnival were things she understood, things she seemed to have prepared herself for unconsciously all her life. But for the fall she might have visualized a dazzling career. And fifty years later it was still a poignant tragedy to her that her career in a circus had been shattered. "They gathered up the poor little broken body," she would murmur softly. With bittersweet longing she gazed back at the irretrievable past. It had not seemed then that there could have been a future.

When the fall from the trapeze ended Suzanne's prospects as a circus performer, she was sixteen. On the offhand suggestion of a friend, she then became an artist's model.

Modeling was a stopgap until she should be in physical condition once more to undertake some other work. But her first appearances at the fountain in the Place Pigalle, where each morning hopeful models of various ages, sizes, shapes, and sexes paraded before the artists, created more than the usual stir. In a very short time she was aware that she had attached herself to something which really mattered to her in a very intimate and precious way.

"I remember the first sitting I did," she recalled. "I remember saying to myself over and over again, 'This is it!

This is it!' Over and over I said it all day. I did not know why. But I knew that I was somewhere at last and that I should never leave."

With glowing excitement and radiant happiness she entered the world that had fascinated her for so long, a world to which she was drawn by an incomprehensible affinity. Tiny, elfin, vivacious, with an ivory skin, soft, luminous eyes, and a superbly ripened figure, she was at the same time the loveliest of children and the most voluptuous of women— considerably more than an artist looking for a model on Montmartre might have hoped for. And beyond her not unimpressive physical attributes she possessed a zestful and original temperament and an enthusiasm for work far beyond the call of duty. Neither the length of time she had to hold a difficult pose nor the question of overtime was of great interest to her; rather, she saw herself as a part of the artist's creation in a vague, metaphysical way. This was her contribution to his fulfillment. Dramatizing her own role, she was even capable of considering herself his inspiration. And so, from the very beginning of her new career she was a resounding success.

Success could not be measured in terms of monetary reward. Pay was poor and notoriously irregular. Models had to haggle over the rates they would receive for each sitting. The hours were long, the "breaks" few and far between. Often after the bargaining and a long sitting the artist would confess that he did not have the money to pay anyway. But painful as these conditions might be, to Suzanne they were compensated for to an enormous degree by the fact that she had become a part of the active life of Bohemia, that the extraordinary personalities she had so fervently longed to approach as a child were now a part of her daily existence, that she was no longer an outsider or freak among the people with whom she lived. Now she "belonged." She would sit in the cafés, listen to or take part in the discussions. She could express her opinions as dogmatically as the next fellow. She could, if she ingratiated herself in the proper quarters, spend time at the circuses, the *cabarets artistiques,* and the dance halls which were the hubs of the life of the Butte. She was always welcome at a studio party.

For all the poverty and struggle, for all Madeleine's sullen resentment and whining, it was a far better life than any she had ever before known. She would rise late in the morning, breakfast frugally on chunks of *baguettes* and coffee, loiter about the fountain in the Place Pigalle gossiping with other models if she did not already have a working assignment for the day; or, if she had an opportunity, she made her appearance at the artist's studio shortly before noon. The afternoon was spent in posing, usually until the light failed. Later might come a visit to one of the cafés for "the green hour," that period of lively relaxation devoted to chatter or serious conversation and the sipping of absinthe. Properly drunk, absinthe was diluted with water, and its bright green color, which gave "the hour" its name, became opalescent. Compounded of medieval-sounding herbs—wormwood, hyssop, fennel, balm mint and brandy at 136 proof—it was the strongest of all alcoholic drinks, and it had the additional virtue of being generally considered a potent aphrodisiac.

The evening was for dinner, again in the joyous company of friends, at one of the *brasseries* on the boulevards or at one of the small restaurants of the side streets, paid for by whoever had money in his pocket. Then on to a dance hall or a cabaret, after which she went home at three or four o'clock—either alone or with a companion.

Nor was Suzanne's life without its creative side. Once more she began to draw, but now the static figures she had once limned suddenly became alive in graceful, fluid curves of movement. As though by magic, the crudity of her childish drawings became certainty, sureness, and power, solidly contained within the limits of bold, savage lines. Her temperament, so curiously absent in early drawings, now found itself in automatic and masterful control of her compositions, which were permeated with joy. For all their savagery they were infused with compassion and even with a touch of sentimentality. Whether they were people, animals, or things, her models were infused alike with her strength and her weaknesses. The sketching which had been hardly more than a momentary release from childhood boredom had now become, miraculously, a manifestation of her burgeoning artistic expression. She was quick to be aware of it. It had come full-blown—from where? She did not know. She had received no tutelage. No one had pointed the way or attempted to enlighten her. She simply accepted it as hard fact and good fortune, and allowed herself secretly to dream of becoming an artist.

Henceforth in the little time she found free between the role she played in the frenzied pace of Bohemian life and her responsibilities as a breadwinner—for her mother was no longer able to produce an income—she worked at her drawing. Considering the little time she was able to spend on her work, her sketches seemed to mature with astonishing speed. Listening to the interminable discussions of artistic problems and observing the methods and techniques of the artists with whom she sat daily undoubtedly had some influence on her development. Anything she garnered from the conversation of other artists or through her study of their working methods she digested. But what emerged bore the stamp of her own invention alone. Groupings of familiar objects, a child combing her hair, flowers, assumed a sensuousness which stemmed not so much from a study of technique as from her own hearty appetite for life. She wanted, she told herself, "to work like mad, not to produce beautiful drawings to be framed and hung, but good drawings which capture a moment of life in movement in all its intensity";

and somehow she managed, in spite of the pressure of living, to apply herself to this end.

But art, in one form or another, by no means filled her life in those years. Far from it. For love is also an important part of the artist's vocation, the fountainhead of his creative life; and Suzanne, living in a world in which all her companions were ceaselessly engaged in affairs of the heart, ranging from frivolous flirtations to the most violent dramas of passion, did not lag behind. Her temperament and her sympathy with masculine society combined to make her amorous. Perhaps the circumstances of her birth led her to think lightly of the virtues of chastity. The sisters of St. Vincent de Paul who had not succeeded in teaching her to read and write were hardly more successful in instructing her in the ideal of immaculacy. When Madeleine protested that being an artist's model was to embark on the road to prostitution, Suzanne replied tartly that even the respectable existence of a village seamstress had failed to provide a father for *her*. As though fathers mattered anyway! What was important was that she, Suzanne Valadon, had come into a way of life which was joyous, and that she was now in a position to enjoy it with the full power of her warm-blooded nature.

Her account of her loss of chastity, given eighteen years after the fact, was calculated fiction, created from whole cloth in order to justify a tragic turn of events in her life. It is altogether possible that her first lesson in love occurred in early childhood and that it was accepted as casually as the nuns' instruction in other fields. Wherever or however it happened, by the time she was sixteen it had given rise to a prodigious show of promiscuity which had many Montmartre tongues wagging. The Breton waiter at Père Lathuile's restaurant, the postman Léconte, Degas' young friend Zandomeneghi, the sailor Guichet—they are but a few of the remembered names of her lovers. A night or two, a week, a month, a sudden disappearance to the forest at Fontainebleau, a rented room above a stationer's shop in the rue Custine, a bacchanale necessitating a call by the police in the studio of Louis Anquetin—such was the substance of her amours, which for all their intensity and animal vitality preserved an aura of playfulness and naïveté. Sensuality and joyousness dominated her love life, uncorrupted by either heartache or the sentimentality natural in a young girl of sixteen. Men? She loved them *en masse*. That she should be faithful to one man was preposterous. Nature had bestowed sex appeal on her in generous proportions; it ill suited her to waste it.

Yet for Suzanne Valadon even the course of promiscuity could not long run smoothly. It was destined to be interrupted by a romantic idyl which lasted almost six months.

Just after Christmas of 1882 she sat for the already eminent painter Pierre Puvis de Chavannes. Today the legend persists in Montmartre that Puvis was the first artist she ever sat to, that it was he, in fact, who started her on her career as an artist's model. The story goes that at the time she met Puvis de Chavannes she was a laundress, and that one day when she was delivering the wash to his studio Puvis saw her and was so struck by her beauty that he prevailed upon her to pose for him. But the fact that only a month or so previous she had so seriously injured her back as to be unable to continue in a circus makes it unlikely that she would have been doing the strenuous work of a laundress at that time. Her own account, as recited to her friends through the years, is somewhat more plausible: that Puvis de Chavannes heard of her success as a model for other artists and sent for her to come to his studio at Neuilly.

Suzanne was seventeen, and Puvis de Chavannes was fifty-seven—a tall, impeccably clad dandy with square shoulders and a proud, imperial beard. One would take him to be a successful lawyer or a politician of the Palais Royale rather than an artist. "At any rate he looks very famous," his friend, the sculptor Rodin, said of him, "and one suspects he had the same imperious beard when he was a schoolboy." Famous he was, at that time certainly better known throughout the world than any of the other Montmartre artists. He was said to be immensely wealthy, partly by virtue of the considerable sums his murals commanded, partly because he was the scion of an old and eminently prosperous Burgundian family. He had been educated at Lyons College and later at the Lycée Henri IV in Paris in preparation for a career as a mining engineer. But when he was eighteen a serious bout with pneumonia sent him to Italy to convalesce. There he became enamored of the placid moods of the *quattrocento* masters and decided to become an artist. Returning to Paris, he studied art under the academicians Scheffer and Couture; and in the Salon of 1852 he exhibited a *Pietà* imitative of the Giotto fresco in the Arena chapel in Padua. In 1852 and 1853 he was rejected by the Salon and did not bother to submit again until 1859, this time with "Return from Hunting," in the uninspired academic style. "It was a very dull picture, and it looked as though I had completely lost interest in easel painting—which I had," he confessed in a letter to his friend Bloy.

Through some family connections he was finally called upon to execute a mural in the library in his native Lyons. The spell of Giotto in Padua was heavily upon him, and he went back to Italy for a month before he undertook his first sketches. Once he began work he realized that the walls gave him room to free himself from the constrictions of academic easel painting. But they did more than that: they allowed him to break from that tendency he feared most—to become caught up in the oncoming flood of Realist-Impressionism undammed by Courbet and Manet. The style which now emerged was purely his own, a heritage but certainly not an imitation of his beloved painters of the *quattrocento*. Simplifying his drawing and muting his colors, he brought to his murals not what his eye perceived but the feelings his observations released. These were reflected in the mood of serenity in which he composed them—the subdued color tones and lyrical lines speaking for the leisurely pace of his brushwork, for the relaxed pipe-smoking and humming he did on the scaffold. Tranquillity was the over-all mood of his work, and it struck a responsive chord in the critics and the public of his day as no other painting had done. And the fact that his art found its being on the walls of public buildings, possessions of the people, and not in the homes of the *bourgeoisie* or aristocracy, endeared it considerably to the democratic public heart. His success was immediate, and shortly his fees became astronomical.

For six months during the autumn and winter of 1882-1883 Suzanne left Madeleine to grumble to herself in their one-room flat in the rue du Poteau and moved into Puvis de Chavannes' apartment at Neuilly as mistress of the famous artist. Although for more than twenty years Puvis de Chavannes had cherished a love for the Princess Cantacuzène, the wife of a Romanian nobleman living in Paris, he was still a bachelor. This romance had been kept alive by a fervent exchange of verse, gifts, and pale pink roses, but, because of the chivalrous convictions of the lover, had reached a no more intimate basis of realization. Dante and Beatrice were reborn in nineteenth-century Paris. Then quite suddenly after twenty years, Puvis de Chavannes had renounced celibacy and had taken to sleeping with his models. This strange turn in behavior had not in the least altered his attitude to the princess: he continued to shower her with gifts, spent long hours composing poetry worthy of her virtue, and continued the flow of pale pink roses. But to one of his aesthetic pupils who had not as yet discovered the new twist in his morality he confessed, "You'll soon discover I'm no saint. There is nothing better in the world than passionately loving women and voluptuousness." By the time he sent for Suzanne Valadon, the student and the rest of his colleagues on the Butte had been more than moderately startled by his amatory exploits.

Puvis, the man of the world, knew the heart of a young girl even though he may have found it increasingly difficult to keep up with the demands of her body. He did not fail to note the light in Suzanne's eyes when she first stepped into the gold-and-white foyer of his apartment, as she took in expanses of the Aubusson carpets, the furniture by Topino, the crystal chandelier, and the bed with the fleur-de-lis patterned silk by Philippe de Lasalle. She might not have recognized it for what it was, but clearly she had never before been surrounded by such elegance. She was standing on the threshold of a girlish dream, and it was within his power to make it come true for her.

"The landscape," he once wrote, "must awaken dreams and strike chords of feeling to summon a mood of solemnity, to delight the eye, and uplift the spirit." For Suzanne he was eager to create such a landscape. In a way he might somewhat bitterly have resented being called "fatherly"; it amused him to observe her reaction to a way of life hitherto alien to her. More practically, he did not want to lose an excellent model, one who was so completely satisfying that he was using her for both the feminine and the masculine figures of his "The Woods Sacred to the Arts and to the Muses," the painting which was currently occupying his attention. It never dawned upon him that in transplanting her to the atmosphere in which he lived he threatened to destroy creative powers which sprang from her savage and unsophisticated way of life.

At first Suzanne was dazzled indeed. The cool, controlled pace of her lover's existence subtly seemed to sap from the young girl all the turbulence which had been the essence of her former life. It was a pleasant new sensation. The tranquillity so much admired in the painting of Puvis de Chavannes was indeed at the very root of his character. Everything he did was suffused with it. He never hurried. He could search for a shirt stud for an hour unruffled, without a flicker of ill temper. He walked "like a monk reading his breviary"; and at his work the long, unhurried measures of his brushstrokes transferred his serenity to his canvas. Gentle, unpedantic, quietly entertaining, he ordered the gentle tenure of their days together, and she was mysteriously without the power to disturb them. Once or twice, with a supreme effort, she was able to rouse a flicker of temper which she thought would disconcert him. It was to no avail. He would not take her to a cabaret? Very well. She would go alone. She would flounce into the street, waiting at the doorway below for him to follow. But he did not come; and after an hour of waiting she would return, contrite and pouting, to find him reading a book. Or she would refuse to pose for him, telling him that his pictures were soulless and bored her, that she wanted nothing more to do with them. Unruffled, he would go on with his work after assuring her kindly that she was probably tired and that, if he really needed a model, he would call another. In a little while she would be back on the model's stand.

For the first time in her life Suzanne found herself dominated by the mood of another human being. It was easy to be passive when one was fairly smothered in amiability, when everything done was in pursuit of tranquil joyousness, when one was always surrounded by beautiful and elegant things, comfort and ease. One lost the urge to control one's own destiny when one was in the charge of a powerful man whose only wish seemed to be contentment. Suzanne did not know by what means this master artist had created the dream in which she now lived, the lovely illusion of peace which had suddenly captured her. In a vague way she had expected her voluptuousness to demean him, not because she was not fond of him but because Youth delighted in the foibles of Age. But he had been neither hurt nor ashamed by their physical relationship. He had merely taken control of the situation and without any great show had steered the course of their lives on another tack.

What he created then was a glowing, tender idyl suffused with soft poetry, as serenely devised and as gently applied as the pale blues and greens and misty grays with which he swathed the poised figures of his murals. She would always remember their many long walks in the twilight along the glimmering boulevards, and chaste suppers in the gracious atmosphere of the Tour d'Argent or Lapérouse, the glitter of nights at the Opera, the rides in an open carriage under the shadows of the lime trees in the Bois de Boulogne, and their occasional visits to cafés of Montmartre frequented by the artists. He gave her her first lessons in gastronomy and taught her the rudiments of wine tasting. He presented her with a little pearl ring.

Long afterward Suzanne suspected that, having created the dream, he also determined its duration. He spoke once of marrying her, but it was in an offhand way which did not allow her an opportunity to give an answer. He continued to send pale pink roses to the Princess Cantacuzène, and Suzanne could recall a couple of instances when she herself posted his letters to his beloved. Strangely, she was not jealous. The letters, like everything else, seemed to her unreal.

And in her memory Suzanne could find no signal for the dissolution of the idyl. Slowly, imperceptibly, it evaporated into nothingness like one of the pallid mists of a Puvis de Chavannes landscape. There were no struggles, no pains, no miserable voids, no sentimental souvenirs to conjure tears. Suddenly she was back in the rue du Poteau with Madeleine in the familiar one-room tenement, Cinderella after the ball; and there were friendly platonic greetings when she encountered Puvis de Chavannes on the Montmartre streets.

She posed for him again in 1884, and in 1886 she sat for the preliminary sketches of the "Life of St. Genevieve," which was later to grace the walls of the Pantheon. In both cases the sittings were on a purely professional basis, and, according to Suzanne, the fees were somewhat higher than normal. She had awakened from the dream, and around her once more was the intoxicating whirl of ecstasy, passion, and self-possession which was her natural element.

Perhaps it was while the idyl with Puvis de Chavannes was dissolving (for it was early in the spring of 1883) that Suzanne was in the Chat Noir on the Boulevard de Rochechouart one evening with a group of old Montmartre friends. During the course of the evening a young Catalan engineering student, one Miguel Utrillo, rose from the table he was occupying with some of his fellow students and, commanding the attention of the rest of the customers, launched into a two-hour lecture on a Catalan dance called the *Bal del Ciri*, performed in the church by outgoing church wardens. It was an extraordinary lecture, peppered with Catalan folklore and wit, and the young man concluded it with an exhibition of leaping *contrepas* and *sardanas* which, to his own tuneful baritone accompaniment, he executed with consummate grace.

Similar spontaneous acts had frequently been performed in the place ever since the Chat Noir had opened its doors the year before. The cabaret was the creation of a theatrical-minded Swiss, Rodolphe de Salis, and was inspired by the thriving business then being enjoyed by another cabaret called the Grande Pinte, which had attracted an especially chic clientele merely by decorating its walls with some historical chromos. Salis' inspiration carried him considerably farther. He re-created the interior of a tavern of the period of Louis XIII, complete with a gigantic open fireplace and great charred ceiling beams. On the walls and from the ceiling he hung copper cooking utensils, armor, and hunting paraphernalia, and he furnished the hall with massive oaken chairs and tables which it required the services of liveried waiters to budge. "God created the world, Napoleon created the Legion of Honor, but I created Montmartre," was Salis' modest boast. There was, however, a grain of truth in his claim: he set the standard for the air of informality which brought the world to the Montmartre cabarets.

At first Salis depended on little more than his own personality to attract the public—his soaring egotism and a mixture of pseudo-seventeenth-century wit and Montmartre argot. The rest of the entertainment he provided was drawn from the good spirits of his customers. With remarkable success he called upon the patrons to display their talents—to render songs, play musical instruments, read poems, perform magic tricks, and act out dramatic sketches. One of these customers, Aristide Bruant, subsequently became one of the greatest theatrical idols of France. The flamboyant Bruant, first a singer of sentimental Montmartre songs, then master of ceremonies, was finally to become the proprietor of the premises. At the peak of his career he broke with Salis; and when Salis moved the Chat Noir to larger quarters in the rue de Laval, Bruant opened his own Mirliton on the old site.

But while Bruant was at the Chat Noir and his lively wit and argot songs depicting the joys and miseries of the dispossessed were enchanting the night-club crowd, the intelligentsia, which considered itself responsible for the success of both Salis and Bruant, withdrew to a room in the rear which became known as "the Institute." Salis, who could not resist any ironic twist, decked the waiters in green livery identical with the uniforms worn by the venerable members of the French Academy. From that point on he left amusement to the patrons themselves. So, while in the main hall of the cabaret the Philistines gathered to drink their beer at sixty-five centimes a glass, in the Institute the customers drank absinthe or cognac at twenty centimes, and amused themselves. Entertainment was of a high order indeed. It was in the Institute that Henri Rivière inaugurated the famous shadow theater after the fashion of the Chinese. There Guy de Maupassant read his stories aloud, Sarah Bernhardt and Coquelin *cadet* performed Shakespearean dialogues, and Stephane Mallarmé and sometimes Paul Verlaine spoke their verses. Anatole France, André Gill, Jean-Louis Forain, Georges Auriol, André Antoine, and young Claude Debussy, too, exhibited their various skills when the mood was upon them, and were roundly cheered by that group of artists, models, musicians, students, and writers who were pleased to consider themselves, according to one of their number, "the only intellectual force of the Third Republic."

Young Miguel Utrillo, with his two-hour lecture on the *Bal del Ciri*, was not out of place in such company. An engineering student at the Institute Agronomique on the Right Bank, he affected the velvet jacket and broad-brimmed hat of the true *Montmartrois*, and together with many of his fellow students spent his hours of relaxation on the Butte. There, as Jean-Louis Forain had put it, "Youth could behave as fantastically as it pleased without being conspicuous." Utrillo's urge to be conspicuous came but rarely, but come it did. He was to be remembered for some time for having ridden into the Moulin de la Galette on the back of a donkey, for having staged a mock bullfight in the lobby of the Boule Noir, and for having arrived among the dancers at the Élysée-Montmartre with a pushcart of fish.

He was the only son of a well-to-do family of Barcelona. Both his mother and his father were "Sunday painters," and a cousin on his father's side of the family was making a name for himself as a portrait artist in Catalonia. Miguel himself had studied art at La Llonja, the Provisional School of Fine Arts, where he was a classmate and boon companion of the painters Santiago Rusiñol and Ramon Casas. In the course of his studies he had switched from painting to architecture; and it was only after five years, during which he received two first prizes, that he decided upon yet another

After the Bath. Pastel drawing by Suzanne Valadon. 1908.
Courtesy of the Lefevre Gallery, London.

Left. Seated Nude Woman with Standing Woman Seen from Back in the Background. Crayon drawing by Suzanne Valadon. *Courtesy of the Art Institute of Chicago. Below.* Family Bath. Drawing by Suzanne Valadon. 1910. *Courtesy of the Lefevre Gallery, London.*

switch, this time to engineering. And it was this that had brought him to Paris.

His lecture at the Chat Noir delighted Suzanne Valadon as much as it did the other habitués of the Institute. Whether or not this was the occasion of their first meeting we do not know. Suzanne often spoke of Miguel's lecture, especially of the *contrepas* and *sardanas* which he subsequently taught her and which she often later performed at parties. However, shortly after the performance at the Chat Noir she was to be found frequently in his company. And it was indeed she (along with Casas and Rusiñol) who trailed him as the push-cart of fish made its way across the dance floor of the Élysée-Montmartre.

It is known that they often ate their meals together that spring beneath the arbors of the Guinguette or in the garden of the Franc-Buveur; and it was presumed by most of the people who knew them that they were lovers. Suzanne's reputation left little reason for any other conclusion. She made no secret of her relationship with the Breton waiter, the postman Léconte, Zandomeneghi, Guichet, Puvis de Chavannes, and a number of others. When in the fall of 1883, therefore, Utrillo and she were still often seen together and she was obviously pregnant, it was generally assumed that he was responsible for her condition.

But among the gossips of the quarter the question of impending paternity was moot indeed. Edmond Heuzé, one of Montmartre's most reliable chroniclers, remembers an old Montmartre hackman shrugging his shoulders and ruminating: "The little one is bitten at last, yes? But which mosquito bit her? Ah, that is the question." And the gossips wondered too. Was it Puvis de Chavannes? Or the young Catalan? Or who in between might it have been?

Suzanne herself was unconcerned or, at any rate, made a studied effort to appear so. She had modeling to do and parties to go to. The serenity of Neuilly behind her, she went her fitful, darting way once more with renewed zest, albeit somewhat misshapen. Never one to be shy of the attention paid her, she was delighted to be the subject of gossip. And when pressed by her friends as to who was responsible for her condition she was evasive and coy. If asked point-blank, "Was it so-and-so?" she merely tossed off an "It could be," or an "I hope so," and went on to another subject. As far as she was concerned, the subject was not worth discussing.

As the birth of the child drew near, Suzanne of course became unemployable as a model. The loss of work apparently did not bother her unduly. She seemed to have money enough to live on. Whoever the father of her unborn child was, he had evidently assumed a decent financial obligation toward her.

She went into labor early on Christmas morning. Madeleine sent for the midwife whose services had been arranged for beforehand. Together in the dingy, cluttered room in the rue du Poteau the two older women prepared for the coming event with that routine of deft puttering which had been a tradition of midwifery for centuries. The patient's agony was unheeded. She flew about the room like a scalded cat or writhed on the bed howling in pain, only to be told with galling casualness that she was not the first woman in the world to have a baby. Toward evening the midwife noted aloud that the birth was taking quite a long time, and Madeleine, muttering that a child born in sin always took longer to face the world, began to drink generously of her brandy. The hours dragged painfully past dawn when the midwife decided that there might be something wrong, and leaving the patient in charge of the by then quite drunken mother, went in search of help. When she returned with a doctor Suzanne was hemorrhaging violently. Meanwhile Madeleine, swaying before her, was screaming at her that her misery was all her own doing.

Shortly after noon on December 26 the baby was born—a frail, jaundiced little boy with a head "that looked like an *aubergine*" and bore the black bruises of the doctor's forceps below each ear. Suzanne was barely aware of the birth. She remembered the little mass of moist flesh somewhere during a succession of violent chills in a blackening room. Within minutes of the child's birth she was in a coma.

It was two days before she regained consciousness and felt the baby drawing greedily from her breast. Madeleine grinned down at her—the first time, Suzanne thought, she had ever seen her mother smile. "The little one, he saved your life. The rest of them are fools," Madeleine said. From then on she was always to insist, "If Maurice had not been so hungry, you would have died."

Suzanne decided to name the baby Maurice because "there is no Maurice who could have been his father and because I like the name." The next day Madeleine registered the child's birth at the Montmartre *mairie*. She gave his name as Maurice Valadon.

Shortly after the birth of Maurice, Suzanne, Madeleine, and the baby moved from the single room in the rue du Poteau to a three-room flat at No. 7 rue Tourlaque, an establishment which the gossips of Montmartre were quick to note was considerably more costly than their former abode. Since at the time Suzanne was nursing the baby and could take modeling jobs only at odd hours, it was evident that she was receiving financial assistance from some source. There was now a nurse for the baby too. It was also to be observed (without surprise) that, except for feeding the child, Suzanne was prone to take motherhood uncommonly lightly. As of old, she was off again on a perpetual round of parties, dance halls, and cabarets; and once more she was the object of masculine attention and was enjoying it as promiscuously as ever. But it was to be noted also that among her admirers Miguel Utrillo still commanded a considerable share of her time.

Then, in the summer of 1884, Miguel completed his studies at the Institut Agronomique and went to Bulgaria. Six months later Suzanne reported that he had been transferred to Germany. From then on she could always be counted upon for news of his whereabouts; and their mutual friends, like the gossips of Montmartre, came to believe that between her and the young Catalan there lay a good deal more intimacy than met the eye.

Nonetheless, she spent little time in pining for him. He had not yet left Paris when Suzanne first posed for Pierre-Auguste Renoir.

Renoir had recently returned from Italy, where he had gone to study the work of Raphael, Tiepolo, and Veronese. "I had gone to the end of Impressionism, and I was reaching the conclusion that I didn't know either how to paint or how to draw. In a word, I was at a dead end," he was later to say in explaining his Italian journey. He returned to Paris now with little taste for the swelling accolade in the rue Faubourg St. Honoré, where the Parisian art dealers had begun to receive impressive sums for his pictures. At the age of forty-one he clung to ramshackle Montmartre and a resolution to acquire the craftsmanship which had given the Italian masters the simplicity and grandeur he so fervently admired. He destroyed as many of his old canvases as he could lay his hands on. So obsessed was he with the importance of elegant lines that he now drew the individual leaves of his background trees in pen and ink upon the canvas before starting to work in color. He no longer painted out of doors, for he was convinced that his preoccupation with light had caused him to neglect the more basic factors of draftsmanship and form. "I am suffering from experimentation," George Moore quotes him as writing. "I'm not content, and I scrape off, always scrape off. I hope this mania will have an end. I'm like little children in school—the white page is to be written upon and *bang!* a blot."

Suzanne knew little and cared less about the perturbation which was marking a turning point in Renoir's career. To her, he was no more important as an artist than a score of others she knew, all heavy with personal artistic problems. When were artists otherwise? Her story of having once encouraged Renoir, when she was a child, advising him to keep up his painting, may be apocryphal. But she did undoubtedly see him many times while she was growing up, and being the gregarious creature she was, she more than likely had a casual acquaintanceship with him. The fact that he, like her mother, came from the Limousin gave them a subject for passing pleasantries. Surely, in her childhood days, Renoir was a fine sight to see—uncommonly handsome, with his peaches-and-cream complexion, his merry brown eyes, his fragile upturned nose, and his tousled black hair squashed beneath the battered felt hat worn on the back of his head. He was honey to the swarms of midinettes, grisettes, models, and laundresses of the Butte, all of whom he treated with a kindly, casual air. Happily he had changed little since those days. Whatever his mental and artistic problems, he was still a rapturous little man, exuding amiability, fun, and boundless love.

"He fell in love with me," Suzanne insisted in after years, "and at Bougival he painted me in his famous picture." This account does not jibe with Renoir's own claim that "Le Bal à Bougival" was painted in his Montmartre studio from sketches made in the Restaurant Fournaise at Bougival. Whether or not Suzanne accompanied Renoir on his excursions to the little river town, or whether she simply posed for the actual painting in his Montmartre studio, we do not know. But in her eagerness to be identified with the famous painting at the source she was well aware of the fact that in the preceding year Renoir had been at Bougival and painted his "Le Déjeuner des Canotiers," and that the model for *its* central figure was a young woman named Alice Charigat, who was soon to become Mme. Renoir. Suzanne was to harbor a dislike of Mme. Renoir for the rest of her life.

In spite of the existence of Alice Charigat, Suzanne did have an affair with Renoir. And brief though it was, she cherished the memory of it into her old age. At no other time in her life had Montmartre borne so romantic an air: never had life been so steeped in charming grace. "The Montmartre Renoir knew," Pierre Courthion writes, "was a rose that still had its natural hues in spite of its proximity to the artifices of the throbbing capital: a rose diamonded in morning dew. It was a home for lovers, an oasis of light reserved for youth which could remain unsophisticated in an atmosphere of carefree gaiety." In its setting a month or two of love could glisten jewel-like throughout a lifetime of less innocent pleasures, and in Suzanne's case it did. Renoir brought her nosegays and presented them with old-fashioned courtliness. When she strolled about the Butte on his arm she knew she was the object of envy of every young woman in the quarter. Such delight was not soon to be forgotten. And on Sundays! Dancing with Renoir at the Moulin de la Galette, or accompanying him on picnics—to Argenteuil, Chatou, or perhaps Meudon. Sometimes they made love in the shadows of the garden in the rue Cortot. Love seemed to breathe about them in a rosy cloud in which they soared high above the common clay. In public they behaved as lovers were supposed to behave—with appropriate cooings and simperings, hand squeezings, and occasional displays of bad temper and jealousy, chiefly on Suzanne's part.

Early in the fall Renoir went to Guernsey, and Suzanne went

with him to pose for a nude which he was later to destroy but which he used in developing the ideas for the classical grandeur of "The Bathers," which took him three years to complete. The face of the central figure of the painting bears some resemblance to Suzanne, but the Goujonesque torso none. Yet Suzanne often claimed that the figure was hers, although by 1887, when the painting was completed, her romance with the artist was long since past and she was not averse to dismissing him with a spitting gesture and the contemptuous expostulation: "Ah Renoir! A fine painter. All brushes but no heart." But with the passing of many years, time was to ease much of the pain she felt at first and to leave it suffused with charm and delight. She could forget entirely that it was while she was with Renoir at Guernsey that he received word that Alice Charigat was coming to see him, and that he had met that situation by ordering Suzanne Valadon to pack up and leave.

III Friendship

ONE DAY IN THE SUMMER OF 1884, WHEN HE HAD CALLED unexpectedly for her in the rue Tourlaque, Renoir had discovered Suzanne at work on a drawing. "Ah, you too," he had exclaimed, "and you hide this talent!" But he had gone no further. He had not asked to see more of her work, had shown no further interest. And in the time they were together he had never again alluded to her drawing. Suzanne was certain that what he had seen of her work had made him jealous of her ability; that she could create vivid, dynamic line naturally and easily, whereas he had to labor over his technique. But in thus slighting her talent, she claimed, it was Renoir who first brought her the realization that she was really an artist.

Back in Montmartre once more and licking the wounds to her pride suffered at Renoir's hands, she was soon once again subjected to the opinions, disputations, theories, and dogmas of her artist friends. Art was the eternal subject of all conversation; and exposed to its jargon and its dialectics all her waking hours, she could not help reach a time when "breathing Art was better than breathing air." But it was her good fortune that she possessed the ability to do something more than pose, listen, and talk. Conversation and chatter led her to test the mettle of her own creative powers, to draw more pictures. This she chose to do secretly, apart from her daily

72

world. And in the very fact that she who was gregarious by nature could remove herself from her friends in order to apply herself to her work was proof to her of her serious purpose. The hours she was able to divorce herself from Bohemia were a secret joy—a fresh facet of independence which she was able to create for herself out of the simple instruments of paper, pencil, and charcoal. Nevertheless, these hours were more than mere retreat. They were productive. Without the aid of a teacher, purely from her own inner resources, and sometimes in spurts so powerful that she could not keep food on her stomach, she was learning to draw. What she might have garnered from conversation in a café or from observation in an artist's studio was being digested and developed into forceful technique and solid composition brimful of her own vivid emotions. But she did not need instruction in the formal sense, she needed badly the encouragement of a fellow artist: within it she would find the boundaries of control. It was this, perhaps, that she had hoped to find in Renoir, and it was his failure to come to her assistance at this time, as much as his physical rejection of her, that accounted for her bitterness toward him in later life.

But Suzanne had, in fact, little time to brood over Renoir's indifference. From two unexpected sources she was to come by help and interest which were to launch her securely as a serious artist. Two artists were to launch her—one a young man as yet unknown, the other the recognized dean, the most successful, the most respected of the Impressionists.

In the spring of 1887 a new tenant arrived in the large studio on the top floor of the building at No. 7 rue Tourlaque —a young would-be artist of twenty-two who had only recently completed his studies in Paris. Toulouse-Lautrec had studied first with the deaf master Princiteau, with whom he had learned to draw and had begun to work in paint; then with Léon Bonnat, "the painter of millionaires," who was to win dubious distinction in future histories of art by telling

the greatest draftsman of his day, "Your painting is not bad
. . . but your drawing is atrocious." Lastly he had worked
with Fernand Cormon, the artist who specialized in painting
prehistoric reconstructions. In Cormon's studio Lautrec first
made friends with Louis Anquetin, Vincent Van Gogh,
Henri Rachou, François Gauzi, and a coterie of other young
exuberants who, for one reason or another, were to become
his good companions for the remainder of his short and
brilliant life.

Scion of the counts of Toulouse, the ancient defenders of
the Albigensian Cathari, and of the viscounts of Lautrec, with
whom they had been united since the twelfth century, Henri
de Toulouse-Lautrec-Monfa was born on November 24,
1864, in the large house, part of which seems to have been
a portion of the old medieval wall, at Albi in Languedoc.
As a small child he showed little disposition toward following
the life of riding and hunting which seems to have been his
father's chief occupation. Apart from a short period during
which he attended the aristocratic Lycée Condorcet in Paris,
Lautrec's early childhood was spent under his mother's direction, either at Albi or at the Château de Malromé at Celeyran,
his mother's country home, where the time not devoted to his
studies was given to drawing pictures—a recreation in which
he seemed to find inordinate pleasure.

When he was fourteen years old he slipped on a polished
floor and broke his left leg. The following year, while walking with his mother near Barèges, he fell again and broke
the right one. Neither leg grew again and, after months of
immobility, the boy's entire physique took on an inexplicably
grotesque appearance. When he came to live permanently in
Paris at eighteen, he was a hideous little man with a body and
head too large for his fragile, shuffling pins of legs. He
walked with the aid of a cane. His nose was large—"big
enough for two faces," the singer Yvette Guilbert observed
upon first seeing him. His skin was dark and oily. A wiry

black beard wreathed his face. "I was horrified," Yvette Guilbert wrote, "until I looked into his eyes. How beautiful, how large, how wide, rich in color, astonishingly brilliant and shining! I looked at them for some time, and suddenly Lautrec, noting my expression, took off his glasses. He was aware that his eyes were his only attractive feature, and he generously unveiled them for my inspection."

Lautrec did not live in the rue Tourlaque. He shared a flat with a doctor friend at No. 19 bis rue Fontaine, but his rue Tourlaque studio immediately became the focal point of his life. There, attracted by the magic of his buoyant personality (and in a measure by the generosity of his purse) foregathered the first of those extraordinary companies of "characters" who for almost thirty years were to symbolize the spirit of Montmartre throughout the world—Adolphe Albert, the etcher; Tristan Bernard, the journalist and playwright; the critics Francis Jourdain, Arsène Alexandre, and the jovial, witty Gustave Coquiot; Maurice Joyant, Lautrec's erstwhile schoolmate and future biographer, not yet a famous art dealer but already a great amateur chef; Louis Bouglé, manager of a bicycle-chain manufacturing company and in off-hours a bicycle rider billed under the name "Spoke"; Aristide Bruant, whose argot songs and ribald wit at the cabaret the Chat Noir were one of the highlights of Montmartre night life, and a host of others. The order of business was talk. There were curses and tirades against the Bonnats and Cormons, boisterous approval or rejection of the work of Ingres or Delacroix, Manet or Degas, Monet or Pissarro. There were endless arguments over the abilities of bicycle riders, prize fighters, the power of the French navy, religion, Rosicrucianism, the virtues and faults of Seurat's Pointillism, or Symbolism, of Degas' "keyhole nudes," of Zola's *L'Oeuvre*, which repudiated Impressionism and which Cézanne took to be a personal attack on himself. The entire new Société des Artistes Indépendants came in for criticism as well as the Academicians and Impressionists. "Interplay of colors," "brushstrokes," "visionary qualities," "luminosity, color, and harmony" shared attention with less abstruse matters, such as the quality of the beer at the Belle Gabrielle, the amatory techniques of "the girls" in the rue d'Amboise, the wrestling matches at the Folies Bergère, the odds on the horses at Longchamps and Maison Lafitte, the disputes between the managers at the Vélodrome-Buffalo, or the performance of the new invention the telephone. The studio vibrated with chatter while Lautrec, a stubby figure dressed in a large white apron and with a towel over his arm like a waiter, hobbled between his easel, where he continued to paint in spite of the confusion about him, and the bar, where he mixed "cocktails" for himself and his friends.

Often he made these mixtures blindfolded. Or he would create the potion numerically by asking one of the company to choose a number between one and ten and another guest to choose a direction, right or left. He would then pour from the number of bottles selected by the first guest from the direction of the bar selected by the second one and pass the resulting drinks around. To prevent overindulgence in water on the part of the company he had goldfish swimming in the carafes. If Maurice Joyant did not oblige by preparing one of his delectable dinners, the evening's repast would be limited to salted herrings to keep everyone's thirst at an active pitch. Sometimes the party would gather up its bottles and proceed to other studios on the Hill (Anquetin was the son of a prosperous butcher and could also afford to supply drinks). Or they would install themselves Chez Bouscarat in the Place du Tertre, or among the Louis XIII trappings of Rodolphe Salis' Chat Noir, at Bruant's Mirliton (where he had recently started in business for himself), or along the railings at the Moulin de la Galette or in the *fauteuils* of the Cirque Fernando. Lautrec drank constantly—to anesthetize the pain in his legs—and in prodigious quantities. Yet he always managed to remain erect and was very proud that he could always outdrink any of his friends.

Sometimes he gave elegant dinners in fine restaurants *"en smoking,"* at other times homey "family" affairs in Père Lathuile's latticed garden in the Avenue de Clichy. He loved picnics and boating parties along the Seine. And frequently he was given to sudden inspirations which reflected the strength of his artistic passions and the originality of his mind.

"Lautrec was giving one of those elaborate luncheons he loved so to arrange," Vuillard, the self-styled "intimist" of the Nabis, tells us. "He knew the specialties of all the Paris restaurants, and so he decided that for this luncheon we would eat each dish at a different restaurant. It would be a veritable feast for kings. Lautrec brought the wine from his mother's cellar. Then, at the end of the meal, when our palates were stimulated to the highest pitch, we wondered what superb touch would conclude such a magnificent repast. Lautrec, inspired, rose and began to lead us—Heaven only knew where. He did not say a word. A bit suspicious as to what whimsical notion might be taking wing in his unpredictable mind, we followed him up three flights of stairs leading to the Dihau flat in the rue Frochot. With the most cursory acknowledgment of the tenants of the flat, he led us before Degas' portrait of Dihau playing the bassoon in the Opera orchestra, and announced with very deep feeling: 'There is dessert.' "

At these gatherings of Lautrec's Suzanne soon became a kind of unofficial hostess. Often she was the only woman present. To Lautrec she was, before all else, a fellow spirit, one who in this wonderful springtime could be a vibrant adjunct to the gaiety his soul craved. On fire for the dramatic and picturesque and openly at war with the commonplace, this little Montmartre model could flout convention as bravely as Lautrec himself. She spoke her mind with the ferocity of the *enfant terrible*. Her wit was pungent, her tongue acid.

She was very beautiful, the object of unreserved admiration among his men friends; and the fact that she was so and at the same time was *his* friend was something for which he was humbly grateful.

Perhaps it was in gratitude to her that he first evinced interest in her development as an artist. In much the same way as Renoir had happened upon her at work in her flat, Lautrec discovered her. He had come to ask her to join him at a party. (It was a source of deep satisfaction to him that she was so tiny that he could appear with her in public and seem less grotesque.) Suzanne was busy on a charcoal sketch. What Lautrec saw on her pad so delighted him that he forgot about the party and stayed, perched on the edge of a chair, watching her and marveling aloud at what she was doing. From that time onward he would often tap on her door with his stick and peek in to demand cheerily, "What is the good work today?" If she had any new drawing to show him, he would come in and, forgetting anything else which might have been in his mind at the moment, would give himself fully to a study of her accomplishment.

He was her first customer. He bought a couple of her drawings and hung them in his flat, where he amused himself by asking his friends to identify their author. Were they Degas' or Steinlen's, Willette's or perhaps Rodin's? It was agreed that they were certainly the work of an artist of stature, an artist who, if yet unrecognized, was certain to be heard of soon.

Often, too, Lautrec would call Suzanne up to his studio to criticize something he had done, for he seemed as respectful of her critical opinions as he was of her artistic ability. Frequently they would sketch together, comparing and analyzing each other's work before they consigned the completed pair of drawings to the fireplace in spite of each other's protests.

Between 1887 and 1890 Suzanne posed for him many times, although he was unwilling to pose for her. Such ugliness as his was a subject fit only for his own satirical brush. She sat for "Gueule de Bois," the hangover—sprawled at a café table. But it was not a pose she executed for money. It was unthinkable that their relationship should be reduced to professional terms: "Gueule de Bois" was a lark, an experience they shared in high spirits, a little private joke that came as an aftermath of one of Lautrec's less inhibited parties. On another occasion he painted her sitting in a straw yachting hat, elegant and youthful, and yet another time in the "Portrait of Suzanne Valadon," which now hangs in the Ny Carlsberg Glyptothek in Copenhagen, in the great butterfly hat he himself had helped her select. Both these sittings were held in the flickering sunlight of the garden of a neighbor of his, M. Forest. In this portrait, alone with the little man who has become her very true friend, the first one to know who she really is and where she is going, she sits pensive, lyrically lovely. He painted her with a gentle tenderness never again to be captured in any of the hundreds of pictures of women he was destined to produce.

As their friendship ripened Lautrec tended to assume a proprietary air toward Suzanne which she would hardly have countenanced from anyone else. He constituted himself her counselor, advised her what clothes to wear, and even went with her when she bought a hat. He told her how to handle her mother, what she should do about the education of her little boy, what she should eat, how she should look after her health. Even when he suggested that she change her name to Suzanne because Marie-Clémentine was too prosaic, she accepted the suggestion blithely and gave him the first drawing she executed over her new signature.

She had, in fact, a more profound reason to accept Lautrec's intimate friendship than he might have guessed. From earliest infancy her son Maurice had been subject to inexplicable fits of rage. Lying peacefully in his grandmother's arms, his body would suddenly stiffen and shudder violently. He would squeeze his eyes shut, bite his lips, and hold his breath until he went purple as a grape. In a panic Madeleine would rush to put him in a basin of warm water, wrap his head in a warm, moist towel, or feed him a *chabrot*, a hot mixture of soup and red wine which was believed by the peasants of the Limousin to be a remedy for many nervous disorders. Soon he would relax and go to sleep. As he grew older the boy would throw himself to the floor, beating it wildly with his fists and feet. He would kick over pieces of furniture, rip curtains or bed linen, smash his grandmother's china figurines. Or he would threaten to jump from the window of the flat or hurl himself before the traffic in the rue Caulaincourt. Equally sudden were his outbursts of grief. He might be quietly playing with a toy or watching the drays and carriages pass in the street below when tears would stream down his cheeks and his small frame would tremble in paroxysms of misery. At the sound of a doorbell, a pot boiling on the stove, or an angry voice directed at an animal he would be overcome with rage or dissolve in tears of sorrow.

Otherwise he was tractable enough—a small, frail, and solemn little boy with deep-set blue eyes and a gentle timid voice given to long rolling sentences which trailed off to a whisper or were left uncompleted. Suzanne, for all the affection she held for the child, was a poor mother. Always short of time and constantly spinning in the whirl of complications and ecstasies which were her professional life, she contributed very little emotional stability to the home. She, too, had her passions, her fits of rage, her bursts of strident laughter, her occasional vulgar humor. They did not make her an easy person to live with; and no amount of impulsive embraces, kisses, pats on the head, toys, and boxes of chocolates could disguise their lurking danger. Not that the little boy feared her or failed to extend toward her the sweetness of his tremulous affection. She had only to open the door and stand in the doorway and he would burst into tears with the joy of seeing her. He adored her. "Oh, my *maman*, how beautiful you are! I love you more than anything in the world!" he would sob. But Suzanne knew in her heart that Maurice could not help but be haunted by the knowledge that the vision of loveliness he treasured could be shattered utterly by her mood of the moment.

It was with his grandmother that he *really* lived, as Suzanne knew. Madeleine, having rejected the affections of her daughter, was determined not to make the same mistake with her grandson. With her Maurice dispelled the apathy she had felt toward the human race since her flight from Bessines, and on him she poured out the love which all her life had been suppressed. The child was her whole existence. She made his clothes. He slept in her bed. Together they played games. As he grew up they developed a special language which was theirs alone. It was she who first called him "Maumau," the nickname which remained with him the rest of his life. And in his turn he loved her with equal fervor. He loved to hold her hand and sit on her lap. He loved the purr of her voice. "Talk. Talk, *grand'mère*. It does not matter what you say—only talk."

Though Suzanne might have been jealous of this companionship, she was not. In fact she looked upon it with considerable tenderness and not without pride. It was as though, at long last, she had a gift to offer her mother which was being accepted with joy. Maurice was her gift. She had finally been able to present her mother with something of her doing which had met with approval. From the time she had been a tiny child she had hoped for this, and now it had come.

And yet she felt somehow that it was ironic that the little boy was not the perfect little cherub she would have wished to offer. One gift accepted in a lifetime should have been flawless. She could not close her eyes to the fact that Maurice was not. Often, bewildered and saddened by some outrageous thing the child did, she would turn to the only friend she knew who might console her—Lautrec, the genial, misshapen one. And somehow, from his optimism, won in the face of such appalling adversity, she would always take heart that in the end everything would turn out all right. There was no cause to worry about the strange behavior of her little boy.

It was Lautrec who insisted that she take samples of her work to Degas, who lived across the courtyard from him in the rue Fontaine. Degas was Lautrec's idol, the man whose work he most admired. Lautrec's enthusiasm for her work was not enough. For all his passionate determination to be an artist Lautrec had yet to create a ripple of interest in his own work. What *he* had to say of Suzanne's talent was meaningless. But if Suzanne was going to devote her energies entirely to drawing, as he thought she should, she ought to submit her work to the judgment of a *real* artist. And of the professionally genuine men of art there was no one whose opinion could be of more value than Edgar Degas'.

Of the thirty young artists who had exhibited in the First Group Exhibition in 1874 (later to be known as the First Impressionist Exhibition) Degas was certainly the one who had come the furthest in critical acclaim and public acceptance. Durand-Ruel, the dealer who had successfully popularized the work of Boudin, Corot, and Millet before the coming of the Impressionists, and who had given over his own gallery at 11 rue le Pelletier for the Second Impressionist Exhibition, had no trouble selling such works of Degas as he could convince that neurasthenic artist to part with. Edmond Duranty, the most knowledgeable of Parisian critics, put Degas' worth a good notch above that of the other Impressionists; and J. K. Huysmans, already a man of literary importance, was his impassioned champion. By the *cognoscenti* as well as by the public, Degas was considered the foremost painter of his day.

Degas had abandoned his study of law to enroll at the École des Beaux-Arts under Ingres' pupil Lamothe. More or less regularly over a period of ten years he had submitted pictures to the Salon, and for the most part they had been accepted and had won applause. But Degas had an intense respect for the creative ability entrusted to man by God, and it was only with chafing difficulty that he could bear to see talent shackled to the impoverished imagination of the Academy teachers. Man's productive powers were limitless: it was criminally wasteful to hold them to formulae.

Otherwise Degas had no fight with the Salon. For himself he was quite happy with the instruction he had received at the Beaux-Arts. To a person of his intellectual powers and originality, however, recognition by the Salon or from any official quarter was quite meaningless. For example, his contempt for Manet, who was frankly eager to receive the red ribbon of the Legion of Honor, was unbounded.

But in spite of his predisposition to chart and sail his own independent course, Degas felt himself drawn to the Impressionists. For all his doubting of their theories, they nonetheless offered a concerted revolt against the rigidity and prejudices of the established order; and his cold, logical mind told him that the group was more likely to succeed than the individual. Cynically confident that the revolutionaries would eventually attempt to hew all developments to their own set of intransigent theories, he was, for the present, willing to join their ranks. He was derisive of their shimmering sunlight and leaves, of the air which they sought to breathe into their pictures. "The air one breathes in a picture is not the air one breathes out of doors," he told Ambroise Vollard. Before a group of Monet and Sisley landscapes in the Durand-Ruel galleries he turned up the collar of his coat and growled, "I hate drafts."

The Impressionist passion for dissolving form into atmosphere infuriated him, for to his ordered mind drawing was

the very core of artistic expression, and he believed with
Ingres that "an object well drawn is an object well painted."
"The study of Nature is insignificant," he wrote; "it is in-
finitely more important to learn to draw from Holbein." To
Degas, the presence of a human being in a picture was worth
the most meticulous draftsmanship: he had no patience with
the Impressionist inclination to treat the human silhouette
accidentally. And although he himself became more and
more dependent upon color for his effects, he maintained that
color was far less important than line. Still, he recognized in
the Impressionist revolt an acceptance of the reality of the
times in which he was living—a modern world distinguished
by its scientific restlessness and eagerness for truth. And it
was from that world, he insisted, that the art of his own day
must come.

The fleeting moment as modern reality thus became the
substance of his art. No poses. No contrived prettiness. He
selected the angles of realistic vision—the view from above,
the view from below, the subject off center, foreshortened;
the unnatural gaslight, the ungainly, even vulgar movements
from which magically beauty springs in the intimacy of a
woman's toilet, at the *barre* of a ballet class, at the ironing
board or wash tub, on a street corner, at a café, in a theater.
His was the camera's click, the instant solidified in incisive,
unfaltering line which precisely rendered the life of the
nineteenth century.

Degas the man was as restless as his day. He was a Royalist
at a time when the monarchy had been forever lost to France.
He was successful at a time when the failures of his associates
bore an aura of nobility and immortality. Even his economic
security was inappropriate: the great work was supposed to
be done by the poor. But while the other artists wore workingmen's corduroys and berets, Degas dressed in tweeds like
an English dandy. Physically he seemed to have come out of
the Second Empire, yet his point of view was so far in advance

of his day that he was already developing techniques for photography, a science which was as yet virtually unborn.

Degas might align himself with the Impressionists and might, indeed, assume leadership in organizing seven of their eight exhibitions, yet he would always be an outsider. It was not in his nature to "belong." He was deeply suspicious of "schools" and "movements." Even in his relations with members of his own family and with his friends he maintained a respectable distance. When he was still a very young man he began to have fits of depression and hypochondria which were to remain with him, growing ever worse, to the end of his life. In 1870, when he was enlisting in the artillery, the doctors discovered that he was losing the sight in his right eye. Nevertheless he was accepted for military service. He never saw combat, but he was billeted uncomfortably and claimed later that the dampness had further accelerated the loss of his vision. The doctor's diagnosis unnerved him: he began to wait for blindness.

In 1886 Degas relinquished the bulk of his fortune in order to help a brother who had lost heavily in American cotton speculations. From then on he was occasionally obliged to sell some of his pictures. He now became painfully frightened. He had always disliked parting with his paintings. Durand-Ruel continually pleaded with him to increase his output; but with Degas it was a question not of meager production but of his unwillingness to separate himself from his work. He wanted to rework everything he accomplished. It had to be perfect; in his eyes he knew it never would be, but he wanted his work around him. He could love a picture trustingly as he had never been able to love a living creature. Many times he would borrow a picture from someone who had bought it on the pretext that he wanted to retouch it. He would then forget to return it. The singer Faure had to go to law in order to recover two pictures Degas had "borrowed" from him eleven years before and had consistently promised to return "in a few days" or "tomorrow." Henri Rouart, another friend, of somewhat cannier substance than Faure, chained and padlocked his Degas pictures to his walls and insisted he had lost the keys.

When he was in Paris he walked—long hours in the back streets where he could escape from the familiar surroundings of his living quarters, his studio, or the cafés he had once known. In his flat he artificially created a sense of movement and instability by constantly shifting the furniture and the pictures on the walls. "It's the movement of things and people which both distracts and consoles me," he wrote to his friend Rouart; "that is, if it's possible to be consoled when one is so miserable. If the leaves of the trees don't stir, the trees are as miserable as we are."

Degas was given to moving fretfully from place to place; he could not stay long anywhere. In 1872 he had stood on the platform of the Gare St. Lazare to bid farewell to his brother, who was leaving for New Orleans. On the spur of the moment, as the train began to pull out of the station, he hopped on: he ended by sailing to the New World. After six months in Louisiana he returned to France—Paris for a while, then to Menil-Hubert near Gace (Orne) to stay with his friends the Valpinçons; then to Dieppe, where he first met Gauguin, one of the few contemporaries whose work he bought for his own collection; to Couteret to take the cure for his asthma; to Mont St. Michel; to Le Havre; to Burgundy, Italy, Sicily, Spain, and Tangiers.

As he grew older his depressing moods increased and he began to speak cynically of his work as "articles"—pieces of merchandise destined for the vulgar marts of trade, the art galleries. And he showed little disposition to finish any work he began. Unendingly his eyesight was a subject of his complaining. "*Ah, la vue, la vue, la vue!*" he whined. Yet his vision was not nearly so bad as he would have people think it was. True, his housekeeper Zoë read him the newspapers each day, but he could spot on the opposite side of the street an acquaintance who happened to miss seeing him, and would complain to Ambroise Vollard, the dealer, that people snubbed him on the streets. He still did the close work of engraving and lithographing. Nevertheless, he was increasingly querulous and contentious. Few who knew him came to see him, and many went out of their way to avoid him. "A great wrangler and formidable debater," Paul Valéry found him, "especially sensitive on the subjects of politics and draftsmanship."

Long before he was an old man, indeed, Degas had become perfectly adamant on the subject of draftsmanship. It was the cornerstone of art, he claimed, just as Ingres had; and, as we have seen, his main quarrel with the Impressionists arose from the fact that they neglected draftsmanship in their obsession for light and fresh air. Degas was unwilling to accept the notion that draftsmanship might be achieved solely by an artist's own efforts, by the development of a natural talent; he felt that it should be studied laboriously. It could be achieved only by endless repetitions and rigid discipline. Furthermore, draftsmanship could result only from a deep appreciation of the great masters of the past—Ingres, Leonardo, and others.

All this Lautrec had heard and listened to. But he did not believe. In proof, he told the Master, he would send him a "natural artist"—one who had never received instruction from anyone and who had probably never even seen a drawing by Ingres or, for that matter, even a painting by Leonardo.

Thus Lautrec laid the groundwork for the meeting in 1887 which to Suzanne Valadon was always to be "the wonderful moment of my life."

"Lautrec's great brown eyes laughed behind his thick glasses, and his mouth was as solemn and grave as a priest's when he told me I must go to M. Degas with my drawings," Suzanne was to recall many, many times. The event had the aura of a Victorian theatrical about it—the young girl for some unknown reason dressed in all her best things, and those things "all wrong." Her hat would not stay straight; there was a gap in the toe of one of her patent-leather shoes, her huge portfolio weighed her down. Then Degas' somber, cluttered house, his formidable starched housekeeper, the interminable wait in his study while she smarted with bitter chagrin over the fact that she had given her name as "Marie-Clémentine" and not as "Suzanne," her artist name. The pictures on the walls were swallowed in darkness: she could not make them out. From the corridor came a sudden blast of tyrannical rage directed at a servant. Finally the Master appeared through the *portières*, a lean little man with quick, shrewd, sunken eyes, high-domed forehead, suspicious mouth. Was he hero or villain? Not until later did she remember having seen him in salt-and-pepper tweeds, swathed in scarves at the Nouvelle-Athènes, when she was a child. But once she remembered, she never forgot the vision. At the age of ten she had mysteriously noticed one who years later would play a large part in the molding of her destiny.

Degas took the portfolio from Suzanne as though it were a package from his tailor, half muttering a "Thank you" in his querulous nasal voice. He moved toward the light by the window, hobbling like an octogenarian and complaining that he was losing his eyesight and was plagued with a cold. With unbearable slowness he went through the drawings—without much interest, she thought. From time to time he looked up from her work to Suzanne herself, and each time she was certain he found something disagreeable in both. His heavy lip seemed to droop, but soon the almost perpetual sneer which flickered about his mouth dissolved. He wiped his eyes with his handkerchief, shifted his weight, and went through the drawings again. At last, turning to face her as she sat in the straight-backed chair at the opposite side of the room, he snapped the portfolio closed. "Yes. It is true. You are indeed one of us."

It was a performance destined to mark the beginning of a friendship that lasted the rest of Degas' life, and the only unbroken one he was ever to maintain with a woman. From that day Suzanne was Degas' "terrible Maria," his "ferocious Maria."

To an artist who, like Degas, spoke of himself as "a colorist with line," Suzanne's drawings could not help but be impressive. They were drawings in pure, savage state. The firm outlines were bold, achieved with economy and certainty. They were totally without refinement, yet they were pliant and graceful. They were free of invention, candidly realistic, but in them was the fever of the artist who created them, also the earthiness.

That earthiness was the quality in her personality which made Suzanne Degas' good and lasting friend. She was the type of woman with whom his social position would not ordinarily have brought him into contact. Degas was pitifully afraid of women of his own class. He could not abide their artifices, their deceits, their intrigues. Alone, of all the women he knew, Suzanne was forthright and honest. While his housekeeper Zoë, with a poor show of diplomacy, warded off the ladies of the *faubourgs* who eternally called to see "dear M. Degas," he pleaded with Suzanne to pay him a visit. "Do not miss coming next Sunday, please." "How are you, my poor Maria? Do let me have news of you." Or, "It is now nearly a month and I have not answered your good wishes for the New Year. I have been confined to my room with I know not what. When fancy takes you, or you have time to come, please do not fail to come and see me."

He wanted to hear what was going on on the Butte and to share the latest gossip. No longer was he capable of being a part of the life which surrounded him. He was ill and aging fast—in his own mind, at any rate. His eyes were worse every day. No one could bring him in such a lively and gay way as his "ferocious Maria" the glimpses he hungered for of that world from which he had resigned. She alone could capture it all for him and deliver it with the spriteliness it demanded. As it came from her lips it would be colorful, mad, passionate, punctuated with the argot of Montmartre, rich in raillery.

But even more than for the lively accounts Suzanne would bring, Degas wanted to see her for her drawings. In his later years he lived a hermitlike existence on the three top floors of an old house in the rue Victor-Massé. The top floor was crammed with his own pictures and pictures he had bought before he remembered that he had no place to hang them. The floor below was his studio. Below it were his living quarters, their walls hung solidly with drawings and canvases. Of these, the drawings seemed to provide his only flashes of delight.

"I look at your red chalk drawing in my dining room. It is still hanging there," he writes to her. "And I always say, 'That she-devil Maria, what talent she has!' Why do you show me nothing more? I am approaching sixty-seven. . . ."

When in 1894, at his insistence, she sent five of her drawings to the Salon de la Nationale, he bought one of them beforehand, and upon arriving at the exhibition the closing day, found the drawings withdrawn. He wrote to her:

"You must have taken your drawings away from the Champs de Mars, Illustrious Valadon. Come and bring mine tomorrow morning. Bartholomé* will have written to you about one of them he was terribly anxious to have. . . ."

---

* Paul Albert Bartholomé, the sculptor and a mutual friend. Degas was unduly pessimistic in this instance. The four remaining drawings were sold at the exhibition. Bartholomé later became an avid collector of Valadon drawings.

But it was not only at the expositions that he watched for her work. He called at the print shops and the smaller galleries.

"Terrible Maria, yesterday at LeBarc I wanted to buy your excellent drawing, but he did not know the price. . . . Come if you can tomorrow about 9:30 with your portfolio to see if you have something better."

Another time he beseeched her:

"I have been in bed and am late in answering you, terrible Maria. Come and see me with drawings. I love seeing those bold and supple lines. Happy New Year!"

Or once again:

"At last, terrible Maria, I am replying to your good wishes. It is influenza. It is bronchitis—everything. You, for your part, are getting along all right? Happy New Year and Good Drawings! You will come soon and show me."

In his last letter to her he said:

"They tell me I am still delicate and must beware of cold on my left side. You must, in spite of the illness of your son, bring me some of your wicked and supple drawings."

It has long been said that Suzanne Valadon owed no debt to any other artist, that hers was entirely a spontaneous and uninhibited talent. Degas himself believed so. Yet today it is impossible to look at her drawings, with their unexpected perspectives, their foreshortenings, their off-center figures, without feeling that her composition was not without its debt to Degas.

Degas supervised her first engravings. They were made in his studio on his press (which, by a curious coincidence, is now used by the artist Demetrios Galanis in the house at No. 20 rue Cortot, which Suzanne so long inhabited). Following Degas' advice, these engravings were made on zinc, a medium much more sympathetic to her broad lines than the more conventional copper. And it was Degas who prevailed upon

Vollard to present an exhibition of these engravings in his gallery in 1895.

To Suzanne Valadon, Degas was always "the Master," the only artist in the world worthy of that respectful title. Whatever he said, it was at once the wittiest and wisest thing she had ever heard; whatever he did was supremely intelligent. To her, his irascibility was charm; his bitterness had the pious air of martyrdom. She alone, of all who knew him, had sympathy with his illnesses, imagined as well as real. In her company she would tolerate no snickering reference to "Degas and his hypochondria." Of all the men she knew, only Degas did she class as a genius. And to her, his genius excused his hypochondria as it did all his other faults. "He has powerful feelings which we are too insignificant to understand," was her blanket defense of him.

When it was suggested that she might have been the model for one of his sculptured dancers, Suzanne was furious. It must be clearly understood that she had *never* posed for Degas, that she was his friend and not one of his models. Their relationship had been on an altogether different plane: artist to artist, mind to mind. There were very few people in the world who could claim to have been a friend to Edgar Degas, but Suzanne Valadon had been. Of this she was prouder than of any other friendship she was ever to have. She had brushed against the angel's wing.

IV   Lovers and the Artist

IN 1888 MIGUEL UTRILLO WAS BACK IN PARIS. FROM GERMANY he had gone to Belgium and had finally returned to Spain to take a position as director of a mining construction company in Cordoba Province. The job lasted only a year. He then went to work with his friend Rusiñol on the construction of a miniature reproduction of the Battle of Waterloo for the Universal Exhibition at Barcelona. The fateful battle of the century was ingeniously reconstructed with the aid of several hundred gallons of oil paint, mirrors, motors, and lighting effects which gave the illusion of acres of battlefield and life-sized fighting men and horses. It was the sensation of the Exhibition.

At the close of the Exhibition, Miguel made his way to Paris, this time to act as art critic for Barcelona's largest newspaper, *La Vanguardia*; and with Rusiñol he took up quarters first in the Boulevard de Clichy, and in the fall of 1891 in a room next to the bar at the Moulin de la Galette.

One evening, shortly after New Year's Day of 1891, he is supposed to have been dining with Suzanne Valadon, Toulouse-Lautrec, and a group of their friends at the Auberge du Clou in the Avenue Trudaine when one of the company asked Suzanne point-blank if she actually knew who was the father of her child. "I've never been able to decide," she is supposed to have replied. "I don't know whether the little fellow is the work of Puvis de Chavannes or Renoir." Where-upon Miguel is said to have exclaimed, "Why, I would be honored to sign my name to the work of either of those fine artists." The story is no doubt partly apocryphal if for no other reason than that so far as is known, her affair with Renoir postdated the birth of the boy. But a few weeks later, on February 27, Suzanne and Miguel appeared at the *mairie* of the 9th arrondissement where Miguel signed the "Act of Recognition," the text of which ran as follows:

"27 February 1891. Act of Recognition of Maurice, Masculine Sex. Born 26 December 1883 and inscribed on the 29th following at the *mairie* 18th arrondissement as son of Marie Valadon and unnamed father. Set up by us, Charles-Paul-Auguste Bernard, assistant to the mayor, officer of the civil state 9th arrondissement, on the declaration made by Michael (Miguel) Utrillo, 28 years of age, journalist of 57 Boulevard de Clichy, who has recognized as his son the aforementioned Maurice. In the presence of Charles Mahaut, 44 years of age, em-ployed, residing in Paris, 5b Impasse Rodier, and of Félix Dunion, 44 years of age, waiter, residing in Paris, 3 rue Saint-Rustique, who have signed with the peti-tioner and ourselves after reading. Paris. 8 April 1891."

It seems improbable that at the age of twenty-eight Miguel Utrillo would have made this extravagant spontaneous ges-ture, which would certainly involve him in the manifold responsibilities of paternity, if he had not had sufficient cause to do so. He was no longer an impetuous boy. After seven years' experience in the world of business, he must have known the full meaning of his signature on a legal document. The fact that the machinery of the Act of Recognition was set in motion at the end of February and did not come up for signature until six weeks later allowed him ample time to reflect on the wisdom or folly of his action. Yet he filed the application, waited the prescribed length of time, and signed the Act. It seems hardly reasonable that he would have done so had the statement of the Act not been true.

At the time Miguel signed the Act of Recognition, Suzanne no longer had need of financial assistance. She had formed a liaison with one of Miguel's friends, Paul Mousis, a wealthy banker. It was rumored that, good man though he was, Mousis wanted to marry Suzanne but refused to accept Maurice as his son. In bestowing his name upon the boy, some people were saying, Miguel acted as much to please his friend as to honor his former mistress. However, since Paul Mousis was quite willing to accept Maurice as a member of his household and (as subsequent events proved) to be a very good friend to him, it is extremely unlikely that it would have mattered to him whether the lad's name were Valadon or Utrillo. If he did not want it to be Mousis, he could hardly have cared what it was. Here too, then, Utrillo's recognition of the child would have been pointless were the boy, in fact, not his own.

As Maurice grew to manhood there was strong physical evidence that he was Miguel's son. The two men were of identical height. They had the same massive skull structure, the thin-lipped line of mouth, the black hair, the deep-set brilliant blue eyes, the long rectangular fingers. Among their studies at school each showed a greater disposition for mathematics than for any other subject in the curriculum. The rolling rhythms of Maurice's speech strongly resembled Miguel's. And men like Edmond Heuzé, Gustave Coquiot, and Raoul Dufy, who knew them both, often commented upon the similarity of many of their gestures—the way they both ended a question with a dead pause followed by a quick shrug of their shoulders; the way they sat pigeon-toed in the cafés; the way they nervously clenched and unclenched their fists when they conversed.

As these resemblances became evident over the years the question was often put to Suzanne—was Miguel Maurice's father? The same question was often asked in respect to Puvis de Chavannes, Rodin, Bartholomé, Zandomeneghi, Renoir, Lautrec—almost every male who had lived in Montmartre during that period. For all such questions Suzanne had enigmatic answers much like the one she had given at the Auberge du Clou. It was therefore extremely curious that when Miguel's name was put forth as a possible father, then and then only did she have a quick and definite response: "No. Absolutely no. Miguel Utrillo is not the father."

If anything, her denial strengthened suspicion. Weren't the boy's eyes exactly like Miguel's? One did not see eyes like them in thousands. Didn't Suzanne remember how Miguel used to open and tighten his fists when he talked—the way the little one does? And when he speaks, the way his words roll along on top of each other and fade away at the end! Did she not remember the young Catalan's voice?

Miguel had been gone from Paris only a short time when Suzanne first told the story she was to repeat again and again throughout her life until she herself believed it and was confident the rest of the world did too. Maurice was, at the time, eighteen years of age, and the circumstances of her life made it expedient for her to account for the boy's strange and tragic behavior. She blamed heredity. Maurice's illness was inherited from his father—a dissolute young man named Adrian Boissy who, indeed, had briefly been her lover before she sat to Puvis de Chavannes and who, in 1901, had conveniently been dead for more than a year.

In her telling of the story Maurice's father and her first lover became miraculously one and the same man. The picturesque Moulin de la Galette was the setting of the melodrama. It was a Monday night, so different in atmosphere from the Sunday afternoon and evening proceedings when mothers and chaperones monitored the deportment of their

Left. Portrait of Suzanne Valadon in the hat he bought for her, by Henri de Toulouse-Lautrec. *Courtesy of Ny Carlsberg Glyptothek, Copenhagen. Below.* Nude Reflection. Pastel drawing by Suzanne Valadon. Undated. *Courtesy of Paul Pétridès, Paris.*

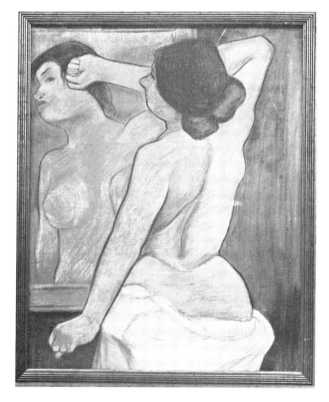

Sacré-Coeur. Oil painting by Suzanne Valadon. 1929.
Courtesy of Paul Pétridès, Paris.

young charges. On Monday nights the Moulin was the playground of the Montmartre underworld. Women and girls
were admitted without charge. And what a crew they were!
—pickpockets, thieves, nymphomaniacs, lesbians, and prostitutes, disporting themselves with the brutes, drunks, dope addicts, hoodlums, and gangsters who were the terrors of all
Paris. Occasionally a group of students, perhaps a little the
braver for the wine they had drunk, would go slumming
among this flotsam. They would take with them their female
companions of the moment—a muscular laundress, a dancer
from one of the cabarets, or one or two of the adventurous
models. According to Suzanne's account, it was while she
was on such a slumming adventure that events led to her
seduction.

There was a brawl, as she remembered it. The music
stopped. The lights went out. There were feminine screams
and flying fists. A knife flashed. And she found herself,
terror-stricken and weak, in the arms of Adrian Boissy, a
drunken accountant from an insurance company. He
bundled her off to his studio flat off the Place Pigalle. There
he plied her with drink which she dared not refuse. And in
the course of one frightful, hideous night he cruelly raped
her.

A couple of years later Boissy suffered two savage attacks
at the hands of apaches whose women he had wronged. Until
he lost his job and his money ran out, he continued to abuse
a string of miserable prostitutes who visited his studio daily
to satisfy his insatiable lusts. After that he became a tramp, a
clochard rambling aimlessly about the Butte, soaked in alcohol
and caked with grime. For a while he slept in a dustbin behind an ironmonger's shop on the Boulevard de Rochechouart. He finally died of acute alcoholism in a tenement
doorway during a heavy snowstorm in the winter of 1899.

For the rest of her life Suzanne insisted that Boissy was the
loathsome villain who had vilely seduced her when she was

hardly more than an innocent child and that Maurice was the child of that unfortunate union. It was from Boissy, clearly, that Maurice had inherited the passion for alcohol that was to develop. Had she admitted that Miguel Utrillo was the father of her son (or that anyone else not addicted to drink was the father) she might have hinted that the source of the boy's malady stemmed from *her* side of his family. She had strong reason to suspect that indeed it did. She had only to cast a glance at Madeleine and her ever-present brandy bottle to know where Maurice's obsession for alcohol may well have come from. Furthermore, gossip had long had it (unjust though it was) that Suzanne herself had an uncommon appetite for drink. Therefore, to admit that anyone who did not have a history of excessive drinking might be the father of her son would have strengthened the belief that she was the one who was responsible for the terrible curse on the boy. In selecting Adrian Boissy as the boy's father Suzanne was confident she had put the responsibility for the curse on Boissy's shoulders.

Only once was she known to have a good word for the wretched insurance-company accountant, and the reporter in this case is Maurice, hardly an unimpeachable source, especially in matters which concerned his mother. "It was in the rue Girardon," he told Francis Carco. "He [Boissy] went by on the pavement with several other 'characters,' and she said to me, 'That's him, down there with the beard . . . a fine drunkard too.' Then she added, 'But I don't ever want you to think ill of him, for in spite of all his vices, to me he'll always be the troubadour who sang of the windmills of Montmartre.'" "The Song of the Windmills" is the title of a poem by a minor Montmartre poet named Gabriel Boissy, a contemporary of Maurice's and, incidentally, a friend of Guillaume Apollinaire and Picasso. Suzanne wanted Maurice to believe her story, and he alone, of all who heard it, did believe it.

But ultimately she was to admit at least on one occasion that Miguel Utrillo was Maurice's father. Two or three days after Miguel's death at Sitges in January, 1934, Berthe Weill, the art dealer and one of Suzanne's close friends, happened upon an obituary photograph in the Barcelona newspaper *La Vanguardia*. Never having seen Miguel, Berthe Weill was immediately struck by the resemblance between the photograph and Maurice Utrillo. Armed with the clipping, she hastened to Suzanne in the rue Junot, where she found the artist depressed and listless. Yes, Suzanne knew Miguel Utrillo was dead. She had received the word directly from Spain. All her old friends were dead. Yes, she had known Miguel "rather well" in the old days.

"*Ma foi!*" Berthe Weill exclaimed, bringing out the photograph. "It's Maurice! The spitting image. The same eyes. The shape of the head. The expression!"

Yes, it was so, Suzanne confessed wearily. Miguel was Maurice's father. And because Miguel was dead now, she spoke long and fondly of the days of their youth when they had been together, of the meals they had eaten beneath the arbors of the Guinguette, of parties at Lautrec's studio, of the night they had pushed the cart of fish onto the dance floor at the Élysée-Montmartre. Yes, Miguel would always be a delight to her.

But within a few days of the interview with Berthe Weill, Suzanne was to deny to Edmond Heuzé that she had ever had anything more than a passing acquaintance with Miguel Utrillo. She had never laid eyes upon the "so-called Act of Recognition" he was supposed to have signed. Everything that was being said about her relationship with the dead Spaniard was senseless gossip. If Edmond Heuzé believed such nonsense, let him go to the 9th *arrondissement* and find any such document as an Act of Recognition! Heuzé went instead to the 18th *arrondissement* and found it.

In Barcelona, however, neither gossip nor the Act of Recognition were being blithely dismissed by the executors of Miguel Utrillo's estate. In April, three months after Miguel's death, his two Spanish sons journeyed to Paris to see Suzanne. Under Spanish law an illegitimate child was entitled to a share in his father's estate unless his claim against it was disavowed by his mother.

Mme. Nora Kars, a close friend of Suzanne for many years, was present when the two young Spaniards arrived in the rue Junot, and has given the writer an account of the interview which followed. Suzanne had called her to witness the proceedings. "It is very important. It may even be historic, *chérie*," Suzanne had warned. Nora Kars's account leaves little doubt that on this occasion Suzanne was acting the part of a heroine in a melodrama, and that the point she wished to make by her histrionics was the point she chose so dramatically to deny.

"The young men stated their business," Mme. Kars relates, "and Suzanne, who had been apprised beforehand of their mission, promptly denied that her son had any claim on their father's estate. She asked for the necessary documents and signed them. The conversation then went on to inconsequential chitchat, which ordinarily would have bored Suzanne. But she sat on the edge of her big chair, squinting with keen interest at each young man as he spoke. It was plain that she was amused not by what the young men were saying but by what she was thinking. The chitchat had continued for some time when suddenly she bounded to her feet. 'Wait a moment!' she cried, and rushed upstairs. She was gone for some time. When she returned she carried a packet of letters—oh, there must have been fifty of them, tied with a colored ribbon. She sat down and untied the ribbon, and from the packet she drew out one letter. 'I will read you something,' she said with great intensity. She read the letter over to herself first, licking her lips and mouthing the words as she always did when she read to herself. Then, just as she seemed on the verge of reading the letter aloud or perhaps passing it to us, she leaped to her feet and tossed it into the fire. She stood before the fireplace with her back to us watching the flames consume the paper. At last, after riffling through the rest of the packet, she tossed it too into the fire. 'No,' she said, facing us again, 'it was not your father. I did not know him very well.' She glanced back at the packet burning in the fireplace and shrugged her shoulders. . . . This is what she wanted us to remember, not the words she had spoken. 'It is all over, now.'

"And when the young men got up to leave she presented them with a set of her drawings which she had promised to give me. They were all nude studies—all except one, which was a portrait sketch of Miguel Utrillo. 'Maybe you would like to have it as a souvenir of this afternoon,' she said. 'I've held onto it a long, long time. I don't have any more use for it.' "

When Maurice was five years old Suzanne enrolled him at the Pension La Flaiselle in the rue Labat. It was a long walk up the hill from the rue Tourlaque which the spindly little fellow negotiated tightly gripping his grandmother's hand. Or if he did not go with Madeleine, it was Catherine, the Breton maid, whose hand he clung to. He was terrified of school and did very badly. His entire day was spent in a long hideous wait for his grandmother or Catherine to take him back to the security of his home. Suzanne was aware of his terror, yet could not bring herself to accompany him to school or to be at the school gate when his purgatory for the day was over. To her, his fears and terror were cowardly and absurd. She could see no connection between the torture he obviously endured away from home and the rages and depressions he suffered, for as he grew older his spells of violence—of curtain-rippings and china-breakings and tearful paroxysms—did not become less frequent or less intense as the doctors had assured her they would. She saw them now as examples of weakness of character—of cowardice, of self-indulgence. And remembering her own fearlessness at the same age, she was more inclined to be ashamed of the child than sympathetic with him.

Yet she could share his triumphs with great pride. When he picked out chords on Lautrec's piano, all Montmartre knew. And when, at the age of eight, he was reading the works of Zola, she bore his opinions of them to the tables of the cafés in the rue Fontaine. She did not confess that it was Madeleine who was responsible for this phenomenon, that it was her mother who had hired a tutor for the boy. But when something went wrong, when there were fits of anger and tears, when Madeleine's china figurines went hurtling through the air, Suzanne vanished from the scene to forget about home with a lover or by joining a group of her lighthearted friends at a party.

Early in 1888 the lover was Paul Mousis. A young well-to-do banker and avowed bourgeois, Mousis had become a nightly habitué of the Auberge du Clou and the Chat Noir, where he had been accepted as "a worthy Philistine" by the convivial coterie of artists for whom he bought drinks with an open hand. It was a short spiritual journey from the Auberge du Clou to Lautrec's studio, and it was there that Suzanne met him—a bemused fish out of water who, by his affability if by nothing else, was able to defend the political policies of Jules Ferry in company which ignored politics, and to ignore the establishment of Antoine's Théâtre Libre in a company which considered the event a major one in world history. Mousis immediately fell in love with Suzanne, and before many weeks had gone by he proposed marriage. She coyly turned down his offer and countered with a willingness to become his mistress. It was an arrangement that Mousis was obliged to accept on her terms, for he was soon aware that in being her lover or "her protector" he was in no wise her master. The liaison had scarcely been established when Suzanne's constancy stood threatened by the appearance of the bizarre figure of the composer Erik Satie.

Once again the meeting place was the Institute of the Chat Noir, where Satie for a short time had been employed by Rodolphe Salis as "second pianist." The son of a minor Parisian composer and music publisher and of a mother who composed for the piano, Erik was a year younger than Suzanne, having been born at Honfleur, Calvados, May 17, 1866. When he was thirteen he entered the Paris Conservatory, where, in contrast to the grim manner in which he pursued his courses, he often entertained fellow students and teachers alike by improvising humorous parodies of the verses of Villon and Ronsard to his own accompaniment. At twenty he interrupted his musical studies to don the uniform of the 33d Infantry Regiment in service at Arras. It was a short military career, for within a few months he evolved for himself and two of his companions a "health-building" regimen of cross-country running from which he contracted severe bronchitis, and was invalided out of the army.

Shortly after his release he published his first two compositions for piano—"Valse Ballet" and "Fantasie Valse," and the following year came "Gymnopédie" and "Trois Sarabandes." Here were harmonic processes which forty years later were to be recognized as the outstanding characteristics of "the Modern French School," but having initiated them, Satie did not develop them further. Once he stated an idea, musical or otherwise, he was virtually finished with it.

He was not a "serious artist." In a sense, he was rather sick of the world and chose to mark his disgust by assuming the role of a bewitched eccentric. He was possessed of devils of a somewhat waggish bent. The peculiar dead-pan humor of Normandy, the *pince-sans-rire* and repertoire of extravagant caprices and idiosyncrasies he acted out with a comic flair; and to the Montmartre of his day he presented, in all, a new type of buffoon—the enchanted intellectual. Cynic and misanthrope that he was, his very disbelief in life left a void which only religion could fill. And since the world was ineffably repugnant, he looked to the occult to dwell in a happier one. His search led him to the work of "Sâr," Josephin Pelédan, and the Catholic Rosicrucian movement known as the "Rose et Croix du Temple et du Graal." "How vain is painting which would have us admire the representation of things which in reality we would disdain!" So ran the motto of the cult.

From 1885 to 1895 most of Satie's compositions were occult-religious in character. In the end, however, nobody else's religion was likely to satisfy him. Eventually he withdrew from the Rosicrucians and organized his own church—the Metropolitan Church of the Art of Jesus the Conductor. At the peak of its membership he had a dozen followers.

At the conclusion of his "turn" at the Chat Noir on the evening of their meeting, Satie left the piano to greet Paul Mousis and Suzanne at the corner table where they were sipping beer. Within a matter of minutes Suzanne commanded his complete attention. He lost no time in informing her that he thought they ought to get married. "I breathe with care, a little at a time, and I dance very rarely," he informed her.

"It was my last chance," he later reflected. "It was then three o'clock in the morning—an impossible time to get to the *mairie*. After that it was always too late. She had too many things on her mind to get married, so we never brought up the subject again."

Within a week they were lovers, and Suzanne found herself caught up in a whirlwind of fantasies, wit, and madness transcending anything she had ever known. So dazed by what now went on before his eyes, even Paul Mousis could not retreat. Cuckoldry held for him amazing facets of fascination. Or was it cuckoldry? True, his "wife" had a lover. Everyone knew it, but so did he. That fact had no bearing at all upon their own physical relationship. She had, he was proud to admit, abundant passion to serve two men.

Meanwhile Satie, bearded and wan, with his long hair and gleaming intelligent eyes behind his thick pince-nez, dressed always in soft gray velvet with shoes and top hat to match and with a flowing gray *lavalière* at his throat, leaped into his newest role—conductor of a bizarre triangle. He bought Suzanne necklaces of sausages. He took her to the Luxembourg Gardens to sail toy boats. He sent an enormous funeral wreath to her son Maurice "so that you may learn the names of the flowers and make up better ones." He wrote passionate letters to Madeleine "because I know you cannot read them." He hired two small Negro boys to march before them beating small drums the night he took Suzanne and Mousis to Fort's Théâtre d'Art to see Pierre Quillard's *The Girl with the Chopped-off Hands*. For her birthday his gift to Suzanne was a paper sack "with all the wonderful smells of the world in it."

While he occupied himself with devising these capers he turned out strange little atonal compositions such as "Real Boneless Preludes for a Dog," "Things Seen to the Right and to the Left (With a Groping Fugue)," "Three Waltzes of Affected Disgust." These he performed in friends' studios, often with Suzanne at his feet. On such occasions he explained that it was she who radiated the love that nurtured his inventiveness despite the fact that she knew nothing about music. "She will never get a rapt expression on her face like a spaniel of a critic, and she has a tender little belch which is often inspiring."

But for all his antics, the pivotal position of the triangle was firmly Suzanne's, and she did not fail to capitalize upon it. To Mousis she presented herself as the will-o'-the-wisp bacchante—the spirit of love as well as the body. To share her, she quite convinced him, was a greater accomplishment than to possess her wholely. She was a gem so rare that a man of his bourgeois background was indeed blessed to have glimpsed her. While she mended Satie's socks and cooked his white meals ("I eat only white food—eggs, sugar, scraped bones, dead animal fat, veal, salt, and coconuts"), ran his errands, kept a chart of his temperature, and slept with him wrapped in blankets on the bare floor of his studio, Mousis was well convinced that she was the only woman in the world who could satisfy him sexually.

Having created this illusion, Suzanne herself was quick to believe fervently in it. It was no time at all before she was convinced not only that both Satie and Mousis needed her, but that in her turn she loved each of them passionately.

It was nonetheless an arrangement not destined to ride long on an even keel. Highly amusing at first though it might be, Mousis' bourgeois breeding would not allow him to accept it indefinitely. He called for its breakup, was refused, and finally went away in a huff. When he returned, six months later, it was Satie's turn to demand Suzanne's undivided attention. Her refusal sent him to seek consolation in the Christian Rosicrucian Movement. He commemorated his return by composing a song, to be dated Easter Sunday, 1893, entitled *"Bonjour, Bigui, Bonjour,"* on the title page of which he executed a prim "authentic portrait" of Suzanne in pen and ink. In 1894, on the eve of her first exhibition at the Salon de la Nationale, Mousis fled once again—this time to Italy and later to the North African coast. Upon his return he and Suzanne moved into the small gray house at No. 2 rue Cortot, two doors from Satie, and it was from here that many people living on Montmartre today remember "Madame Mousis" driving forth about the Butte in her trap drawn by a mule with little brass bells in his mane and with his tail plaited with bright silk ribbons—a pair of wolfhounds at her feet and a parrot in a cage beside her.

In Satie's bare room at No. 6 Suzanne painted Satie's portrait, her first in oils. And it was there that they had their final breakup—on what specific grounds no one was ever to discover, but that it was a violent and dramatic one the neighbors in the rue Cortot often attested to. Speaking of it to one of his disciples in later years, Satie recalled: "The Master was the most melancholy of humans. He bawled and he threw himself to the floor to weep bitter tears. Suzanne was the only one in the world from whom he could draw the spirit his soul required. She was the anchor to his sanity. If she left him, all would be lost. He sobbed and fainted."

But when the scene was over, she left. Immediately he sat down and wrote her the first of the letters he was to write for almost thirty years in which he protested over and over again that his love for her was indestructible and eternal, that there was no life without his Bigui.

Five years after this parting, Satie left Montmartre pushing a wheelbarrow containing his effects (two wooden benches, a small rectangular table, and a wooden chest) down the hill and across the southern reaches of the city to the grimy little suburb of Arceuil-Cachan and a room over a bistro. No one else ever set foot in that room except to remove his corpse in 1925. "There are mosquitoes here which have certainly been sent by the Freemasons," he wrote, "and the disgusting smells of the tanneries which are too precious to ignore."

Without the distraction of Erik Satie, Suzanne was able to give time to her work. If her appearance at the Salon de la Nationale failed to impress the art world, it at least produced an amusing anecdote which put her name on the tongues of the Parisians. It seems that a mediocre academician, Jules Valadon, was also among the exhibitors at the Nationale. By mistake he received from the critic of the *Argus* a laudatory letter intended for Suzanne. In due course he forwarded it to her, at the same time writing to her to demand what she intended to do about any future confusion arising from the fact that they bore the same surname. He had decided, he informed her loftily, that henceforth he would sign his work "Jules Valadon, Chevalier de la Légion d'Honneur." To which Suzanne replied immediately, "You might also use the signature 'Merde'!"

The Salon of the Société Nationale des Beaux-Arts organized under the leadership of Meissonier and Puvis de Chavannes had come into existence in 1890 after a battle over the question of awards to exhibitors within the Société des Artistes Français, the annual "official" Salon. As early as 1884 a group of artists under the leadership of the young and fiery Georges Seurat had signaled their dissatisfaction with the official Salon by forming their own "Société des Artistes Indépendants," to which any artist who paid the modest fee might belong and might exhibit in what was hoped would be a yearly salon. There was no jury and there were no awards. But, even more than evincing its distaste for the politics of the Salon, the new organization spoke for the tremendous surge of new ideas and new concepts which were now sweeping aside the old. Impressionism, like a lovely crystal goblet, had been shattered by the clamorous voices of Divisionism, Symbolism, Neoclassicism, Synthesism, the Nabi movement, and a host of individual expressions unallied with other movements. In the short period of twelve years between the First Impressionist Exhibition and the Eighth (and last one) the course of Impressionism had been brilliant and incandescent. On the Realist side it had spoken for the nervous technological changes which had altered the life of the city since nineteenth-century man had put his faith in the machine; on the purely Impressionist side it had brought a new concept of light and a renewal of vision. The singularity of the instant was the basic emotional experience of the men and women of the day. Man was the sum total of the individual moments of his life. And this obsession with the significance of the moment the Impressionist painters had couched in terms of elegance and fastidiousness despite all the bleating by their critics about their "disorganization" and "sloppy brushwork."

There were no tears at the breakup of the movement. The artists themselves were eager to be free of it, to refortify their creative powers independently, and to dedicate themselves to new ideas. To have stayed together longer as a group would have meant to become an academy themselves. Already the critics, hostile at first to the movement, talked of it in doctrinaire terms as a set system by which they measured the worth of the rising generation of artists. It is certainly to the credit of the Impressionists that, although they had begun to enjoy monetary reward for their work, they chose to turn their backs on financial success rather than submit to sealing up in a vacuum the living ideal which had been the substance of Impressionism. With the exception of Monet and Sisley, who continued to paint in the Impressionist style, though in doing so they were ruled by their sensibilities rather than by a desire for gain, they became a part of a modern renaissance. Color architecture, the expression of emotion through color, abstraction, symbolism, and the unconscious mind became the fields to which they now directed their interests. Cézanne retired to Aix and Gardanne in the South to undertake endless research in "the strong experience of nature." Renoir, who in 1883 had already wearied of painting out of doors, occupied himself with classical traditions which the critics attacked as cold and dry just as vehemently as once they had taken exception to his "rainbow palette." Degas, who had always refused to paint from nature and who in organizing, with Berthe Morisot, the last Impressionist Exhibition, had insisted that the word "Impressionist" be dropped from the publicity, continued to explore the unexpected angles of vision which were to become such an important part of the graphic arts of the next century. Berthe Morisot began to search for form at the expense of the exquisite light of her early painting, using long, flexible brushstrokes that followed her forms, in place of the strokes which ran in all directions that characterized her Impressionist period. Camille Pissarro joined the Pointillists. And on the threshold stood the new independent spirits—Seurat, Van Gogh, and Gauguin and with them Lautrec, Bonnard, Signac, Valloton, Redon, Denis, Bernard, Sérusier, and the other young men whose names were later to be identified with the Postimpressionist Period.

Postimpressionism was a historical epoch rather than an artistic movement. It represented no clearly defined "ism" and claimed no homogeneity. It was merely the chronological boundary for the formation, dissolution, and re-formation of a host of schools, movements, and groups which appeared on the scene in the wake of Impressionism. Such groups as existed within the limits of its dates bore no clearly definable relationship to one another or to a greater whole. Yet there was among both the groups themselves and the artists who remained apart from them a constantly shifting interplay of ideas which was a continual source of influence upon the work of all.

In the shiftings Suzanne remained apart. For all the enjoyment she found in their society as a model, she was uneasy about her association with artists on an intellectual level. She was conscious of the fact that she was untrained, that as yet she had done very little painting and had actually produced few drawings. Then, too, she was intellectually incapable of understanding the multifarious new concepts about which the artists seemed to live in constant turmoil. The history of the development of art was a subject about which she knew nothing. To her, art was purely a personal expression, the product of her emotion. Before any theory she believed in her own natural gifts and her own physical power to express her feelings in her drawings. Capricious in almost everything else, in one thing alone she remained constant—to make her work expressive of her turbulent passions. She realized innately how, to one of her temperament, that constancy might be disrupted by intimacy with her fellow artists. She could envision its possible devastation of her sensibilities. Perhaps she remembered that day not so long past when Vincent Van Gogh had brought one of his paintings to Lautrec's studio in the rue Tourlaque. It was one of those occasions when the "cocktails" were flowing and Lautrec's friends were lounging about wrangling over the past, future, and present of Art. Van Gogh, then thirty-three (an old man!) had recently arrived from Antwerp to be near his brother Theo, who managed Goupil's Gallery around the corner in the rue Caulaincourt. The Dutchman was full of art now, as once he had been full of Christ, whose words he had tried to bring to the horrible coal-mining district of the Borinage in Belgium a few years before. His green eyes burned with the sacrificial fires of dedication, and he wanted nothing so much as to be accepted as an artist among artists. The fury of his own words made his hands shake. He was too old, too furious, and too humorless to be a part of the exuberant company of Lautrec's studio. He came now because he felt that the only language he knew was the language these people he was among understood, and because the little dwarf had kindly invited him. Years later Suzanne described the scene. "He arrived," she said, "with a large canvas under his arm which he set up in a corner in a good light. And then he waited for it to be noticed. No one looked. No one said anything. He sat in front of it, watching for some expression from his fellow artists, trying timidly to coax a word of encouragement from their conversations. Then at last, wearied, he left, taking his picture with him. You painters are cows!" Suzanne exploded.

However, at the Exposition Universelle of 1889 Suzanne stood face to face with the work of an artist whose power she was unable to resist. The language he spoke she understood: it was before her in several canvases only recently brought back from Martinique. The artist was Paul Gauguin.

She attended the exposition with Degas, who spoke glowingly of Gauguin's passionate dedication to his art and quizzically of the sacrifices he had made in order to pursue it—how he had given up his job in a stockbroker's office and left his wife and family. In 1886 he had gone to Pont-Aven in Brittany, where with a group of friends he had evolved a theory of art which he called Synthesism. Here simplified forms, color as intense as it possibly could be, shadowless drawing, and "a free treatment of nature" combined to speak as a symbol for the artist's thoughts as well as his emotions. The following year, with a young painter friend, Charles Laval, he had fled France with an undigested notion that he might be able to participate in the building of the Panama Canal and at the same time paint the intense colors of the tropics. In Panama he went to work as a laborer, but the strenuousness of the work left no opportunity for painting. After a few months, and with a bit of money for his labor, he moved on to Martinique, where he and Laval set up their establishment in a hut in a cocoa plantation among the Indians, Chinese, and Negroes. There Gauguin painted the seventeen canvases he was to show at the Exposition Universelle. But by the beginning of 1888 Laval came down with malaria and in one of his deliriums tried to commit suicide, and Gauguin became wretched with dysentery. They decided to return to France together.

Gauguin was nursed back to health at Montrouge, where his friend and former associate in the stockbrokerage office, Émile Schuffenecker, now had a house and a studio. In the summer he returned to Pont-Aven, where he painted with Émile Bernard, Laval, and Serusier at the Pension Gloanec. In October he answered Vincent Van Gogh's plea to join him at Arles: for three tortured months he attempted to reason the desperate Dutchman from insanity. Fleeing finally after the violent outburst when Van Gogh cut off his ear, he arrived in Paris in time to organize the opening of the art exhibition at Volpini's during the Exposition Universelle. There, an extraordinary figure in his long blue coat with mother-of-pearl clasps, astrakhan cap, green and yellow collars, and white kid gloves, he prowled the galleries. The pictures including paintings by Émile Schuffenecker; Émile Bernard, who under the name of "Meno" also exhibited some "pictures done with gasoline"; Louis Anquetin; Léon Fauché; and Louis Roy. Volpini's café, where the exhibition was held, was on the Champs de Mars in front of the Press Pavilion and in the shadow of the Eiffel Tower (which was built specially for the occasion). It was held in a hall painted in pomegranate-red, and the pictures were all framed in white. In competition with this attraction Signor Volpini directed the public's attention also to the presence in his café of a "Russian" orchestra comprised entirely of women violinists and a male trumpeter under the direction of a "Princess Dolgouska." Among the visitors to the café the princess proved the bigger attraction.

But what Suzanne saw on the pomegranate walls was deeply moving. The sinuous, heavy black lines of the arabesques which gave the painting of Gauguin and his associates at once the quality both of primitive art and of the sophisticated Oriental cloisonné enamels was to her the "glorification of the decorative plane." Here was the direction in which the firm line of her drawing might lead. The Symbolist ideal, however, she dismissed as she was wont to dismiss anything she did not understand. There was in her no urge to adopt the Pont-Aven techniques in order to create some mental cerebration or an imaginative suggestion of her dreams. Whereas Gauguin and his friends strove to create in their canvases an intellectual or a spiritual adventure, Suzanne was determined to reduce her own experience purely to visual and emotional terms. Years later she was to sum up her reaction to the show when she admitted to Gustave Coquiot that she had been "impressed much by the techniques of Pont-Aven," but that she had then decided "to pursue them, but without the vestiges of aestheticism or artiness."

Shortly after the exhibition at Volpini's a group of her drawings of Maurice as a naked child were shown in the exhibition called "Impressionists and Symbolists" held at the gallery of Le Barc de Boutteville in the rue Pelletier. Her work stood in company with Gauguin, Bernard, Daniel de Monfreid, Anquetin, and that of a new group—the Nabis— philosopher-painters led by Bonnard, Vuillard, and Maurice Denis. Denis had already issued the manifesto of the Nabis, the oft-repeated phrase of the next fifty years in the history of painting: "A picture—before being a war horse, a nude woman, or any subject at all—is essentially a flat surface covered with colors assembled in a certain order." This was strange company indeed for a young woman who believed, above all else, that her painting was the instrument of her emotions. Yet to some degree Suzanne's decorative style was akin to the Nabis' two-dimensional conception of space even though her passion for life was revealed in her bold lines. Her elemental human drawings must have been difficult for the Nabis to reconcile with their misty beliefs. Yet the drawings were so beautifully composed that they seemed to be in complete harmony with the other painters' work. All of them were sold. Francis Jourdain, the art critic, then but a youngster helping Le Barc hang the show, was struck by their power—"Suzanne Valadon's line was crude but firm, executed with undaunted courage which gave her studies unexpected character and revealed a mania for truth."

Degas, who had been responsible for her appearance with the Impressionists and Symbolists, had also been responsible for her first one-woman show at Vollard's the year before.

Recently arrived from Réunion Island, Vollard opened a gallery-cellar in the rue Lafitte, where in addition to exhibiting the works of new artists he prepared succulent casseroles for friends and customers. The place was quick to become a hub and forum for the artists of the Butte. At Vollard's Suzanne exhibited twelve remarkably supple and dynamic zinc etchings, nudes in various attitudes of their toilets, prepared in Degas' studio with the Master himself supervising the work. Degas was wretched. By now his eyesight was very bad. "It is too difficult," he kept moaning as he went over the plates time and again with a magnifying glass. As far as his own work was concerned he had practically given up painting altogether. He worked in pastels almost exclusively or modeled small figures of nudes and dancers in clay without bothering to have them cast. But mostly he puttered over his enormous collection of paintings and drawings by his contemporaries, many of whom, he was convinced, had taken the paths he had discovered and had long ago overtaken him. The series of anarchist bombings which shook Paris in the spring of 1894, culminating in the assassination of President Carnot at Lyons in June, terrified him. He saw nothing but disaster ahead—for himself and for the world. When he could muster enough courage to venture out of the house in the rue Victor-Massé he fled to the country, visiting the few friends he could still tolerate.

In October, Colonel Henry's revelation in *La Libre Parole* that Captain Alfred Dreyfus, a Jew, had confessed to charges of communicating military secrets to a foreign power unleashed a wave of anti-Semitism. Degas roused himself enough from his misanthropy to add his voice to that of the anti-Semites. Immediately his health and his eyesight took a turn for the better; he had, at last, something tangible on which to pin his misery. Within less than three years he had cut himself off from a twenty-five-year-old friendship with Pissarro, who was a Jew, and Claude Monet, who was a

Dreyfusard, and a host of his old acquaintances, to say nothing of the young artists, who were in the main passionately pro-Dreyfus in their sentiments. It was perhaps as well that his Suzanne "knew nothing about such things."

As a result of the exhibition at Vollard's a number of small galleries began to take an interest in Suzanne's work and to send her orders for etchings. Vollard ordered a hundred additional prints of her "Two Girls Drying Themselves," observing to Degas that most of the etchings he had sold had been bought by artists. Artists had little money and could buy only what they believed in. They did not pay much for the etchings of Suzanne Valadon, but they bought them because they believed in her art. On the Butte people were heard to speak of her as "Mme. Valadon the artist."

V   The Curse

BUT THE PATH AHEAD HAD BARELY BEEN SEEN WHEN THE course of Suzanne's life veered from it. In after years Suzanne put the responsibility for this shift upon Paul Mousis. Even before Erik Satie had been removed from the scene, Mousis had begun to lose his taste for Bohemia and to maneuver himself back into the bourgeois atmosphere whence he hailed. His wild oats sown, he was ready to create for himself that domestic tranquillity prescribed by the society of his day for the life of a banker. And having won himself a talented "wife" and having accepted generously the responsibility of providing for her family, he felt it his due to enjoy the aura of approbation which could never be his in the hedonist world of the Butte.

In the spring of 1892 he took the first step in the direction of reclaiming respectability by leasing a house in the village of Pierrefitte, some twenty-five kilometers north of Paris in the Seine valley. Ostensibly the place was to serve merely as a country retreat for himself and his family for weekends and holidays, but almost immediately, using Maurice's unstable state of health as an excuse, he established Madeleine and the boy there on a year-round basis.

The geographical shift was a bitter blow to Maurice. From the Pension La Flaiselle, he had gone to the Collège Rollin, where his scholastic record had begun to show marked improvement, owing particularly to prodigious performance in mathematics. Coupled with the fact that his stepfather provided him with a generous spending allowance, his proficiency in mathematics earned him the respect and friendship of his schoolmates. In a short time Maurice had become one of the most popular boys in the school. Although he could still be made wretched by a harsh word or a snub, he had already learned that a quick smile and not-too-hearty laughter were armament against pain, and that he had in himself the power to muster them. For the first time in his life Maurice recognized the possibilities of human companionship. No longer did he bolt from the school gates to the shelter of his home. He lingered among his companions, smoked cigarettes with them, and drank beer in the cafés after school, and on one or two occasions loitered long enough to send Madeleine scurrying frantically through the darkening streets to search for him.

This pleasant way of life was disrupted, of course, by the move to Pierrefitte. Not until he was a grown man did he speak of it, and then hardly with resentment: it was for him only one more bewilderment in a pattern of life he never understood.

Madeleine, for her part, was sublimely content to have her grandson to herself and to find about her, once again, the lazy tranquillity of a small town. By this time she was well into her sixties, shriveled, gnarled by rheumatism, and fretful. She had never liked the city, had always been a stranger to the Butte; and the restless Bohemian existence her daughter led had been a long, thorny trial to her. Whether it was her age or whether it was because she still drank steadily, she moved about in a vague, babbling daze in which the sole point of reality seemed to be the little fellow, her grandson, now entrusted to her care. Only when she was with him did the querulous tremolo leave her voice, her dull watery eyes catch the light of life, and her bodily movements assume their peasant stolidity. The old woman and the boy shared a secret world which she had created. It was built of private little jokes and interminable silly games and a language which was theirs alone. Except for the few hours he spent in the village school, it was uninterrupted. A deep coziness permeated their lives together. To anyone who observed them strolling through the village or sitting in cane chairs in the garden on a summer afternoon as the boy read aloud to her and she clucked happily between naps, the affectionate calm of their lives would have been impressive. But the old woman knew how fragile such moments were. For all the outward peace of their existence, she was more than ever unable to control the terrible moods which had dogged Maurice since infancy and which, now that he was alone with her in the country, seemed to be becoming more frequent and more violent. When such fits of rage or grief possessed him she was powerless. The *chabrot* no longer worked its charm. She would give him a glass of wine instead, even though she soon noticed that wine was as likely to aggravate his seizure as to dispel it. At such times he would scream "More! More! Or I'll run away and never come back." Panic-stricken, she would give in, filling one glass after another until he was insensible and she could put him to bed, hoping above all else that the neighbors had not heard.

In the summer of 1894 Mousis began to build a new house on the crest of the Butte Pinson, which divided Pierrefitte from the adjoining village of Montmagny. Ostensibly it was a business project, an investment in real estate, but by the time it was finished, Mousis had pretty well convinced Suzanne that if she was going to be a serious artist she would have to dissociate herself from the frenetic atmosphere of Montmartre. How seriously Mousis actually took her work we do not know; how much of his plea was flattery it is impossible to say. We have it from Maurice that "this man whose memory I respect, lived in an atmosphere that had nothing to do with artistic matters." But the fact that Mousis was among the very first to interest others in Maurice's art and that, eager though he was to divorce himself from the Butte, he was still willing to allow Suzanne to maintain the studio in the rue Cortot, indicates a certain sympathy not easily found among the Philistines. At any rate, there was enough truth in Mousis' plea to convince Suzanne that the "artiness" which surrounded her was destructive to her talents, and that in order to bring her powers to maturity she would have to tear herself away from the distractions of the Butte.

It was not easy for her to leave. Though she repeatedly told herself that she would be able to arrange her daily life so as not to interfere with her work, that Madeleine and the Breton maid Catherine, and whatever other help she wanted would be quite able to run the household, that Maurice would be out of the way in school nearly all day, when the time finally came for the move she was frightened. She was, at core, a creature of the twisted streets. The *brasseries*, the bistros, the butter-and-cheese shops, the bare-armed laundresses, scurrying grisettes, the pushcarts, the pigeons in the gutters, the cats on the crumbling walls were all a part of her bloodstream, more so perhaps than the urge to draw and paint, more certainly than the swarms of artists with their high-flown theories and arguments, egocentric drives, and protean verbiage. She was a *Montmartroise*, not by adoption or affectation but because Montmartre was the only world she had ever known. To her it was not picturesque. She did not want to paint it, catch its lights, romanticize its moods. It was home, ugly and cluttered as a kitchen. And even though she could convince herself of the necessity of deserting it momentarily as an expedient, she sensed that deep within her lay the conviction that her future was inexorably bound to it, that somehow she would return to draw from it the ultimate glory of her work.

The house at Montmagny, rectangular and massive, with its green tile frieze of entwined garlands below the eaves and its cement urns in the Grecian style atop its pediments, looking out through a hillside grove of young chestnut trees to the sweep of valley and blue zinc roofs of the village, was a monument to acumen in banking. Suzanne now stood at the palace door, and the palace was hers. There was a rose-marble foyer, a parlor and dining room with their bulging satin-upholstered furniture reproductions in the style of Louis XIV, their vitrines stuffed with Grandfather Mousis' gold and purple Sèvres porcelain with Imperial N's on them, alabaster statuettes, ormolu chandeliers and mirrors, walls hung with stuffed trophies of the chase, and oil paintings depicting scenes from the victories of Napoleon I. Did Suzanne dare to refuse to enter?

Perhaps unconsciously for some time she had been preparing herself for such an environment. Apart from the emotional factors involved, the liaison with Mousis had given her economic security, and she was now sufficiently convinced of the importance of her creative work to appreciate the advantages of security. Being a breadwinner, for all her apparent casualness, had been a heavy drag on her productivity. The long hours spent in studio gatherings, parties, and café disputations and discussions, all inseparable from her work as a model, had likewise interfered with her progress as an artist. In both cases Paul Mousis offered release. But from the first Suzanne also realized that in accepting Mousis' help she would eventually be subject to his will. A successful banker was not likely to tarry overlong in a studio in Montmartre. Ultimately she would be faced with the decision of either letting him go his way—in which case she would be left to face the same struggles she had had before he came into her life—or else going with him. And even though he appeared to have a genuine interest in her life as an artist, she knew that secretly he harbored the hope that in moving her to Montmagny he was establishing a permanent and respectable ménage of which she was hardly more than another graceful adornment.

He had counted on her zest for life to fill the void created by her desertion of Montmartre. He understood her temperament well enough to know that, faced with a new situation, she would not waste time mourning the past. He calculated well. Before very long Suzanne had assumed a domestic role and was acting it out wholeheartedly to the delight of his friends and business associates, to say nothing of their middle-class neighbors. The pair were mammoth fish in the little pond. Their home, the most pretentious in the area, was also the most animated, the most lavish, the most gracious. Staffed now with a cook, a butler-coachman, a corps of gardeners, and two housemaids besides Catherine, the Mousis kept something of a perpetual open house, with weekend house parties, elegant luncheons, elaborate dinners, and musical soirees. Over them all Suzanne presided with the air of a miniature young duchess—lovely, exuberant, her personality now flushed with authority and well-being. A cool, slightly theatrical grandeur dominated her social manner. As a hostess she seemed to combine the most desirable attributes of both sexes, to exhibit simultaneously masculine directness and feminine tact, a woman's voluptuousness and a man's sense of humor. Her temperament, full-blooded as it had always been, in its present aspect appeared attractively astringent rather than brash or diabolic. She cultivated a taste for fine food and wine, and kept a close eye on the kitchen and wine cellar. If she failed to read the latest novels of M. Daudet or M. Ohnet, she remembered enough of what was said of them at one gathering to be able to talk about them knowledgeably at the next. Her reading was pretty well limited to *La Vie Parisienne, Modes Parisiennes,* and the *Journal des Modes.* With such literary ammunition she was able to chat airily with the ladies about the latest designs of Worth, Creed, or Coucet, Mme. Colas' lingerie or the *chapeaux* of Mlles. Romain. Her own wardrobe was chic and simple.

Toward men she maintained an attitude of genteel politeness in keeping with her position as wife of a banker. It was an air perhaps a shade too neatly drawn, for by its rigidity it suggested that she had formerly been of quite another disposition. A similar hint was to lurk in her attitude toward the collection of furniture and bric-a-brac which surrounded her in her home. It arrived haphazardly in bulk shipments from dealers in Paris or Chantilly, to be disposed of as free floor space or free shelf space alone decreed. She collected in order to fulfill one of the functions of her class, because it was expected of her—with little interest and no affection. A subtle eye would have noted that she had but recently been quite comfortable in sparser quarters.

There was, in fact, a murmuring restlessness underlying her air of authority. Today it would be called an inferiority complex. But she was resolute enough in purpose to keep it fairly well under control. It found no expression in irascibility or contentiousness. She never preached. Her conversation was always good-humored, albeit sporadically salted with cynical observations or waspish criticism. But in the perfection of her role there was a constant current of nervousness. That she would remain permanently and securely as she was—ladylike, even-tempered, lighthearted—few who knew her believed.

However, her life at Montmagny was not wholly an accomplishment in stagecraft. Suzanne still found time for her creative work, less, it is true, than in her most productive Montmartre days, but she succeeded in completing several sets of drawings, etchings, and lithographs. At first she worked only in the studio in the rue Cortot which Mousis retained for her, journeying back and forth to Montmagny in the little dogcart drawn by the mule Mousis had given her upon his return from North Africa. But as time went on, and particularly when the weather was severe, she worked at "the Château of the Four Winds," as Mousis had dubbed the big house on the Butte Pinson. She became quite fond of the little village with its gray, hall-like main street, its blue-smocked workingmen and bulbous ambling housewives, its perpetual bakery smells, and the voices of its ever-crowing cocks. She began to paint in the woods and fields about the village; in Montmartre she had never drawn or painted out of doors. Later she prevailed upon several of the village people to allow her to paint their portraits in their own homes or in their gardens. It was at Montmagny that she developed the simple palette which was to serve her for so long and which was to be developed so brilliantly by her son—two chrome yellows, vermilion, Turkey red, and white zinc. She also turned her hand to furniture designing—large undecorated pieces of yellow oak and walnut, the last sort of furniture one would expect from one who lived surrounded by reproductions of Louis XIV. In connection with this furniture it is interesting to note that Mousis was enthusiastic about it, if not artistically, commercially. He installed it in his office, whence he proceeded to sell it to his colleagues. These poor men were obliged to keep it at their places of business: it was unwelcome in the houses of wives who aspired to lovely furniture like Mme. Mousis' in the Château of the Four Winds.

At Montmagny Suzanne developed the passion for flowers, fierce and constant, which was to remain with her the rest of her life. From earliest childhood she had inherited the Parisian's love for a little bowl of color, a pot of greenery. At Montmagny she was to know flowers in the forests and in the fields, alone in poignant splendor, in grassy blankets, or in surging sweeps of vertiginous color. She could not be out in the countryside or in the village streets for a quarter of an hour without discovering some kind of root which was certain to turn her garden into a miracle of splendor. With the jealousy of a governess she brought it home to consign it to its place in the informal variegated masses she grew in the English style. She spent long hours in the garden, pruning and planting and squabbling with the gardeners. And the children of the Butte Pinson, peeking in at the gate and seeing her clad in brown corduroy pantaloons and a blue workingman's smock, reported at home that Mme. Mousis had "a little Chinese working in her garden."

Her performance as wife of a banker might have jogged along uninterrupted a long time. The aura of pleasure, once constructed, was agreeable enough and quite durable. There was something of the indolence of convalescence about it, and to one who had never before known the luxury of relaxation it was fraught with benign possibilities. But hardly had half a year gone by when Suzanne's peace of mind received a severe jolt. Maurice ran away from home, and after a twelve-hour search the police found him dead drunk, with three drained wine bottles, in the forest.

At first Suzanne refused to believe the incident had occurred. She accused her mother of having neglected the boy, intimated that Madeleine had been drunk herself and had urged the child to drink and flee the house. Mousis, taking stock of the boy's surroundings—the doting grandmother, the unstable mother, the foreign atmosphere of the house itself —and appreciating (perhaps from his own experience) the disturbing effects of dislocation upon an adolescent, prescribed the boy's return to the Collège Rollin.

His decision seemed immediately to bear heartening results. Maurice was visibly delighted with this latest shift in his fortunes. The last day he went to the village school he wept all day for happiness; and the first reports from the Collège Rollin were more than encouraging. He enjoyed commuting between Montmartre and Montmagny. Still small for his age, and frail, he was deeply thrilled at the size and power of the locomotives, hissing their white clouds of steam, their enormous boilers throbbing with the burning of crimson coals as he stood beside them in the station shed. The black sheen, the bright brass pipes, the clang of couplings fascinated him as living things. Then to be on the train! To be riding through the tunnels, through the long corridors of grimy, crumbling buildings out onto the sweep of the valley with its low-lying fields and tiny plowmen, propelled by the fantastic power of that tremendous giant, the engine—certain, relentless, and furious! It was a vision which was to stay with him always. For the rest of his life he never saw a train without being once again caught up in the ecstasy he had known as a small boy standing on the platform of the Gare du Nord, or with his face squeezed tightly against the cool of the compartment window as the train tore, powerful and relentless, across the valley of the Seine. Many years later, when he had grown up, his mother bought him a toy electric train; and playing with it for hours, he recaptured those delightful memories of commuting with such intensity that beyond the little track before him the world ceased to exist.

However, neither the fascination of the trains nor the facts that he was doing passable work at school, that he was well provided with pocket money by his stepfather, and that he was living once again with his adored mother, was enough to draw Maurice away from the bewitchment of drink. At the cafés the waiters would serve him *rouge* as though he were a man. At the little round marble tables he would stand drinks for those of his schoolmates who would join him. When he ran out of money, he would travel third class instead of second as his stepfather's allowance provided. The wooden benches were small inconvenience for the number of *pinards* the money would buy. Wine was cheap, but he also liked cognac and absinthe. But, curiously, neither of these more potent drinks seemed to satisfy him as wine did, especially red wine. And although later in life he would drink eau de Cologne, fuel alcohol or even ether in his desperation to escape from the world about him, it was for the *rouge* only that he actually thirsted, and he drank only *rouge* if it was available.

Once the first report came from the Collège Rollin that Maurice was making satisfactory progress and, indeed, notable strides in mathematics, Suzanne paid little attention to his activities or his moods. She scoffed at Madeleine's oft-repeated stories of his drinking during the time they had been alone in the house at Pierrefitte. The old woman talked less and less sense as she grew older. That Maurice behaved a bit strangely sometimes Suzanne had to admit. He was given to protracted periods of brooding silence. He never laughed or smiled. There was often a vague, faraway look in his eyes. He was forgetful, shy, and nervous. But these lapses, she was certain, were characteristics of adolescence; they would pass. And when the school reports showed a deterioration in the quality of his schoolwork, she dismissed them with a guffaw. At his worst, she was sure, he was a better scholar than she had been at her best in the hands of the sisters of St. Vincent de Paul!

Finally came word from the school that the masters had reason to suspect that Maurice was attending classes in a state of intoxication. The first of these reports aroused Suzanne to scornful laughter. How preposterous could schoolmasters be! A second and a third report served only to heighten her derision. But it was derision born of fear, and ultimately she could not resist the impulse to bespeak her suspicions to the boy. The results hideously confirmed what she had refused to believe. Maurice flew into a violent rage. He tore his shirt and began to howl like a dog. Panic-stricken, she tried to embrace him, only to be thrown brutally against the wall. In an effort to avoid his flailing fists she stumbled, and he tried to kick her. Cowering in a corner before his maniacal rage, pleading desperately for him to calm himself, weeping, shivering with terror, she heard herself offer him a glass of wine. It was a moment she could never again entirely wipe from her consciousness. He was calm immediately, waiting for her next move, the blue flames of his eyes boring into her—commanding. She fetched him the wine and poured a glass for him. He took it and smiled. Then with measured calm he drank it off and quietly demanded another. She poured it for him, and in doing so she arrived at the turning point of her life.

Until now Maurice had certainly been a minor force in her existence. Equally obsessed with the need to give expression to her artistic power and to draw from her environment the fullest degree of pleasure, she had been unfettered by maternal feelings. From time to time she would take her son for a walk or for a visit to the studio of one of her artist friends. Toulouse-Lautrec gave him a comic drawing of a cow and at another time a sailboat. Degas was uneasily kind. Otherwise there was little beyond a kiss for him now and then, a hurried impulsive embrace; and she was gone—the lovely butterfly vision vanished. He was out of her mind entirely.

Now with dramatic swiftness, as any emotional shift was bound to come with Suzanne, her entire relationship with the boy was changed. For all her laxity and apparent irresponsibility, nature had given her a deep love of human companionship. Far more sincerely than most people she longed to engender well-being and pleasure in others. If until now her life had been untouched by actual tragedy, she had the generosity which made her eager to offer the best of herself to a fellow human being in distress. How much stronger must this impulse be when the person involved was her own son! The vigor of her spirit welled up in a tidal wave of compas-

sion and tenderness toward the child whom she now recognized as a desperately sick boy in need of her ministrations.
And as in everything else into which she threw her energies,
there was a suspicion of theatricality about her passionate
reaction. Suzanne Valadon became, all of a sudden, the she-
wolf defending her young.

Obviously it was only a question of time before she would
be torn between her loyalty to the man she lived with and her
new devotion to her son. From the start she was completely
frank as to what her decision would be if pressed to the
choice: unhesitatingly it would be Maurice. And there can
be little doubt that her candor went a long way toward
breeding in Mousis a tolerant and indeed sympathetic attitude
toward his stepson. On the whole he was extraordinarily
patient and made the most of the few hours of tranquillity
allotted to him in his own house. To neighbors, business
associates, and guests he remained cool, affable, and poised.
Nothing in his bearing betrayed the domestic horrors surrounding him—Maurice coming home drunk from school
every evening, Suzanne's acute nervousness and tension, the
violent scenes of rage and tears, recrimination, and hysteria
that shook the household upon the drop of a word or the
slightest gesture of reproof. They were bitter pills indeed
to a young man with a large suburban house, a beautiful and
talented wife, and all the other marks of "success."

When Maurice was fourteen Mousis convinced Suzanne
that there was nothing more to be gained by keeping the boy
in school; not only was Maurice bored with it, but going to
school was, in fact, contributing to his illness. How much
better off he would be with a job and an opportunity to prove
himself manly in a man's world. With a job he might have
an opportunity to gain full self-confidence and no longer
feel the need for alcohol to bolster him. In final proof he
laid the proposal before Maurice. At once the boy brightened.

So in rapid succession over a period of about three years

Maurice was a shipping clerk in a furniture-polish factory, a delivery boy, a messenger for a process server, and a fitter in a lampshade factory. In each case some pretext was seized upon for his dismissal; at the bottom lay the real reason— drunkenness. Finally, through Mousis' influence, he landed a job in the bookkeeping department of the Crédit Foncier, where for several months his skill at figures gave promise of rapid promotion. Thanks to Mousis' generosity, he now sported custom-made clothes and a bowler hat. "I liked that bowler hat," Maurice was to sigh in later years. For longer than ever before, things went well. He stopped drinking entirely, strode the boulevards, and went to the bicycle races with his associates at the bank, or at Montmagny wandered about the village tipping his bowler to the ladies and dispensing sous to the small children. But then one day at work, for no apparent reason he suddenly seized his umbrella and beat the manager of his department into unconsciousness. Thus ended his banking career.

Events now rushed to their terrible climax. Maurice lost all desire to work and spent his time floundering about the house and the village drinking anything he could lay his hands on. If he was not given the *rouge*, he stole it—from his step-father's cellar, the kitchen, a café, or a wine shop. For weeks he was unshaven. His clothes reeked of vomit. His fits of rage were now wilder than ever. There were rows with the shopkeepers during which he hurled their stocks into the street and reviled them with obscene taunts. He abused the servants at home until they quit. The sight of a pregnant woman particularly enraged him; he would loudly hurl abuse at her. Such outbursts would be followed by dark fits of depression during which he would sit despondently for hours with his chin in his hands and tears streaming down his cheeks while Suzanne would try to coax some rational response from him. All such scenes would end in the same way, with protestations of remorse, ineffable lassitude, and again the plea for another *rouge*.

Suzanne was certain that some day these outbursts would pass and the boy would be miraculously cured. But she did not resign herself to the arrival of the miracle. If there was to be a cure, she was determined that she, his mother, would be able to claim the major share of it. She left no stone unturned. She consulted all sorts of doctors and psychologists. She tried to pursue each course prescribed. She even took to reading books on psychology. All, of course, in vain. If there were any signs of a change in Maurice's condition, they were for the worse.

Then one evening in the midst of an explosion Maurice ran into the kitchen threatening to kill himself with a meat knife. It was the beginning of an orgy of destruction. He ran through the house like a wild animal, overturning furniture, slashing curtains and upholstery, flinging crockery, glassware, and kitchen utensils in all directions. On Mousis' order Catherine ran for the police and a neighbor, Dr. Ettlinger. By the time they arrived Maurice had torn off all his clothes and was defecating on the staircase.

The doctor was finally able to administer a hypodermic sedative and put him to bed; and for several days Maurice was confined to his room under the influence of the drugs. In the meantime there were consultations with medical men and psychologists, at the conclusion of which an exhausted and terrified Suzanne reluctantly signed the necessary papers committing her son to the care of Dr. Vallon at the Asylum of Sainte-Anne. Maurice was then not yet nineteen years old.

While Maurice lay under sedation in his room overlooking the garden at Montmagny, Suzanne received word that Toulouse-Lautrec had died at Malromé at the age of thirty-seven. Suzanne had last seen him a little over a year before—

in May, 1900. From February until April of the preceding year Lautrec had been incarcerated in a sanatorium in the Madrid suburb at Neuilly as the result of a mental breakdown owing primarily to the effects of excessive drinking. It was his release from Neuilly he was celebrating when Suzanne saw him for the last time. He was giving another of his famous parties—an informal exhibition of his latest work in his studio. The invitation had borne an uproarious cartoon of the host-to-be in his high-crowned bowler hat milking a cow and bidding the invited guest "to come drink a glass of milk with me."

On arriving at the studio Suzanne was appalled to see her old friend—his face the deadly gray of putty, the beautiful eyes he was so proud of sagged in dull mists behind his heavy glasses. Teetering pathetically on his two stubby canes, the wraith of the ugly little man struggled manfully to re-create that air of incandescent gaiety which had once enveloped him. But his speech faltered, and he did not seem to hear much that was said to him. "It was terrible seeing him like that," Suzanne recalled. After a very little while she slipped quietly from the studio.

Lautrec was much on her mind during the three months Maurice remained in the sanatorium of Sainte-Anne. If Lautrec's untimely death was the result of drink, what was in store for her Maurice? What would happen to the boy once he was released from the asylum? Was his mind already destroyed by his morbid appetite for alcohol? Yet while Maurice was in the hands of the doctors she could do nothing more for him than promise herself that once he was released she would devote her life to his care. To have to wait at Montmagny for the boy's release with nothing to do but conform to the hollow inanities of the life of a banker's wife was an insufferable prospect. She had to throw herself into hard work. She had to do something to fill the vacuum of her days.

So it was that she spent most of her time in the rue Cortot at work on the magnificent series of nude drawings for which she served as her own model. During those three months she executed hundreds of drawings, only a dozen or so of which met with her critical approval and are preserved. Nothing of her mental exhaustion or perturbation is to be found in them. They are deft, forceful, and supple, as nothing she had ever done up to that time had been. In them her tiny wiry physique somehow assumes an almost statuesque quality, and she begins, for the first time, to *portray* rather than to reproduce her subject. Touchingly the drawings bespeak the role she has devoutly assumed for herself—the tower of strength. There are grandeur and vibrant mysterious hope in the rhythmic linear arabesques which finally and unalterably lift her drawings into first rank. When Degas saw them he is said to have remarked, "If there were any tears left in me, I'd be happy to shed them for one of those drawings."

After three months Maurice was released from Sainte-Anne's "looking better than he has for years—and so beautiful," Suzanne reported ecstatically to a friend. His thirst for alcohol was gone. But he was spiritless, dull—as though life had been drained out of him. He moped about Montmagny doing nothing. He shrank from contact with everyone and rarely spoke. Sometimes he roused himself to read a book, and then for days he would be lost in it—a technical scientific work which he could not possibly understand. Francis Carco tells us that he put down these scientific books only at mealtimes, and that when he was not reading he spent long hours staring at a spot on the floor or just stroking the cat. If he wandered down the hill to the village, he was likely to be lost for hours, and Suzanne would have to summon the police to find him.

It was their neighbor Dr. Ettlinger who suggested to Suzanne that some sort of manual therapy might improve Maurice's state of mind. He suggested that she try to interest him in painting. An early Freudian psychologist, the doctor was much concerned with "a number of eccentric gestures of an erotic character" which he had observed in Maurice's behavior. Later he suggested that Maurice's first alcoholic excesses were connected with a morbid sexual development. But as to what such a development was, and as to what extent it may have continued during the rest of his life, he offered no clue. Subsequently other doctors, notably Dr. Revertegat at Sannois and Dr. Vicq at Aulnay-sous-Bois, attempted to probe these sexual aberrations, but their findings were inconclusive, and in later life Maurice was unwilling to submit to psychological testings which might have produced concrete results. Whatever aberrations possessed him, Maurice kept them subjugated to alcohol throughout his life and took the secret to his grave. Beyond an occasional visit to a prostitute —but never to a *maison close*, always to a dark room—his active sexual life was virtually nonexistent. In his own autobiographical sketch he tells us that he was twenty-eight before he had his first sexual experience with a woman and that it was painfully shameful.

He did not respond miraculously to the idea of painting. He seemed at first to have no interest in art. It was something for women or for sick old men like M. Degas or cripples like "M. Toulouse." He much preferred being left alone to wander about as he pleased or to "read" his scientific books or histories of his new-found idol Napoleon. Only the ultimate threat that he would have to paint or else be reincarcerated at Sainte-Anne's for further treatment moved him to take up brush and palette.

Then the miracle occurred. Suzanne taught him to paint —a few months of daily lessons, to which he seemed to remain glumly apathetic. When he was not with his mother he now began to sit alone at the window of his room, his chin in his hands, staring for long hours at the village at the foot of the hill and at the play of light hovering over it. What did he see? When Suzanne asked, he said he did not know. He had no further interest in his scientific books, and even a short walk about the garden seemed to command all his strength. Then, with ineffable weariness and no conviction, he began to paint by himself—to put colors on his canvas, to set down almost as though they were columns of mathematical figures the relationships as he saw them between blues and greens and reds. He used the palette his mother set up for him.

The first awkward efforts, the heaviness of his palette, the crudity of his brushwork soon gave way to a spontaneous buoyancy, clarity, and impeccable mastery of technique. In a surprisingly short time he was completely his own master. Over these first works there lay a magic glow of tenderness and freshness, of astonishing originality which had its source apparently in instinct alone. The problems of the painter's craft—color relationship, chiaroscuro, tone, and perspective —resolved themselves in his subconscious mind and the picture appeared on his canvas as from the unfaltering hand of an expert. His movements as he painted seemed automatic, involuntary, never deliberate. As Maurice Raynal was later to observe, "the art of painting was as unthinking as that of the pianist who improvises while he carries on a conversation or reads aloud." From the beginning the substance of great painting was in him, the craftsmanship intact and solid, given wing by ingenuous sincerity and a secret fountain of gentle poetry.

That he should reject mankind was a logical expression of his temperament. His shyness was an insurmountable barrier to the human understanding which must be the essence of the portraitist's art; his timidity made any adventure into the moods of Nature hopeless. Still, if Man was forbidding and

Nature awesome, he saw in the *work* of Man a display of holy things. Man's achievements surrounded him—his locomotives, his houses, his churches, the thousands of works he had wrought by his hands out of his imagination and necessity. Of all of these, nothing his eyes fell upon had for Maurice the compelling fascination of a wall. To him, a wall became man's most meaningful creation, and the most beautiful. Wherever he went he saw man-made walls—battered, flaked, crumbling; solid, forbidding, soaring; cruel, sheltering, comforting—with their tortured surfaces, their mosses, and their scraps of advertising posters, their stains of animal urine. The sky, the sun, the fog, and the snow existed only as their background, and they were most lovely when they took on the grayish tones of walls. Human figures, pathetic daubs that they were, existed only to accent the terrible solidity of walls. Walls became the protagonists of his vision.

The part which walls were to play in Maurice's art can, of course, be explained in modern psychological terms as an obsession with shelter and security. It can also be seen as an outgrowth of man's emotional history, as a poignant victory over the assailing forces of nature which surround him. But in Maurice Utrillo, who in a few years was to be roused to the very depths of his being by the sight of a little gilt figure of Joan of Arc, the stirrings of mysticism were uncommonly deep. And in view of the future developments of his life, they alone can be cited logically to account both for his inability to rouse himself to normal human relationships and for the seemingly automatic expression of his art. To him, walls were the direct knowledge of God's desire to protect his children. They were the manifestation of the divine gift—the ability to build, to construct. And even as with the little statue of Ste. Jeanne, with the innumerable man-made crucifixes, rosaries, medals, books, and religious pictures which became the anchors of his later faith, he approached them with artless humility, awe, and profound love.

In this first spate of painting he found sound health and security at last. He was able to make frequent excursions to Montmartre, where he remembered there stood the most beautiful walls in the world. He no longer needed alcohol to shield him from the tortures of the world. In two years he produced over 150 paintings, many of them masterpieces.

Now it was time to go and live among the painters, for surely he was one of them. He took up permanent residence in his mother's studio at No. 2 rue Cortot. He was twenty-three years old and he was brave at last.

VI   Threshold of Revolution

SNOW PLAGUED PARIS THROUGHOUT MARCH, 1896. ALONG THE boulevards gray, soot-sprinkled drifts lined the curbs to be dusted white by the next snowfall. The roads were a morass of slush and horse manure which kept most of the feminine population of the city indoors. Traffic was, at best, desultory. Business was in a sorry state. But on the afternoon of the 23d Suzanne and Paul Mousis journeyed into the capital by train to go to the theater.

The word had already spread wide of Montmartre that at Lugné-Poë's new Théâtre de l'Oeuvre a bombshell was about to be dropped which would revolutionize the whole world of art. After tonight Montmartre would be changed completely. The Prince of Poets, it was said, was already preparing to welcome "the victims of the Revolution" back to the Latin Quarter. Despite the weather the evening promised to be one which would not soon be forgotten. Many Parisian intellectuals journeyed a distance longer than from Montmagny in order to be at hand for the historical occasion. Clearly Lugné-Poë's publicity men had done their job thoroughly.

"Merde!" The monosyllabic obscenity thundered out over the footlights, the first word of the new play *Ubu-Roi* by the young Breton, Alfred Jarry. The speaker was Ubu, a monstrous parody of a bourgeois humbug—monumentally gross,

138

brutal, lewd, hypocritical, and respectable. He moved like a giant marionette across a stage peopled with grotesque masks (scenery, costumes, and masks were designed by the author), among scenic changes announced by the posting of placards. A single soldier played the part of a regiment, and when the hero was to mount a charger he merely hung round his neck a sign announcing that he had accomplished that feat. The play was greeted with hisses, boos, catcalls, and applause. The audience rose to its feet. Men and women shouted and screamed, spat and shook their fists at the fallen curtain. "Ubu will become a popular legend of man's instincts—vile, greedy, and unclean," wrote Catulle Mendès.

Alfred Jarry was twenty-three, sodden with absinthe and ether. He lived in a world of fantastic hallucinations and spent much of his time on a bicycle, yet somehow he managed to remain in the regular employ of Remy de Gourmont by writing witty, satirical, and lucid essays for *l'Imagier*. A tiny bowlegged man with "irregular, wolfish teeth," he made his home with two tomcats and an owl in rooms in which he had had the ceiling lowered so that tall people would have to come in on their hands and knees. He always carried a revolver, and without warning he would stop on a crowded street to shoot pigeons and sparrows. "Filthy beasts of nightingales!" he would scream. He fancied that he had been created to lead an intellectual revolt against the world. Ill-mannered, hostile to common sense, overbearing, and misogynous, he now settled on the Montmartre hill to plot his own weird brand of satirical revolution.

Despite the fanfare of the opening might Ubu was taken lightly by the subsequent audiences at the Théâtre de l'Oeuvre—a pea shot at the walls of Jericho, too bizarre to be taken seriously. But on the turbulent Butte, Jarry immediately assumed the stature of a sage, an animated symbol of the intellectual and artistic forces which threatened to annihilate all vestiges of bourgeois complacency. Under his sardonic patronage fresh and original evaluations of the meaning of art were to burgeon and a new intellectualism to flourish. Whether in the end he was symbol, patron, or prophet, by dint of his fanciful eye and curious imagination Jarry contributed considerably to the change in the mentality which now crept over the Butte. But he was by no means alone in bringing this to pass.

Of itself the "golden age" had gone a long way to plot its own extinction. While Lautrec and his friends strove to keep bright the last flickering of their high spirits in the gaudy gaslight of the cabarets and dance halls, the Nabis as a group disintegrated. Serusier, Verklade, and Denis veered toward the mysticism which was to make of the first a theoretician rather than a painter, of the second a monk, and a religious painter of the man who once had warned his fellow artists, "Remember that a picture, before it is a horse, a nude woman, or any subject at all, is essentially a flat surface covered with colors assembled in a certain order." Pierre Bonnard and Vuillard pursued their separate courses by seeking in the everyday lives of the common people to create "Intimism," while Félix Valloton evolved his own highly personal aesthetic. The men who, with Seurat, had forged Neo-impressionism out of scientific theory—Signac, Redon, Gross, Angrand, Dubois-Pillet, and later Pissarro—struck out, after Seurat's death, to develop Pointillism according to their individual forms of expression. In Tahiti that restless spirit Gauguin, plagued by syphilis, wrote home to Daniel de Monfreid that his imagination "had begun to cool"; he was thinking of moving on to the Marquesas. Monet and Renoir (who still lived in the rue la Rochefoucauld) were becoming rich men. And Degas, his eyesight failing, continued to shuffle about in his house in the rue Victor-Masse cataloguing and arranging his pictures.

Something of the revolt which Jarry deliberately strove to foment through the strength of his personality and acid language Cézanne had already stirred up through the power of his brush. A shy, clumsy man, thickset, short and very dark, churlish and proud, a bourgeois conservative who went to Mass every Sunday, hungered for the ribbon of the Legion of Honor and observed all the conventions of his class, Cézanne might have been a pale shadow of Ubu-Roi. Instead he was something Ubu did not know existed—a painter, not a person. Whatever he truly was his pictures reflected. "I thought that one could do good painting without drawing attention to one's private life," he wrote. "Surely an artist tries to lift himself as high as possible intellectually, but as a human being he should remain in the dark." He was to be seen purely through his own eyes on the canvas. In his paintings stood his visual experience, his sensations set in the mirror of his mind, constructed in the most refined terms of honesty, the fruit of long hours of "research," each painstaking stroke of his brush a solid brick shaped and hewn by his intellect and heart.

Beginning as an Impressionist of sorts, Cézanne first aimed "to make of Impressionism something as solid and durable as the paintings in the museums." He arrived at the age of twenty-two in Paris, where he studied at the Académie Suisse and first met Pissarro. By this time he had finished his formal education, tried studying law to please his father, abandoned it, and subsequently rejected a paternal offer to admit him to the family banking firm, Cézanne et Chabessol, in his native Aix-en-Provence. Dissatisfied with his progress in Paris, Cézanne returned home in less than a year. But after a few months he was back again, to associate gingerly with the Impressionists. In 1871 he returned to Paris, having hidden out at l'Estaque to avoid military service. This time he deflected from the Impressionists completely and occupied himself with a series of weird theatrical orgies, heavy with sexual overtones, set to canvas in wild torments of gloomy color.

It was only a phase, after which Cézanne settled down to

the long work of evolving an aesthetic system based, as he put it, on "the strong experience of nature" rather than on the mere effects of light or his own emotional instability. Finally the repeated antagonism of the critics, discontent with the Impressionist personalities, his own doubts, and his distrust of people in general forced him to leave the Paris scene entirely. "Honors can be created only for the cretins, the jackasses, and the crooks," he said.

He retired to Provence, where he was equally irritated by the advent of electric light, road repairs, "modern" architecture, provincial society, and the "stupidity of the peasants." His wife and son, unable to tolerate his irascibility, spent the greater part of their time in Paris. "What remains for me in my condition," he wrote, "but to rusticate quietly?" Nevertheless, in the familiar landscape which was so dear to him he could at least paint. He could wander off into the green and copper countryside among the pines and olive trees which always kept their foliage, with his boxes of paints, his canvases, and his easel, and set himself up in the clear white sunlight "to express simultaneously objects and the air that envelops them, form and atmosphere." "The sun is so powerful," he wrote to Pissarro, "that I have the impression that everything stands out in silhouette, not only in black and white but in blue, in red, in brown, in violet. I may be mistaken, but it seems to me to be the opposite of modeling."

Systematically Cézanne worked to arrange and order what lay before him until it loomed big, balanced, and serene, until light and shadow were no more and color expressed everything. His "method" and "logic" meticulously created "the picture," the structure of forms and tones which, as he saw it, were no longer the mood of the instant, the passing thing, but Truth, solid and eternal.

"I must always continue to work, not, however, to arrive at that perfection which wins the admiration of the stupid. . . . That perfection, which the public esteems so highly, is nothing but the result of technical knowledge, and makes every work that is thus created inartistic and commonplace. I must try to arrive at perfection solely from a desire to be truer and more artistic. . . . I work stubbornly. I see the Promised Land before me. Shall I feel like that great Hebrew leader, or be able to set foot in it? . . . Is art really a priesthood which requires pure men who are given to her body and soul?"

Cézanne's work threw up before the world an intellectual and spiritual adventure so magnificent in its prospects it revolutionized the course of painting. While the critics carped and the public snickered, a few of the minds which had themselves come through the fire stood in awe before his paintings at Vollard's. "My enthusiasm was nothing compared with Renoir's," Pissarro wrote to his son. "Degas himself is captivated by the spell of this refined savage—Monet, all of us. The only ones who are not subject to Cézanne's magic are precisely those artists and amateurs who have already shown by their own errors that their sensibilities are at fault."

And so the nineteenth century passed into limbo and the twentieth began. Pablo Picasso (or, as he was then, at nineteen, Pablo Ruiz y Picasso) arrived in Paris in 1900, appropriately inaugurating the new century of art in which he was assuredly to play the chief role. He stayed only two months, selling three of his drawings to Berthe Weill, who had recently opened a gallery and whom the artists already called *"La Merveille"* (la Mère Weill). In December he returned to Barcelona—where he had studied at La Llonja, the Barcelona Province school of Fine Arts—for "a warm bed and a good feed." He was back in Paris again for a few months the next spring. During his stay Vollard held a small exhibition of his work which created little excitement, and after his return to Spain fifteen of his paintings were exhibited at Berthe Weill's gallery. The following year Picasso returned to Paris for six months, and in April, 1904, he moved permanently, taking up residence at No. 13 rue Ravignan in a great jumble of rickety rooms and dark corridors dubbed "the Bateau Lavoir," because externally it suggested one of the laundry boats to be found along the Seine. In the five years he lived there, until 1909, the "Bateau Lavoir" became the nest from which the art of the twentieth century took wing. The other tenants of this warren of dark and dirty cubicles included an "ether salesman," a costermonger, a laundress, a couple of prize fighters, an artist's model, a picture framer, an unfrocked priest, and a young woman who insisted that she was a milkmaid. They came and went with mysterious irregularity and in varying degrees of insobriety. The Dutchman Van Dongen was its first artistic inhabitant; and shortly after Picasso moved in came the two Spanish sculptors Paco Durio, who had been a friend of Gauguin, and Manolo; the writers Pierre MacOrlan and André Salmon, who were to be among the most brilliant historians of this period of Montmartre history; the poets Pierre Reverdy and Max Jacob (Picasso's great friend and former roommate, that extraordinary cynic and mystic); the mathematician Maurice Princet, whose imaginative calculations were later to form a cornerstone of the Cubist movement, and later Juan Gris.

When it did not overflow into the little bistro Zut—whose walls, during his second sojourn in Paris in 1901, Picasso decorated with blue nudes—or into the Closerie des Lilas, another haunt, the place seethed with discussions, inspirations, and manifestoes. Artists like Braque, Matisse, Derain, Dufy, Marie Laurencin, Jean Metzinger, Modigliani, Louis Marcoussis, and Vlaminck were there always, singly or in groups. Alfred Jarry was the center of the company; and it was to the "Bateau Lavoir" that the mourners were to come "to sing, drink, and eat sausages" after seeing Jarry's "wine-and-ether-soaked remains" interred in the Montmartre Cemetery on a sunny November Sunday in 1907. "A barbarous sight like a scene imagined by the fellow we were putting into the ground," so spoke Guillaume Apollinaire of the occasion. Jean Cocteau, Maurice Raynal, Gustave Coquiot, and Apollinaire himself, whose "aesthetic meditations" were often the basis for much of the talk, were always there, certainly on Monday nights, when Max Jacob held forth on classical literature, acting pages of Racine from memory and passing out ether and tinned sardines to his guests. And, of course, there were the ones who failed to make names for themselves—the youths who ultimately retreated to the careers their families hoped they would pursue, the discouraged, the ungifted, the dilettanti, the wastrels. There, too, were the American brother and sister Leo and Gertrude Stein—Leo, who Max Jacob said looked like "St. Francis of Pennsylvania," and Gertrude, who sat to Picasso eighty times in the "Bateau Lavoir" for the portrait of which the artist said, "Everybody thinks that it is not like her, but never mind, in the end she will look like the portrait." Paul Fort, the theatrical impresario, was a frequenter, as were the actors Harry Baur and Gaston Modot, the art dealers Vollard, Clovis Sagot, Louis Libaude, Daniel Henry Kahnweiler and Berthe Weill, the German collector Wilhelm Uhde (he was to be one of the first to write a book on Picasso), and the Russian Shchukin.

Picasso worked at night after the confusion died down, "small, black, squat, restless and inspiring restlessness, with somber eyes, deep, piercing, and strange—always staring. He seemed almost awkward in his manner, and dressed carelessly. A thick lock of hair, black and shining, slashed across his intelligent forehead. Part Bohemian, part workingman." He was concerned with life's outcasts, the poor, the miserable and homeless who thus became the dramatis personae of what has since been called his "Blue Period." Soon his style was to mellow to the melancholy sweetness of the harlequins, acrobats, and jugglers of his "Rose Period." Then suddenly his agile intelligence was off to strange new vistas.

It was Cézanne who had said, "Everything in nature is based on the cone, the sphere, and the cylinder." The cube, reasoned the mathematician Princet, was the cone, the sphere or the cylinder reduced to even more absolute terms. Was not the straight line the beginning of all things? Might not, therefore, humanity and everything else which came within the artist's visual frame gain its fullest power and greatest artistic significance when it was reduced to purely geometrical solids—that is, to cubes? Picasso wondered, too.

Then, at the opposite pole, Henri Matisse studied the architecture of color of Cézanne. (In 1899 he had bought Cézanne's *Bathers*, which later, in 1936, he was to present to the Petit Palais. At that time he wrote, "I have appreciated it for thirty-seven years. To it I have pinned my faith.") Together with a group of young friends—Maurice Vlaminck, André Derain, Othon Friesz and Albert Marquet, and later Georges Braque, Cornelius Van Dongen, Jean Puy, and Louis Valtat—he sought to achieve space-construction through color by creating "strange visions of green skies, vermilion rivers, lemon-colored trees and emerald green faces." The group had first exhibited its paintings at the *Salon des Independants*. It is said that when the critic Louis Vauxcelles spotted a small statue of a child's head in the Florentine manner, by the sculptor Marque, in the room with these paintings, he exclaimed, "Ah, Donatello among the wild animals." The name "Fauves" (Wild Ones) stuck.

The two directions, Cubism and Fauvism, were in the making when Cézanne caught his fatal chill on a muddy country road near his home in Provence. The following year Jarry died. It was Jarry who, in rage against the world he loathed, had called for the "unfolding [of] a new universe that supplements our own." With his compassionate love of mankind, Picasso could hardly have sought the same objective from the same motive. If now he painted his extraordinary picture *"Les Demoiselles d'Avignon,"* in which "the lines, the angles, the strange juxtaposition of the planes announced a new direction in modern painting," he painted because he believed in man's ability to understand and love.

Matisse had already exhibited his "Luxury, Calm and Voluptuousness," which was to chart the course of the Fauve movement.

Revolution was in the air.

As far as Maurice was concerned, Montmartre had not changed when he settled down there in 1906 at the age of twenty-three. It was still a place of twisted, weather-worn streets, bricks and mortar, plaster, tiles, cement, and wonderful stone and roughcast walls. When had he first fallen in love with these visions? He did not remember. In a nebulous way they spoke to him of nostalgia and of a happiness he had never really experienced as a child. They suggested that in those faraway days his life had been bathed in gentle golden light and soft shadows. The fear and the rage which had bewitched his boyhood were forgotten entirely, the melancholy suffused tenderly with his joyous illusion of the past. It was the Montmartre of these memories which he now began to paint.

If only there had not been people! If only there had not been those terrifying faces of the monster children of the Pension La Flaiselle, the big, merciless bodies of grownups in bustling crowds, the strident voices, the questions, the answers, the laughter, he would have been profoundly happy and would have been able to work calmly at his painting. But they were there now as they had been in other days— setting his nerves on edge, vile, tormenting, driving him to distraction. He wanted to slaughter them, all of them, with one great sweep of his mighty arm. It was not enough to try to ignore them—to leave them entirely out of the pictures he painted. He had to shut them out of his mind entirely or else meet them head on with titanic rage. And in order to be able to take either course he had to drink.

His driving urge to paint saw him through the daytime in peace. Sometimes he suffered excruciating hangovers, but he could bear them as long as he could paint. He painted, as we have seen, automatically, with miraculous precision and speed, hardly aware of his own movements. Suzanne had warned him that he must visit art galleries, and he went dutifully, especially to Durand-Ruel's, where the Impressionists were now a regular feature. He avoided the Louvre because there were too many people there, but he would go to the Luxembourg. "When the attendants were not looking," Carco says, "he would caress the works of the Impressionists with his fingertips." What he carried away from the galleries in his mind it is hard to say. His biographer Tabarant says that he was influenced particularly by the work of Sisley. Yet the incisiveness of his design and the solidity of his structure belies any such influence. His own commentary to Gustave Coquiot on his work at this period is perhaps nearer the truth: "When I believe that what I've done is good I say, 'It's good, eh? Sisley, maybe!' Why Sisley? I don't know. I've never seen any of the work of this master, but I've heard my mother speak of him. So I repeat the name. . . . A beginner is very stupid, isn't he?"

If Maurice owed a debt to any other painter, it was probably to Adolphe Monticelli, that brilliant painter of circuses, masquerades, and *fêtes galantes* who had died when Maurice was three years old. Monticelli's thick layers of paint ("the pudding") and invented pictorial light ("I am the luminous center: it is I who light") are clearly evident in Utrillo's early painting. But, here again, how much of it was conscious awareness of the master's technique and how much his own painting instinct it is hard to divine. One could never tell with Utrillo when he was studying and when he was stupefied. For the most part he was singularly uninterested in the work of other artists; and beyond their application to his own work he had no critical faculties. For his own work his standard was very high, but otherwise his taste was bad. If he had an ambition, it was that he should be thought as "great" a painter as the hack Raffaelli. He believed that Raffaelli's "Clemenceau Giving an Account of His Mandate to the Voters of Montmartre at the Cirque Fernando" was a great picture, and when pressed to explain this singular judgment he replied, "It is very big, and Clemenceau is very heroic." Once he told Francis Carco, "It was Raffaelli who impressed me most. My greatest hope was that one day I'd be able to paint as well as he did." Then he added, as though he were talking only to himself, "But Suzanne kept me away from him, and I had to hide my opinions."

Anyway, outside influence on his art was negligible. He pursued his own unique course, transferring what stood before him, decrepit or banal, into terms of his personal rapture. By the laws he alone established for himself he controlled his impulses and exaltations. Yet they allowed him a wide field for experiments. With the primitive ingenuity of a child, for example, he tried to intensify the tactile quality of the buildings he painted by mixing plaster, sand, or glue into his paints, by pasting sticks and bits of burlap to his canvas. Was he here stepping unconsciously toward the colleges of a decade later? In any event, he drew back: it was as far as his laws allowed him to go.

Each day now saw Maurice in a different place on the hill at his easel—before the Moulin de la Galette at any one of a dozen angles, in the rue du Mont-Cenis facing the roof tops of the northern suburbs, facing the rue Cortot, where he now lived in his mother's studio at No. 2, on the pavement of the rue Norvins looking toward the Place du Tertre, Montmartre's heart, before the church of St. Pierre, before Notre-Dame de Lorette, along the Place Blanche or the Place Pigalle; and how many times and from how many vantage points before the cool Byzantine white turrets and dome of the still-unfinished basilica of Sacré-Coeur! The canvases, one a day, are his diary of those first years of his return to the Butte.

But his nights were horrors. Beginning innocently enough with a glass of *rouge* as he sat alone at a café table straining his ears to pick up the threads of the lively conversations around him, he would finally be sufficiently fortified by his wine to introduce himself at one of the tables. "My name is Maurice . . . Maurice Valadon," for he obstinately refused to accept the name given him by the Act of Recognition signed by Miguel Utrillo. "Never call me that other name—Utrillo. Never. My friends call me 'Maumau,' " he would add. His manner was charming, slightly formal: the flicker of a timid smile, the gentle roll of his soft speech, the fun in his blue eyes, the patrician lift of his shoulders—all gave promise of geniality. His conversation was rather whimsical and delicate; it startled him to find that people were amused by it. But, as the talk about him grew more animated, he began to lose himself. His eyes shifted restlessly from one face to another. He quickened his drinking, often ordering the waiter to bring him half a dozen glasses at a time. Around him the talk spun like the uncontrollable pieces of colored light in a kaleidoscope: he could not follow it. After a while he understood nothing, only the furious hostility which these jabbering faces and cacophonous voices now assumed—toward him. If he was among painters, he heard words like "Cézanne" or "Matisse," "research," "expression," or phrases like "our geometrical problems," "organized brain." He knew nothing of this language. He was "a simple painter fellow." One didn't talk, one painted. Why did people have to talk about something that came out of their souls?

In his desperate confusion he imagined that he was being mocked. People were laughing at him, shoving him around, spitting on him. And then, all at once he would explode. He would scream and curse, smash the glassware, swing his fists, and reel out into the night—on to more wine, more bistros, more hideous, hostile people, more pain, more violence, more wine, more . . . more. . . .

"Don't you even prepare your canvas?" Maurice looked up. A young man stood at his shoulder looking at the painting on the easel—an immensely handsome fellow with light hair, the ghost of a golden beard flickering about his broad full-lipped mouth, pipe stuck between two rows of small, even teeth. "I'm André—André Utter. I paint, too."

Maurice grunted and went back to applying paint to his canvas. The young man stayed where he was, watched silently for a quarter of an hour. Then all at once Maurice turned to him. "I'm called Maurice."

It was to be his first genuine friendship. André Utter, nicknamed "Dédé," was three years younger than Maurice. The son of a plumber who had his shop in the rue Caulaincourt, he had gone through the École Communale in a blaze of brilliant scholarship which gave his mother the idea that he was headed for one of the learned professions, possibly law or the priesthood; his father expected him to take over the plumbing business. But the boy had made up his mind that he wanted to be an artist. For several years while at school he had spent all his spare time on the Butte—watching the painters at their easels, running errands for them, helping them to clean up their studios, listening to their discussions. At thirteen he began smoking a pipe and sampling absinthe. By the time he left school he felt as if he were one of them.

He could paint very competently, as he could do whatever else he put his mind to. And there was in everything he did a dash of breathlessness and brilliant imagination. In a full-blooded happy-go-lucky way he was the leader of a group of young painters and intellectuals, lads like himself who had grown up in Montmartre and who saw in the artists' carefree atmosphere a possible escape from the drab succession to their father's business. Self-taught as painters, writers, and in one or two cases as musicians, they undertook to give themselves full courses in the sensual pleasures of life. They learned to drink absinthe and ether so that they might live in feverish dreams. They learned to eat hashish or to smoke opium (hashish was the more easily available and the more popular), and, quite naturally, they delighted above all in exploring the mysteries of love. Here Utter was "Pope," the leader of the priesthood in whose charge stood the sacred altar of Venus.

Utter credited an aunt, his father's spinster sister Louise, with having crystallized his interest in art and given him direction. "Living in the Faubourg St. Germain, in the rue Madame, and dividing her time between her religious devotions and museums, she determined my vocation. On the first Friday of every month she came to Mass at Sacré-Coeur and then to lunch at our house. One Friday she came as usual and happened to ask me what I had been doing with myself. I told her that the day before I had been to a museum. 'Excellent. Which one?' 'The Luxembourg,' I said. 'Good! But that isn't the place to begin. You should begin at the Louvre. Next Thursday I'll take you there.' " Thereafter he went with her regularly every Thursday.

In the Louvre he studied the old masters. Among the Leonardos and Titians, the Raphaels, Van Eycks, Velasquezes, and Rembrandts he began to form his own ideas and tried to incorporate them in his painting. Driven by insatiable curiosity, he delved into history and the problems of technique, from which he developed his "philosophy of art"— "simplicity, courage, and elemental emotion." Max Jacob thought him "highly original" and for a short time shared a room with him. Through Jacob he was introduced at the "Bateau Lavoir," where, as "a real *Montmartrois*" and a bright intelligence, he was warmly accepted by the group. Gustave Coquiot spoke of him as "one of the coming 'greats.'" Although he ignored most of the audacities of his contemporaries, Utter was temperamentally a Fauve, and had he not eventually constricted his creative power with the weight of intellectual restraints, he might have been an important painter.

Thanks to his mother's willingness to let him go his chosen way, and in spite of his father's opposition, he moved into the studio room which had been Satie's at No. 6 rue Cortot, a few steps from Maurice.

Soon after they met, Maurice and Utter became inseparable. André Utter's boyish enthusiasm, his unaffected warmth and friendliness, the sense of fun that emanated from him put Maurice at his ease as he had never been before. In the daytime they painted together. Utter loved to talk while he worked, sounding off on his "philosophy," registering his observations about color, light, technique. Maurice was the perfect listener. "Yes, yes," he would mutter from time to time as he went on his automatic way, almost rhythmically transferring his pigments from the dirty palette to the canvas. Now and again he would smile at his friend, timidly, gratefully. If they had money, they would go off for dinner at noon to a restaurant somewhere on the hill—the Mère Catherine, or the Belle Gabrielle, or perhaps to the Bonne Fraquette in the rue Saint-Rustique, to sit quietly at one of the garden tables where the Impressionists once ate and where Van Gogh painted his "La Guinguette." In the evening they would pick up Jules Depaquit ("the quick drinker") and Tiret-Bognet ("the greatest painter alive—have you seen his latest picture of Napoleon in *l'Illustration?*") or Robert Naley, the Swiss, and sell what canvases there were among them to buy drinks. Then, arm in arm or falling over each other, they would make their high spirits felt wherever it suited their fancy, invading a friend's studio or one of the *maisons closes* near Notre-Dame de Lorette, settling in a café or bistro in the rue des Saules, the Place du Tertre, or on the precipitous steps of the rue Muller. Only Maumau would go beyond the fun. As the others' spirits rose, his plummeted. As the gaiety increased, he became more miserable. And ultimately he would wander off by himself to abuse passers-by, to send stones crashing through windowpanes, to fall into a gutter, to end up bloody and filthy in the police station.

After a particularly violent bout the police would send for Suzanne, and she would take him back to Montmagny, where she and Madeleine would nurse him back to health for a few days. And then he would return to Montmartre.

It was apparently while Maurice was at Montmagny that André Utter first saw Suzanne. He was painting in the street with another friend, Edmond Heuzé. "She passed by, ignoring us," Utter wrote, "but I began to dream of her."

And well he might! She had never been lovelier—a tiny, voluptuous figure, cool and detached, a touch of poignant melancholy about her eyes. The ripened vigor of her spirit was in her walk, in the long unfaltering stride so strangely incongruous to her size, in the lift of her breasts. She at once exuded fine sensuality and robust grandeur. She was far too subtle, too complicated, too dangerous to fire the desires of the callow. To Utter she was immediately and passionately a challenge—to his vigorous masculinity, his intelligence, and his profound sensibilities. If he were to live a hundred years, he knew, he would find no one else like this.

They were to meet finally at Montmagny. By 1908 the pace at which he had been living had begun to tell on Utter. His weight had dropped to barely one hundred pounds. Alarmed, his parents packed him off to a convalescent home in the country, which, by a curious coincidence, was at Pierrefitte-Montmagny. There he found Maurice. "I set up my easel beside him," he wrote many years later, "and when our painting session was over I walked with him to the gate of the big house overlooking a magnificent stretch of country-side. It was the home of his stepfather, M. Paul Mousis, where he was staying with his mother and grandmother. . . . That evening Maurice told his mother about our meeting. His mother was pleased. Apparently she thought I should be a good influence on him. . . . The next day Maurice introduced me to her. . . . She was the young woman I had been dreaming about! . . . She showed me two of her paintings, some pastels, some drawings, and some etchings. . . . I left on a cloud."

It was a fateful meeting.

The bourgeois life of Montmagny had begun to pall on Suzanne. Mousis had evidently seen the danger signals, for shortly afterward he expressed his willingness to leave his big house and establish his family on the Butte, staying at Montmagny only weekends. He rented an apartment and studio recently vacated by the Catholic writer Leon Bloy on the first floor of the old seventeenth-century building at No. 12 rue Cortot. Poor Mousis! His cause was by now hopeless. The last years at Montmagny had been too strenuous for Suzanne. It was only a question of time when the "marriage" would come to grief. During the first years it was held intact by the ardor of their youthful passion and the novelty of their social life. Even then they sometimes quarreled. But as the trouble with Maurice increased, the differences between them rose more and more to penetrate that veneer of well-being to which the big house on the Butte Pinson was a monument. Living as she did in a feverish state of apprehension over Maurice—never knowing whether to give him free rein or to coddle him, torn between her duties as a mother and her surging creative urge—Suzanne had been compelled to assume interest in the endless trivialities of a housewife's life, to create an illusion of well-being which, in her own sense of the fitness of things, was completely false. She wilted. The more frivolous her life appeared to be, the deeper became her real anxieties. True, she dramatized her predicament somewhat; otherwise she would have been able to resolve it and make a clean break. But, in an obscure way, what she saw ahead was as depressing as what she was living through. If she gave up her present position, she would only be catapulted into a struggle for economic survival, and then the problems of Maurice and of her artistic expression would still be with her. To live on what she was able to make as an artist was impossible; even modeling jobs were not likely to come her way as they had fifteen years before.

Not that Suzanne coolly determined these matters in her mind—she was far too agitated. They were but desultory thoughts in her confusion. But the Montmagny years (and sometimes she had an oppressive feeling that it might be age too) had filled her with a lassitude which was not easily cast off.

Had she known what to do about Maurice, she might have made the plunge. Despite all her savage determination to save the boy, she could see herself losing the battle. She was always torn between a desire to shield him and a fear of being overprotective. Sometimes she was convinced, in a mystical way which was certainly alien to her character, that the boy's salvation could come only through her absolute rejection of him; then immediately she knew that she was the only prop he had.

In her actual contact with Maurice she was patient and sympathetic. She did not chide or nag him. Nor did she fail to show her disapproval or her pain. She made the most of his rare periods of sobriety—talking to him about his work and his friends, going for walks with him, taking him out to dinner. It was such a pitiful bit to offer, and yet it was all that was possible—to be there when he wanted her. Where would she be, she asked herself, if she broke with Mousis? With a living to make and the fight to hold a household together, how much would Maurice be able to come to her then?

And still she longed to escape from the life she was living. No amount of reasoning could deaden the feeling of pain that she felt in keeping herself chained to this practical power of money. If only she had the strength to tear herself away! For the first time in her life she lacked courage, and no one knew it better than she. It was knowledge which only added to her confusion, her distress.

If anything, her discontent was increased by the environment in which she now lived. She might have suffered less in Montmagny, with parquet floors, lace curtains, and shopping lists. But instead she was in the rue Cortot. This was the Montmartre of her carefree days, and she was entertaining bankers! The contrast was bitter.

So matters stood, one day after they had moved into No. 12 rue Cortot, when young André Utter passed by in the street and Suzanne called to him. The consequence of this encounter was the painting of that curiously barbaric and solid "Adam and Eve," * for which Utter posed for the figure of Adam. The picture was shown at the Salon d'Automne, which had been inaugurated some years earlier in the basement of the Petit Palais on the Champs Élysées by Matisse, Francis Jourdain, the architect Marquet, and Pierre Bonnard —a show then dominated by the Fauves. But more important to her at the time than her appearance among this dynamic group of revolutionaries was the fact that next to her "Adam

* Now in the Valadon-Utrillo Room in the Museum of Modern Art, Paris.

and Eve" hung "Pont Notre Dame," by Maurice Utrillo V.,* and that Maurice spent hours each day strolling through the rooms at the Petit Palais with a sly smile on his lips, his shoulders straight, and a cane under his arm. Once again her hopes soared.

Despite her anxieties it was, all in all, an optimistic period for her. While she painted "Adam and Eve" Utter became her lover. Brilliant, beautiful, inflamed with glowing youthful passion, it seemed to her he was everything she had all her life been hungering for. That he was twenty-one years younger than she—three years younger than her own son— she airily ignored. The force of his youth made her young, imbued her once again with the buoyancy she had had when she first went to the fountain in the Place Pigalle. Now, closing her eyes to everything but her own sensations, she knew to the very depths of her being that she had found the love of her life. Nor was Utter less moved. His boyish dreams had come true. He stood in possession of a mature and magnificent woman with a superb body, an original mind, a temperament at once extravagant and impassioned. In every one of her changing moods—her intensity, the shimmer of raillery, her bursts of lusty humor—she seemed alive as no woman he had ever known was alive.

The years 1909-1910 saw them caught up in a cloud of happiness. Utter now shared a studio at No. 5 Impasse de

---

* Maurice had begun to use this signature in 1905, having previously stubbornly signed all his work "Maurice Valadon" or "Maurice U. Valadon." The reasons for this change of heart have never been probed by his biographers. It was about this time that one of Miguel Utrillo's closest friends, the artist Rusiñol, painted a charming Impressionist picture, "Suzanne Valadon and Her Son Maurice Utrillo at the Moulin de la Galette." It seems that Rusiñol would not have so entitled his painting had he not had Maurice's permission to do so. There is also room for conjecture that during the painting of the picture Rusiñol might have gone a long way toward prejudicing the young man in favor of the elder Utrillo's name.

Guelma with Maurice, and here the lovers enjoyed rendezvous which they were at pains to see could hardly be called
"secret." In the rue Cortot they posed for each other. At the
café tables they held hands and were lost in tender attitudes.
Even their rows became public spectacles, for from the beginning they enjoyed a fight. They were a continual delight
to each other and were pleased that the world should know
it.

Suzanne's art found renewed strength and sureness. Spring-
ing partly from the release of emotional forces which had
been stifled during the final Montmagny years, partly from
the optimistic prospects of the future, the new power yet
owed much to Utter's highly sensitive feeling for painting,
his intelligence, instinctive good taste, and tremendous enthusiasm. From the first he regarded her art as even more
important than their personal relationship. It was something
in which he believed with all the terrible brutality of his
youth. "The Valadon Drama," he called it, "a kind of divine
magic which moves of itself." But even in his awe he was
aware of the direction in which her energies must bend in
order to give that "divine magic" its might. That her drawing was beautiful he knew; but he was also perceptive enough
to realize that she had already carried it as far as it could go.
Nowhere in it now was the promise of further development,
of a rise to new horizons. Instead, she must paint. To direct
her power to painting, he pointed out, was to refresh her
aesthetic spirit, to give it free rein, to create for herself a vast
new field in which she would reflect the full potency of her
temperament. She accepted his judgment as a loving pupil.
How could she do otherwise, knowing that in him she had
someone who fervently believed in her genius?

In turn, it was her confidence in him even more than her
love which in 1909 made of her break with Mousis a light

thing.* She packed Madeleine and her collection of china pieces off to the Impasse de Guelma, and within an hour followed with her own effects. Maurice had just received the news that his application to enroll for study at the École des Beaux Arts had been rejected. He was drinking like a fiend. There was no money. And yet Suzanne was sure that she had never been so happy.

Shortly after Maurice's return to Montmartre a merry, round little man named Clovis Sagot ("Sagot the Madman"), who had established himself in a former chemist's shop in the rue Laffitte and handed out to the artists, in exchange for their pictures, the drugs and medicines left on his shelves by his predecessor, had begun to buy Maurice's pictures, or rather to exchange them for medicines of high alcoholic content. Ultimately he paid money—from five to twenty francs, depending on the size of the canvas. These paintings Sagot shipped to Switzerland, where they passed into the hands of the type of international tourist who buys oil paintings in gift shops. But Sagot doubled his money.

It was at Sagot's shop that Louis Libaude, art critic of *L'Art Littéraire*, first saw Maurice's work. Libaude, of whom André Utter was to say "he wouldn't hurt a lion," had recently shifted his talents from the auctioneer's stand at Tattersall's, the Neuilly horse market; and Émile Bernard, the editor of *L'Art Littéraire*, was delighted to have come by such cogent critical talent in so unlikely a place. Libaude's job seemed, on the surface, to have little connection with big money-making, which was his confessed purpose in life. However, it did allow him a good deal of time to frequent the government auction rooms at Hôtel Drouot. There he in-

* Mousis has often been referred to as "Suzanne's first husband." A thorough search of the *mairies*, both in Montmartre and at Pierrefitte-Montmagny, has failed to produce any record of marriage or of divorce. It has always been assumed by all of Suzanne's friends that her "marriage to Mousis" was figurative rather than literal.

vested shrewdly by purchasing antique furniture, paintings, porcelain, and sculpture. His flat at No. 6 rue Baudin was filled with these purchases, and everything, including the bed he slept in, displayed a sales tag. Francis Jourdain gives us a fine description of the man: "Thin, bilious, with a greenish-yellow face . . . he lurked in the auction rooms at the Hôtel Drouot like a shadow. I often met him there, and each time he tried to throw me off his track by talking about nothing but horses. 'I want to talk to you,' he would say. 'Where can I see you? I'd invite you to lunch, but I don't eat or drink. My stomach is bad, my liver is awful.' "

Libaude's method of buying Utrillo paintings was characteristically devious. In the back of his mind was the idea that once it became known that Libaude was buying them, others would offer more than he did. By promising to stage a one-man show of the canvases, he did business with Suzanne under a pledge of secrecy. Not even Maurice (least of all Maurice, who was likely to spill anything when drunk!) must know that the art critic of *L'Art Littéraire* was buying his pictures.

To Francis Jourdain, however, must go the credit for being the first critic to recognize in print the importance of Maurice's art. Shortly after the Libaude show Jourdain published his first brochure on the artist: *Maurice Utrillo.* But by that time a few wise collectors could already boast of having Utrillo paintings in their collections. One day in 1909 Manzana Pissarro, the Impressionist's son, came upon Maurice with one of his pictures under his arm standing under a Montmartre awning in a rainstorm. The picture interested him, and he persuaded Maurice to let him see more of his work. A few days later young Pissarro appeared at Maurice's studio, where he found the painter at his easel eating pickled herrings to increase his thirst as he worked. Pissarro bought ten canvases at fifty francs apiece.

A year later Francis Jourdain was in the Galerie Druet

when Maurice, drunken and filthy, brought in several of his canvases and tried to show them to M. Druet. Druet would have none of them, but Jourdain was impressed. Finally the firm's accountant, overhearing the critic trying to persuade the dealer to reverse his judgment, asked him whether he thought it might not be a "bit of business" to buy one of the canvases for fifty francs. "I told him to go ahead," Jourdain recounts; then adds, "And my commission was a grateful smile from the poor wretch." He himself then bought two paintings of the Montmagny period, and soon his enthusiasm brought several of his friends to Libaude's flat and the new gallery which he had just opened in the Avenue Trudaine. These visitors included the Kapfeerer brothers, who were collectors; Paul Gallimard, the publisher, and his brother-in-law Duche, the novelist; Octave Mirbeau; and the critic Élie Faure; all of whom bought paintings. Libaude lost no time in having word spread about that these eminent personages were buying Utrillos from him "at from 250 francs upward." At the Hôtel Drouot he passed out leaflets—"M. Louis Libaude sells privately and at retail his collection of modern pictures. . . ." He was at the time paying Suzanne a flat rate of fifty francs. "This price must remain confidential," he wrote to her in a letter dated "at ten minutes to noon." "I buy few works by young artists, but I am prepared to make an exception for your son because his talent particularly interests me."

Had the money been handed over to Maurice, it would have gone for wine only. No longer driven by a desire to paint, he now did so only to drink, staggering from bistro to bistro offering his still-wet canvases in exchange for a few glasses of *rouge*. Two or three glasses were enough to make him reeling drunk; if he still had money then, he would throw it into the sewers. Now he floundered about, sometimes miserable and weeping, sometimes absurdly belligerent, sometimes trying to be comical by making erotic and obscene gestures, often sick. Hounded by ruffians, tormented by yelping urchins, abused by night revelers, he could find escape only in stupor or coma. When he fell into some merciful dark corner, young brutes stripped him of his clothes or emptied garbage buckets over him. So many were the debauches that ended for him in the police station that the gendarmes always had brushes and colors on hand and made him produce a painting before letting him go home. It no longer seemed to matter whether he was drunk or sober when he painted. The automatic production went on. Canvas after canvas seemed "to happen" before the listless strokes of his brush. Nor did he have to look at what he was painting. Often he set up his easel to command a certain street scene and then, facing it, he would paint an altogether different one —one in his mind.

For the most part he worked from picture post cards picked up in souvenir shops! From these he measured angles and perspectives with a ruler, but what happened in the finished painting bore no relation to the post card in front of him. The scene was now suffused with affection and radiance, with the harmony of his uncanny technique, radiating security, magic, and glory. His famous "White Period," that of his greatest painting, belongs to these years, roughly between 1908 and 1914. Here, by using massive blocks of blues and browns he brought to his white walls, in contrast, a solid grandeur and poetry never before seen in painting, or equaled since. On the meaning of those walls, on their emotional impact upon the hearts of men, he staked his worth as an artist.

Only at the Lapin Agile did he find a measure of peace. This tiny single-storied pink building on the northeast corner of the rue des Saules and the rue Saint-Vincent, looking squarely at the high wall of the cemetery across the street, had since 1902 become the meeting place of the "Bateau Lavoir gang" and a great many of the other Montmartre

artists. The building had a romantic history. Originally supposed to have been the hunting lodge of Henri IV, it was in
the eighties the home of André Gill, the great political carica-
turist. In remembrance of its original purpose Gill painted
a rabbit above the door in the manner of sixteenth-century
taverns. As a result the house became known as "Le Lapin
à Gill." In 1885 Gill blew out his brains in the kitchen, and
soon afterward the place was converted into a cabaret frequented in the main by local thugs. The proprietress was "*la
grosse* Adèle," a former model and friend of Suzanne
Valadon. During her regime the cabaret was known as "Les
Assassins." But in 1901 Adèle established herself in a restaurant at the top of the hill facing the church of St. Pierre—
The Moulin Joyeux—while Frédé Gerard, who had owned
Zut in the Place Ravignan when Picasso painted the mural,
now took over the cabaret, changing its name to "Le Lapin
Agile," a pun on the name it had borne in Gill's time. Just as
at the Zut, Frédé, with his heavy beard, his flaming velvet
vests and tasseled nightcap, looking for all the world like an
operatic bandit, once again sat astride a barrel strumming his
guitar and singing "Cherry Time" and "The Coster's Wife."
Cramped at the benches and tables around him in the small
main room decorated with paintings by Picasso, Modigliani,
Utrillo, Rouault, and others, and with a large wax crucifixion
by Wasselet, the customers would drink their Corsican wine,
join in the choruses of Frédé's risqué ballads, and continue
the arguments which had been broken off the previous
evening.

It was the only place where Maurice could feel that there
were understanding and affection around him. No one tried
to change him. No one ridiculed him; in fact, he had a feeling
that everyone admired his strange independence of spirit.
"He is one of the greatest French painters," Picasso was later
to say of him. For the present, being a painter was enough.
As such, he was entitled to behave as he wanted to. If he fell

asleep, they let him snore through the evening and then took him home. If he stormed off in a drunken rage, they shrugged their shoulders rather than murmured in pity. They knew that he wanted to be one of them, that he tried to make sense of their high-flown language and their complicated aesthetic theories, but that in the end it was easier for him to insult them all and get roaring drunk. They did not mind. There was not one among them who did not have the urge to do the same thing every once in a while.

Modigliani alone would go with him.

Born in Leghorn in 1884, the son of a Jewish banker whose bank had failed and a mother who was happy for her son to be an artist, Amedeo Modigliani was sent to study at the Florentine and Venetian academies before he arrived in Paris in 1907, when he was twenty-three. He came to the Butte with an exaggerated conception of the artist's life, in his mind's eye and the intermittent fever of tuberculosis in his body. A tall, indolent figure, aristocratic and poised, he dressed in corduroy suits and brilliant purple and orange scarves, and affected the wide-brimmed black hat which had been the mark of the artist before the turn of the century. Uncommonly handsome, with the lithe and powerful body of a Ghirlandajo stripling and the emotional drive of a satyr, he plunged at once into all the dissipations of Montmartre. He seems to have made a beeline for Pigeard, the notorious dope peddler, whose small house in the Impasse du Delta, fitted to resemble the current idea of a Chinese opium den, was the gathering place of the hashish addicts. Fifteen francs bought enough of the drug to last a fortnight.

It was at one of Pigeard's "hashish and alcohol parties" that Modigliani met André Utter, who later introduced him to Maurice. And it was during the evening of this meeting *chez* Pigeard that Modigliani is supposed suddenly to have shouted, "I've found the way!" and shown the company a sketch he had just drawn of a woman's head with the almond-shaped eyes and swanlike neck which were henceforth to stamp his painting. Whether or not this vision of sickness, refined, decorative, and gentle, which now began to permeate his work stemmed from the delirium of the addict it is hard to say. Surely the cool air of death was upon Modigliani always; it was in the natural course of things that it should be in his art. But, far from depressing him, it heightened and quickened his desire to experience all sensual pleasure at its most ecstatic pitch. Desperately he loved women. Willfully he became addicted to wine, to absinthe, to drugs. No dissipation was too wild for him to hurl himself into it with rapture. "I have been through Dante's hell tonight. Ah, wonderful hell!" he once exclaimed to Suzanne Valadon.

But there was also at the core of Modigliani's character a deep compassion for the dispossessed, the humble, the simple people. The melancholy which he found in their weariness, in their drawn faces, in their loneliness was the restraining anchor to the dark forces which possessed him. It is the melancholy which haunts his pictures. He could burst into tears at the sight of a sick child, or insist that a ragged little girl take the last sou in his pocket.

In Maurice, Modigliani found an outlet for all these emotions as well as a fellow who could share his appetite for alcohol. They were two gentle men. Furthermore, Maurice was a painter, while as yet Modigliani had not been able to give direction to his work. For although the "Bateau Lavoir" gang listened to his theories, mostly only half formulated, and a few of the minor art galleries paid him a franc or two for some of his drawings, the only public attention his work had had was when Berthe Weill received a summons from the police for exhibiting one of his nudes in her window. "I work at three pictures a day—in my head. But what's the good of spoiling canvases when no one buys my work?" he complained. To him there was something glorious in Maurice's astonishing ability to produce endlessly wonderful pictures in spite of his debauchery. Even selling them for twenty francs was marvelous. In his eyes Maurice was a kind of hero of Bohemianism.

There was, as far as Modigliani was concerned, a glow of lighthearted humor in his carousals with Maurice despite all the disgust with which the Philistines viewed them. There was, for example, the night on Montparnasse when the two of them astounded the clientele of a restaurant by suddenly whipping out their paints and brushes and executing an enormous mural of Montmartre, Utrillo doing the landscape and "Modi" the figures, while the waiters rushed about with their trays and the *patron* made feeble threats to call the police, only to be checked each time by the cheers of his customers as the scene on the wall developed.

Or there was the occasion when the two friends collected the dregs from all the glasses and bottles on the tables and toasted one another.

"You are a great painter, Dédo."

"I'm very honored, Maumau, but you are a greater painter than I."

"No. You are the greatest."

"I protest. Don't contradict me!"

"I protest!"

At this point they began to fight.

On the way to the police station the argument continued.

"Well, who's the greater painter now—you or me?"

"You."

"You lie! It's you."

"You call me a liar?" And again the fists began to fly.

However, for each good-humored episode there were a hundred sordid ones—of nights when they would be beaten up and robbed by ruffians, of nights when they slept in the gutters, of nights when they were lost in the rain or the snow and Modigliani would be racked by his hideous tubercular cough, of nights of abysmal depression obsessed by thoughts of death and suicide.

Sometimes their bouts were solitary, and Modigliani would finish by rolling himself into a corner at the Impasse de Guelma with Suzanne's great German sheep dog and sleep off the effects of his orgy. Or he would clatter up the winding stairs, shed all his clothes on the landing, and burst into the flat naked, dancing wildly. Suzanne and Utter would stand him in a tub of water in the kitchen and clean him up before putting him to bed. Suzanne understood drunks. To her and Utter he was, like Maurice, not an object of scorn, not just a noisome alcoholic. He was a gifted spirit, a fine artist battered by demons, and they loved him. If he were mad, so to a point were they also touched with madness. Every artist was touched with it.

In the Impasse de Guelma Suzanne and Utter lived in a sort of miniature "Bateau Lavoir" of their own. Here everyone was an artist—Raoul Dufy, Georges Braque and his wife (and his flute), the bombastic Tuscan Gino Severini, with his sandals and wild unmatched socks. There were no keys to any of the studios, but there were hundreds of empty wine bottles on the landings. Interminable arguments about art filled days and nights, and there were gay uninhibited parties. Vagabond poets and artists streamed in and out at all times, tramps slept on the stairs. Suzanne kept a goat in her studio, where she said she fed it bad drawings. They lived on money borrowed from Dufy, who had a regular employment designing fabrics for Paul Poiret, the couturier, or on the sale of their pictures, which was rarely enough to keep them in food for two or three days once Dufy was paid back. But if Modigliani needed affection and encouragement, Suzanne and Utter gave it unstintingly. Their studio was always open to him as one of their family. "My elected mother" he called Suzanne as he poured out the troubles of his soul, sitting at her feet while she painted. After he left the Butte for Mont-parnasse he carried his canvases and drawings across the city for Suzanne and Utter to see; their admiration was impassioned and sincere. He loved to bring them armloads of hothouse flowers, on which he spent all he had received from the sale of a picture. "Ah! But they are our beautiful Italy!" he would cry. He would sing them boat songs of his native Leghorn and recite for them passages from his beloved Dante. At other times, in less lyrical mood, he would steal one of their paintings and sell it, using the proceeds to launch a spree. Once he brought in a prostitute and camped with her on the studio floor for a week, consuming quantities of hashish pills and engaging in a protracted sexual orgy. Even when he fought with them, smashing one of his canvases on Utter's head because he would not give him money for dope, Suzanne and Utter felt no resentment. Whatever Modigliani did, they understood and loved him.

But, discouraged by failure to win recognition, he became increasingly bitter, and his dissipations became more violent. "Ah! To have the world at my feet as Maumau has!" he would exclaim. And then in a jealous fury he would revile his friend. When he was sober he was surly, quarrelsome, and sadistic. Once accepted by the artists of the Butte as a charming hedonist, he ultimately became a pariah. Too much meanness, too much bitterness. His friends shunned him. He became so objectionable that even the genial Frédé refused to allow him into the Lapin Agile.

Then in 1913 he deserted the Butte for Montparnasse, where he found a kindly oasis in the studios of the Jewish immigrant artists—at Kisling's, at Pascin's, or at the boy Soutine's. And somehow, when he was among these aliens bitterness left him—for a while at any rate. Women were generous to him. And it was on Montparnasse that the Polish poet Leopold Zborowski befriended him—Zborowski, who was to go into debt to buy paints and dope for him, who sheltered him like a child and bore the full brunt of his worst tantrums, and who believed so passionately in his art that he gave up his own literary career in order to sell his pictures.

When he came back to Montmartre it was either to bully some money from Beatrice Hastings, the English poet who lived in the rue Norvins and had been his mistress, or to be with Suzanne and Utter for a little while—to talk, to laugh, to sing them his songs of Leghorn, to take them with him to where his heart was—"*Cara, cara Italia,*" dear, dear Italy, where he was not a stranger, an alien. "*Cara, cara Italia.*"

VII "Unholy Trinity"

"Homage to Yadwiga!" "Honor to Rousseau!"

The hall was festooned in red, white, and blue bunting with French and Mexican flags. On an easel at one end of the room stood an oil painting of a nude woman lying on a couch surrounded by trees and greenery. This was Yadwiga, a memory of first love. A few feet from her, sitting in solemn dignity on an improvised dais, was her creator—small, plump, sixty-five-year-old Henri Rousseau, whom his friends called "the Douanier" because he had once held a job as a minor customs official at a tollgate on the outskirts of Paris. He had had two brief careers in military service: the first in 1866, when he had served as a drummer boy with the 52d Infantry Regimental Band in Napoleon III's disastrous gesture to save Maximilian in Mexico; the second in 1870, when as a sergeant he had, so he said, "saved the town of Dreux from the horrors of civil war" by his "presence of mind in a crisis," and had been cheered by the grateful townspeople with cries of "*Vive le sergeant Rousseau!*"

After he retired from the Customs and Excise Service, Henri Rousseau opened a tiny stationery store, and it was here that he began to paint—strange, primitive visions of commonplace scenes, peopled with stiff, comic personages and toy animals. No one bought his paintings, and few bought the stationery. Once again he retired, this time to a

171

room over a foundry in the rue Pernelle, where he posted a notice on the door: "Instruction: Elocution, Music, Painting, and Solfeggio." A lady and her four children seem to have been his only steady pupils. Here he held "literary and philosophical soirees," during which his pupils performed on the mandolin and clarinet and he himself played his own compositions on the violin. Afterward the company soaked bread in wine, talked, and sang, and then went home "all happy." "Holding that complete freedom of production should be given to any beginner whose turn of mind aspires to achieve the Beautiful and the Good," he exhibited each year in the Salon des Indépendants. It was there that, in 1885, he met Seurat, Toulouse-Lautrec, Gauguin, Redon, and Gustave Coquiot, who were amazed and delighted at the naïve splendor of the two pictures which he exhibited. Ten years later Alfred Jarry "discovered" him and ultimately brought Apollinaire, Picasso, Max Jacob, and others to his soirees.

On this particular night of the year 1908 he sat under a red candle which was dripping wax, and a little inverted cone gradually appeared on the top of his bald head. Apparently he felt that it would be unsoldierly to move. Before him an uproarious "banquet" was in full swing. Given by Pablo Picasso for thirty of his friends, its stated purpose was to celebrate Picasso's acquisition of "Yadwiga," rescued from a secondhand furniture shop. Actually it was in honor of "the brave *douanier*." Somehow Picasso and the caterer had gotten their dates mixed, for, except for the fruit tarts, no food arrived until the following day. But the wine was there, and before the evening was over so was most of the population of Montmartre. Frédé from the Lapin Agile arrived with his guitar and his donkey Aliberon. André Salmon pretended to have a fit, chewing a cake of soap to produce a terrifying froth. There were calls to Gertrude Stein to sing some Pennsylvania Red Indian songs. Marie Laurencin, then twenty-three and with the grace of a fairy, managed to alight in the middle of the dish of tarts, after which, dripping fruit and juice, she sang old Provençal rondels. The highlight of the evening, however, was the extempore recitation of a poem composed by Guillame Apollinaire which recalled Rousseau's military career among the mangoes, pineapples, and monkeys of Mexico. The poem concluded:

> *"Nous sommes réunis pour célébrer ta gloire;*
> *Ces vins, qu'en ton honneur nous verse Picasso,*
> *Buvons-les donc, puisque c'est l'heure de les boire,*
> *En criant tous en chœur: 'Vive! Vive Rousseau!'"* *

The cheers, "*Vive Rousseau!*" lasted the night.

The "bravest of customs officials" then rose to sing a number of his own songs—"*Clochettes*" and "An Angel's Dream" among them—and to play a few solos on his violin, concluding by delivering an address on his Mexican war experiences of forty years before. And at some time during the evening Rousseau is supposed to have told Picasso, "You and I are the two greatest living painters, I in the modern style, you in the Egyptian."

The "banquet" was the climax of thirty years of rollicking fellowship which had made Montmartre the Mecca of the young in heart all over the Western world. From this time onward, the painter-philosophers, the painter-sociologists, the painter-theoreticians, the painter-poets, the painter-psychologists—the heirs of Cézanne—began to drift away from the Sacred Hill as mysteriously as, in the seventies, the artists of Light had followed Manet toward it. Rousseau died of gangrene, the result of a badly dressed cut on his leg, in

---

* "Thy glory we are together to celebrate;
These wines in thine honor are bought by Picasso.
Let's drink 'em—it's time now to down 'em
And cry in a chorus, 'Long life to Rousseau!'"

September, 1910. The following month Picasso left the "Bateau Lavoir" for his large studio on the Boulevard de Clichy, and shortly afterward moved to Montparnasse. Some said it was the commercial fever generated by the theaters and dance halls of the Place de Clichy and the Place Pigalle that drove Cézanne's men to the broad boulevards of Raspail and Montparnasse. Others said it was the motor buses of tourists who arrived every quarter of an hour before the basilica of Sacré-Coeur or in the Place du Tertre; others that it was the sight of the new apartment houses, with the names of un-imaginative, stuffy architects etched on their uninspired façades, that drove anyone with aesthetic sensitivity to desert the Butte. The very picturesqueness of what remained on the scene seemed to impel others to leave. Whatever the reason, the artists departed, and with them went the brilliant light which had ushered in "their" century. Soon most of the eager, the brave, the hopeful young artists followed them. And in the lengthening gray shadow in their wake the weather-torn sails of the last of the windmills turned slowly, and people said that Montmartre was finished.

Above the door of his studio at No. 12 rue Cortot, on the floor above the one Suzanne had maintained when she was living at Montmagny, Émile Bernard had posted a notice: "He who does not believe in God, Raphael, and Titian does not enter here." The words were still there when Suzanne, Utter, Maurice, and Madeleine, two tomcats, the German sheep dog, and a goat moved in.

"If we cannot be as exclusive, at least we shall be better painters than Bernard," Suzanne laughed. It was no idle reso-lution. With the full powers of her creative being unleashed, and filled with the exquisite turbulence of love, she hurled herself at her work with every fiber of her vitality. If there was talk in the cafés and studios of an artistic exodus from the Butte, she did not hear it; nor, if she had heard it, would it have altered her course. She did not believe in "schools" and "movements." To her, art was an expression of private passion, uncomplicated and irrational. Its theories were imposed by nature, not by group thinking. "Above all," she was to say later, "I believe that the true theory is the one imposed by nature—first on the painter and then on what he sees."

Suzanne loved the confraternity of artists in an anarchic, emotional way because she shared their eccentric tempers, not because she hoped to draw upon their thought processes or align herself with their aesthetic credos. In any case, most of what she heard was over her head. She had no intellectual training. She never read. The charge of her own emotions had always been too mercurial for her to be able to control her thinking responses. Intelligent enough to appreciate superior mentality, she nonetheless to a certain extent despised it. This was true particularly in the case of her lover. Utter's fund of knowledge, his curiosity, the daring thrusts and somersaults of his lively reasoning, his ability to pierce to the heart of almost any subject dazzled her, but at the same time she convinced herself that his cerebral prowess did little to enhance his artistic worth. Yet in the beginning she found it somewhat flattering that, in much the same way as in their physical relationship he ignored the difference in their ages, he accepted her rational powers as the equal of his own.

Her physical enjoyment of Utter's presence was slavish. In his youth, in the sound of his voice, in the smoke from his pipe she found a source of profound exhilaration. To have him near as they worked at their easels in the studio was a tonic to her painting, and she was irritable and frustrated when he was not around. "They flirted like schoolchildren," Utter's boyhood friend Edmond Heuzé says, "and she was always devising pretexts to stay close to him." So together they spent hours at the Louvre and the Luxembourg—"on Thursdays, in honor of my aunt Louise." They went to all the exhibitions, visited the galleries. When they could raise the money, there were the theater and the ballet. They saw Nijinsky dance "The Specter of the Rose," and Suzanne told a friend that "the dancers all seemed to dance very well." In Max Jacob's dark and mysterious room in the "Bateau Lavoir" they listened to Guillaume Apollinaire ("the bastard son of a cardinal," so he said) read the poem called "*Alcools*" and discuss aesthetic objectives and Cubism. At Severini's they heard the manifesto of yet another movement—Futurism ("we extol aggressive movement, feverish insomnia, the double-quick step, the somersault, the box on the ear, the fisticuff"). And at Picasso's new studio on the Boulevard de Clichy the painter Pascin would juggle with Freud, or Matisse in his cool, incisive way would speak of "chromatism" and "zones of color." That these occasions had a genuine importance to Utter, that on them he was able to draw for either his character or his art she could not believe. She could attribute his interest only to youthful exuberance, and accept it docilely with whatever verve she thought necessary to muster.

There were financial difficulties. They were desperately poor. Libaude continued to buy Maurice's paintings, but he complained that there were too many of them. "Since early April you have brought me a picture every other day. It is too much." To make matters worse, he kept payment a bit in arrears. Their own canvases Suzanne and Utter sold for twenty-five or thirty francs—when they could sell them at all. It was better when they could trade them at the butcher's.

A few months after they moved into the rue Cortot, Utter, with a weather eye to the machinations of the wily Libaude, persuaded Clovis Sagot that there were sensational possibilities in a joint exhibition of the paintings of mother and son—Valadon and Utrillo. Suzanne exhibited "*Maurice, la Gran'mère et le chien Pierret*," the vigorous "Portrait of

Below. Suzanne Valadon with her husband, André Utter, in 1920. *Photograph courtesy of Mme. Georges Kars.*

Above. Suzanne Valadon at the age of twenty in the hat Toulouse-Lautrec bought for her. *Photograph courtesy of Gazi-I.G. Below. From the Left:* Maurice Utrillo, Suzanne Valadon, and André Utter, in the studio in the rue Junot. *Photograph courtesy of the Musée de l'Art Moderne, Paris.*

The Valadon Family: *From the left:* André Utter, Suzanne Valadon, Madeleine Valadon, and Maurice Utrillo. Sketch for oil painting by Suzanne Valadon, 1913. *Courtesy of Paul Pétridès, Paris.*

Maurice Utrillo. Drawing by Suzanne Valadon. 1925. *From the collection of Mme. Yvonne Vigneron, Paris.*

Maurice" which now hangs in the Valadon-Utrillo Room of the Museum of Modern Art in Paris, two of four large white nudes which she had done at the Impasse de Guelma, five still lifes which she painted for the exhibition, a pastel portrait of André Utter, and some drawings. Maurice's share of the show was greater—thirty-seven paintings, all of them Montmartre scenes, and a few pencil drawings. The two portraits of Maurice and five of the paintings, including his "Rue Ravignan" and "Renoir's Garden," were shown that year at the Salon des Indépendants and were subsequently sold. But the exhibition at Sagot's was disappointing. Sagot blamed the apache disturbances: the newspapers were full of stories of robberies and brutal murders. People were afraid to go into the streets in their own neighborhoods, much less venture into the dark and narrow Montmartre purlieus. At Meudon, Rodin had a loaded revolver in every room in his house and an armed bodyguard beside his bed at night.

But if Sagot failed to profit much financially, he had the satisfaction of watching Libaude lurking in the doorways across the street, and to Sagot, the merry little "madman," it was a sight that compensated for the failure of his show.

However, neither poverty, intellectual pursuits, nor private calamities had the power to shake the inner citadel of their happiness. Maurice still drank heavily, and there were frequent calls to the police station. For a while he stayed with Suzanne and Utter in the rue Cortot, apparently quite happy with the domestic setup—his beloved mother, his "wonderful best friend," and his darling *gran'mère* all together. "How practical and original we are!" he kept repeating. "How charming!" But eventually he grew restless. "It is too stuffy. I prefer to sleep alone." And so he began to move from lodging to lodging, or, as he put it with the gentle irony he delighted in, "I go from this *hôtel de luxe* to that one." But each morning, in varying stages of sobriety, he returned to the rue Cortot, and in the little room adjoining his mother's studio he painted his scenes of Montmartre from post cards pinned to his easel.

Even when, one spring day in 1912, Maurice was found in a violent state of delirium tremens in the *pissoir* near the Place des Abbesses, Suzanne and Utter took this setback in their stride. Utter sold all his own canvases to Libaude, and they were able to put Maurice in a private sanatorium at Sannois under the care of Dr. Revertegat, a specialist in alcoholism.

Though at first resentful of his confinement, Maurice sat on the stone bench in Dr. Revertegat's small garden staring at the iron gate, his moods varying between apathy, depression, and frustration. Finally he sent for his paints and post cards. Immediately he began to improve. Furthermore, his painting ripened. He began to work less rapidly. His brushwork no longer seemed automatic, and his canvases lost much of the gloom which had so far characterized his "White Period." His sensitivity sharpened. He cleaned his palette of everything but the essential materials. His pictures seemed to take on a fresh suppleness and sobriety.

By the beginning of the summer Maurice was released, and Suzanne and Utter took him to the little village of Ouessant in Brittany. To Suzanne, Brittany was Gauguin, to whom she had for some time formed a sentimental attachment, crediting him with her artistic heritage in much the same way as she had heard the other Montmartre artists credit Cézanne with theirs. She painted with great fervor "in homage to that fine artist," while, less enthralled, Utter worked beside her. But for Maurice there was no spiritual or emotional anchor in Brittany. He longed for Montmartre as one longs for a lover—for the walls, the plaster, the familiar buildings, the poetry of the rain-soaked and weather-beaten streets. He had been away from them too long. He had nothing to paint.

The fields of flowers, the starched white coifs, the pony carts with their English tourists, the fog-enveloped cottages meant nothing to him. He gazed at them listlessly, grew sullen and morose, finally irritable. Soon work became impossible. Suzanne put away her paints, and Utter wandered restlessly over the red iron soil of the countryside. Maurice's unhappy moods dominated the days. The last weeks of the holiday were spent waiting for an explosion.

The summer was charged with forebodings anyway. Even the Montmartre hedonists, resolute refugees from the affairs of the world, were buying newspapers, peeping over the wall, as it were, at the curious behavior of Europe's statesmen. At the tables of La Rotonde on Montparnasse, two saturnine Russians, Lenin and Trotsky, spoke of the coming of war and "the crisis of imperialistic capitalism." In a maneuver to bring Morocco into a French "protectorate," in case Germany should challenge the solvency of the Franco-Russian Alliance, the government sent troops to Fez. The Kaiser countered by sending gunboats to Agadir. War was in the air. But Caillaux, the French premier, had gone farther than his nerve would carry him. The wind rushed out of his sails, and he scrambled together a policy of appeasement that for the time being saved the day.

Back on the Butte at the end of the summer, the pattern of life in the rue Cortot resumed its old course. Meanwhile Sagot had died, and Libaude was quick to put Maurice on a small monthly retainer in exchange for the exclusive right to handle his paintings. The arrangement eased the financial situation somewhat. Later in the year Libaude gave Maurice the long-promised one-man show, where, thanks to the support of Jourdain, Mirbeau, and Faure, the majority of the paintings were sold at prices between 100 and 120 francs.

But Maurice was not interested. Sitting at the edge of the gutter before Libaude's gallery with a couple of wine bottles, he enjoined the pedestrians to drink with him and to extol "the divine art of M. Raffaelli."

In the course of his wanderings this year Maurice had found a silver-painted statuette of Joan of Arc in a market. The little figure was with him always now. If the passers-by before Libaude's showed no disposition to talk with him about M. Raffaelli, Maurice invited them to converse with "his" saint. At cafés almost anywhere on the hill customers were likely to see his wavering, unkempt figure speaking aloud his part of an imaginary conversation with the little statuette, confessing his sins to it, or kneeling before it in supplication. When he fell asleep, huddled in some dark alley or at the foot of a tree, he would be clutching the little figure. Sometimes he cradled it in his arm as he walked, and, the tears streaming down his cheeks, croaked lullabies to it.

Summer saw Maurice on holiday again with Suzanne and Utter, this time in Corsica, where, as he told Frédé afterward, "On the hills there were wonderful bouquets of houses, white as if for weddings." It was a happy, relaxed time. The three painted together in the unpaved streets of the little villages. They took long walks along the surf. Everywhere the crisp bright colors blazing under the clean blue skies delighted them. Inspired by the sight of the Corsican fishermen at work at their nets, Suzanne made the first sketches for her *"Les Lanceurs de Filets,"* that large, strangely self-conscious canvas which now hangs in the Museum of Modern Art in Paris, for which Utter posed for the three figures. The food was strange and good, the wine (drunk in moderation) was excellent, the Corsicans were friendly and warmhearted. Within two months Maurice had gained ten pounds and was spending a couple of hours each day on a bicycle "to build muscles."

But not long after they returned to Paris with the two little donkeys to which Maurice had become attached, Maurice had to be confined again, this time in the insane asylum at Villejuif. Here his sadistic keeper smudged his paintings, and his cellmate ate his paints. He responded with astonishing patience. "Here I am, stumbling among all sorts of vexations," he wrote to a friend, the ex-police sergeant M. Gay. "I'm dying with impatience to be free, to work, to paint, and to be reasonable."

Had he cared anything about what happened to his pictures once he had painted them, he might have taken heart from the results of the sale which took place at the Hôtel Drouot shortly after his release from Villejuif in February. A society of Parisian businessmen called "The Bearskin (*La Peau de l'Ours*)," which for some years had been collecting paintings by contemporary artists, put their collection up for auction. Among the pictures, which included works by Matisse, Picasso, Dufy, Derain, and Rouault, three of Utrillo's canvases brought 120, 150, and 270 francs, while a view of Notre Dame commanded 400 francs.

Maurice was standing on the threshold of acclaim and fortune. He could not have cared less. Once again he was floundering in the nightmare of his alcoholism, reeling through the same shabby streets which his brush would transfigure in the new day's light, full of alcohol, rage, and misery. Around him, in the little squares which he loved so tenderly when they were empty, masses of hostile humanity chattered and laughed and sang. Their merrymaking stalked his lonely zigzag course. All he wanted was escape—escape from people, escape from himself.

That year the spring was especially sunny, and along the Champs Élysées the chestnuts were in leaf a month earlier than usual. King George V and Queen Mary and later the King and Queen of Denmark arrived for gala state visits. The city buzzed with American businessmen and their wives looking for the works of Impressionist and Postimpressionist painters to take home. At fetes and costume balls people were turkey-trotting and bunny-hugging to orchestras featuring the new moaning horn of Adolphe Sax. Count Camondo's collection of Impressionist paintings, including Manet's "*Lola de Valence*," Degas' "*L'Absinthe*," and Lautrec's "*La Clownesse Cha-U-Kao*," was installed in a dark corner of the Louvre.

On June 28 the heir to the Austrian throne and his morganatic wife were shot dead in the streets of Sarajevo while making a St. Vitus' Day inspection of the town. People said the incident meant war.

Mme. Caillaux, the wife of the ex-premier and present Minister of Finance, went to her hairdresser's for a hairdo and manicure, after which she proceeded to shoot and kill Gaston Calmette, the editor of *Figaro*, who had charged her husband with corruption in office. Her deed was done with style, and even Caillaux's first wife came to court to support her. Everyone was delighted when, on July 28, she was acquitted.

Three days later Jean Jaurès, the Socialist leader, was assassinated by a monarchist fanatic while he sat in a café.

On the 4th of August the German army invaded Belgium.

On Montmartre the bugle call held a ring of gaiety. "I have loved art so much that I'm an art-illery man," sang Apollinaire. Let others prate about "the lamps going out all over Europe," the exuberant young men of the Butte, charged with cynicism, patriotism, or romance, hastened to don the blue uniform of the Army of the Republic. To the cynics, war spelled the end of bourgeois impedimenta. Food and shelter would be free. It mattered no longer whether one was "successful" or not. Landlords, bill collectors, critics, and dealers were left to prey upon one another. To the patriotic, France stood as the glorious defender of mankind against the loathsome bestiality of German imperial ambition. To the romantic young men like Apollinaire, war was a new frontier opened to their abilities, their stamina, and their sensitivity.

It was a world of fresh ideas, of experiment, of action. But whatever their motives, the young men flocked to the recruiting stations by the hundreds.

André Utter was among the first. He went off in a detachment which included his neighbors at No. 12 rue Cortot —Galanis and the poet Reverdy, Guillaume Apollinaire, Louis Marcoussis, Charles Laborde, and Edmond Heuzé. At first they were billeted in improvised barracks on the Esplanade des Invalides, but after a few days Utter was assigned to the 158th Infantry Regiment at Fontainebleau. What impulse carried him it was hard to say. Afterward he insisted he had volunteered because he knew he would be drafted. But, like millions who fought with him, his disillusionment when he returned was so intense that it masked forever any idealism which might have propelled him into the struggle.

Utter's going was a cruel blow to Suzanne. Nor did the fact that before leaving he insisted on marrying her lessen its impact. She went to the *mairie* depressed and disconsolate. The brief ceremony, for others a beginning, to her spelled the end. Behind it was the happiness of five years—an idyllic ecstasy, as she saw it now, in which together they had started on the road to fine achievement. Always she had hated separation from him. This, she told herself, was because she enjoyed having him close to her. But now, seeing him go off with the others, sharing their lives, being a part of something in which she did not exist, she knew she was afraid of losing him. It was a disastrous admission, for with it came a host of doubts and questions, of which the most cogent was probably: What powers did she have to hold him? Her art? Her mind? She was not deluded.

Her body? Here Suzanne ran into a problem she had never faced before. Utter was twenty-eight years old, and she was forty-nine. Until now it was he who had made a point of refusing to acknowledge the difference in their ages; of course she had been willing to humor him. He had made her keenly aware of her fascination, encouraging her to exploit her voluptuousness, her fine sensuality, her passionate temperament, her lusty humor—all that he loved best in her. And, with the wisdom born of her experience with other men, she shifted the light from one facet of her personality to another with such subtlety that he was always enthralled. It was a game she loved—a triumphant substitute for any deficiency she felt intellectually. As long as Utter was beside her she would feel certain of the power she held over him. Had he had the broad experience of love of which she had been the climax, she might have been confident that he would remain constant. But he was young, in the full bloom of virility, tormentingly handsome in his blue uniform; and in spite of the legal ties which now bound them together, Suzanne was haunted by fear of what would happen to their relationship.

"She was always too young for her age," Nora Kars, who met her at the close of the war, observed. Outwardly Suzanne had changed very little since André Utter first saw her. Tiny still, with a beautifully ripened figure and an enormous amount of animal energy, she had lost none of the appeal she had always had for men. Yet she was not reassured inwardly. Her age had become her adversary, and she was fighting a desperate battle against it, using all the artifices associated in her mind with youthful feminine allure. Her movements became birdlike flutterings. She giggled and tittered in a high-pitched, excited voice. "Suzanne," said a friend, "chirps like a robin." Maurice had to call her by her first name. The year of her birth changed repeatedly, and soon all the events of her past life followed suit. Only when Maurice came to her in the mornings did she paint, for play was the badge of youth. Her studio was rarely empty of friends. The evenings found her the vivacious center of some café or cabaret gathering, or, in a friend's studio, the life of the party. Even her fidelity to Utter had to be sacrificed occasionally so that she might prove her body had lost none of its vigor.

Still Suzanne missed Utter every hour of the day, missed him even more than she had feared she would from the moment he had announced his intention to enlist. Part of herself had gone with him, Heaven only knew where. What was left on the platform of the Gare Montparnasse as the train carrying her young husband pulled away was seared with the pain of years. Age struck savagely from the cold draft of the departing train. She was ineffably old. A violent chill overcame her, and by the time she reached the Metro her teeth were chattering uncontrollably. But by the time she reached Lamarck-Caulincourt the chill had passed. Ruefully and wearily she climbed the long hill to the rue Cortot. Somewhere ahead, she told herself, there must be hope for an aging woman. Utter must come back. And youth would be with him, always.

One day in February, 1915, Maurice too presented himself at the army recruiting station in the rue Ordener and volunteered for military service. The officer accepted his application and instructed him to proceed to the training center at Argentan. Maurice was delighted. For six months a depression had hung over him as he saw young men of his generation leaving for the front. Hatred of the Germans coursed through his blood. Only fear that people might ridicule him if he were not accepted for service had prevented him from appearing at the recruiting station earlier. Now it was done: he was in the army. This called for a celebration, which in turn became a binge, and he arrived at Argentan in such a wild, drunken fury that he was flatly rejected.

The next two months began one of the darkest periods of his life—days of hallucinations, nights of maniacal screaming and window-breaking, rabid tirades against the Germans. His hatred of pregnant women became obsessive again; frothing at the mouth and howling madly, he lurched about the streets in pursuit of them. In one of his few periods of comparative calm he painted his indictment of the German savagery—"*La Cathédrale de Reims en Flamme*," the cathedral where his revered Joan of Arc had accomplished her earthly mission by crowning the dauphin. He had never seen the cathedral: he copied it from a post card and enveloped it in flames of his own imagination. At last one day the police picked him up in the Place de la Bourse, where he had outraged a crowd of citizens by his particularly unlicensed conduct. He was taken to La Santé prison and the judge ordered him to be confined as a lunatic at Villejuif.

In June, Madeleine died. The long unloving relationship of mother and daughter had run its course. Dwelling on thoughts of what their lives might have been, Suzanne was able to weep; and since she happened to be in possession of a little money at the moment, she purchased a family burial plot in the cemetery at Saint-Ouen. She felt Madeleine's passing keenly. However detached the relationship between her mother and herself had become, contemptuous and hostile as her feelings had grown to be, Madeleine's death could not but intensify the sense of loneliness that gripped Suzanne after Utter's departure to the war, a departure now all the more poignant because even Maurice was not with her.

It was six months before Maurice was released from Villejuif and returned to live with his friend César Gay. Gay, the retired police sergeant, ran a small bistro called the Casse-Croute in the rue Paul-Féval, a few steps from the Place du Tertre in one direction and the rue Cortot in another. Since early 1915 a small room above the Casse-Croute had been one of Maurice's "*hôtels de luxe*." One night he had lingered there very drunk, and had astonished Gay by insisting on tallying the daily receipts in his account book, which he did with amazing speed and accuracy. From then on he returned nightly "to do his bookkeeping." Gay finally let him rent the little room which Maurice began to call home, and hung some of his pictures (with price tags of 100 francs on each) about the walls of his bistro. And when he found a likely customer for one of them, he applied all he knew about salesmanship, which was usually considerably more than the customer could resist.

With patient devotion Gay assumed a fatherly role, to which Maurice responded with affection. The old sergeant was no prude: "I gave him his liter of red wine whenever he finished a painting. Only I tried to keep him from downing it in one gulp." There was admiration in his voice when he called him "Monsieur Maurice." He liked to sit beside the artist while he painted, and talk about his experiences in the police force. He was delighted when his lodger offered to teach him to paint. It was small pay for what Gay was obliged to put up with, but he did not complain. Something of a lighthearted, play-acting formality permeated their relationship up to a point; what came afterward Gay accepted with resignation. As long as it was practical to be firm, he was so unflinchingly, but once matters were beyond his control his retreat was good-humored and kind. With ceremonial dignity they made "agreements" which they always sealed solemnly with a toast.

When he was thirsty Maurice would stamp on the floor and Gay would leave his bar and come up to see what he wanted. The "agreement" was that Maurice was to be given his wine when the painting he was working on was finished. Now, in the middle of the job, Maurice demanded three liters. The ex-sergeant was firm. Then Maurice threatened to drink his turpentine. Clearly there had to be a new agreement. So they toasted it. Another time they had an "agreement" that Maurice was to give up drinking entirely. Within a matter of hours he appeared at the bar of the Casse-Croute roaring drunk on Mme. Gay's eau de Cologne. There was the written agreement which Tabarant, Maurice's biographer, speaks of: "I agree to stay at M. Gay's without going out until the end of September." This would have been for three weeks, but before the day was over Maurice had jumped out of a window into the street and made a getaway. "What can I do?" the old sergeant wanted to know. "He gave me his word in writing and swore by the head of his mother to be serious about it, and by the time the day was over he had gone. Perhaps I should have tied him up, but that wouldn't have done any good. He'd have ended by cutting the rope with his teeth. What a pity! And such a fine painter!" And when Maurice finally returned, his face swollen and bleeding, his clothes covered with filth, he stuck his head in the doorway and asked plaintively, "Do you want me back?"

There were countless agreements that he would stay locked in his room for various periods of time. These, too, had to be revised when he kicked in a panel of the door, or threatened to set the building on fire, or screamed to passers-by in the street to come and rescue him, or again jumped from the window and disappeared for several days. There was the agreement that he would write his autobiography, to expiate his past misdeeds and to take his mind off his obsession. Maurice began with what he first considered a prologue but which later became an epilogue—a testament to the virtues of the noble man who was his friend. The rest of the material was a miscellany of drinking bouts and confinements in disjointed, wandering prose.* A few pages and he was off on another binge.

While at M. Gay's he had to be locked in a room in order to paint; in the rue Cortot he was free to come and go as he

---

* There is, however, one interesting statement in the sketch. Here for the first time he states that he was born on Christmas Day, a fact which in the later years of his piety had some obscure but nonetheless profound meaning to his religious belief, just as the statuette of St. Joan had. Actually he was born on December 26, as the record in the Montmartre *mairie* shows. He dismissed the validity of the official record with the contention, "God keeps more accurate ones. He told me I was born on Christmas Day."

chose, and there he worked most of the time. It made little difference what the preceding night had been for him. He came in the morning as he had been doing for years, with a mischievous ghost of a smile about his lips. Suzanne painted with him now in the big studio where she had painted with Utter. It was only because he came that she painted at all, she used to say. Not that she was really apathetic to her work. When she was at her easel everything fell into its old way again. Strangely, she did not even miss Utter then. The old powers asserted themselves as strongly as ever; it was simply the desire to get to work that had slackened.

Only in these hours with her son did she find any happiness. The studio teeming with people who brought their own food and a great deal of wine and picnicked on the beds, the hilarious impromptu parties, the gossip of the cafés were only an antidote to the malignant disease that threatened her—old age. Maurice's visits were a tonic, not because he and Suzanne had much to say to each other, but because Maurice's presence gave meaning to Suzanne's rudderless life. Circumstances had long since tamed her fierce protective impulses toward him. She had been forced to accept his wish to be alone, to rove as he wanted. Independence is the very soil from which any artist draws his strength; without it, Suzanne was now convinced, Maurice would be trapped and his future hopeless. The wild fire of genius that burned so unsteadily in him needed freedom, or else it would be quenched. He needed his art; it was the only medicine that could keep him alive. In time, therefore, the full flourishing of his artistic powers became more important to her than the tortured course of his personal life. "Ah, if my son had not known how to render light in his painting, how I should have suffered!" she exclaimed to Jacques Guenne. It was here, then, in the work he was doing, that she could be of practical help in directing him to the only objective which could, in the end, save him from disaster.

She could not believe in the strange automatic development of his art. He had learned to paint from her. It was impossible for her to accept the fact that he had long since outreached her. "If it is not right," she told Jean Vertex, "I insist on his doing it over again. And he does." She was certain that she was the dominating influence in his art. At the 1924 Valadon-Utrillo Exhibition at the Bernheim Jeune Gallery, André Utter made the observation (later supported by Coquiot) that in the pictures of both mother and son, during the period 1910-1912, one found "the same organization, the same materials, the same method, the same harmonies: that only the subjects, the motifs differ." Suzanne was quick to reply, "But of course! And it is the Valadon palette."

Against the ravages of Maurice's obsession, on the other hand, everything Suzanne could do seemed useless. She might plead with Marie Vizier at the Belle Gabrielle not to give him wine, or with M. Gay to keep him locked in his room. She might go to the hospital or the police station in the middle of the night, as she often did, to bring him home, or sign the necessary papers to confine him in a sanatorium— all with a heavy heart. But all this seemed to do no good. To be able to tell him that his drawing was not as certain as it should be, that his palette was muddy, or that he had caught beautifully the melancholy of a church spire was to give him the only help that meant anything.

Without ambition for himself or his art, with nothing else prodding him except an unaccountable urge to paint, Maurice was virtually unaware of his mother's desire to influence his development. "She was too great an artist herself," he would say, in later years, "to interfere with another, even her own son."

To Maurice it was not what she was to his art that mattered; it was what she was to him. He adored her. He came to the rue Cortot to work beside her because it was painful to him to be away from her. She was everything that was right, everything a woman was meant to be. He had never been able to outgrow the thrill of seeing her. He wrote of her:

> *"Suzanne Valadon, ma mère ainsi se nomme.*
> *C'est une noble femme, et belle ainsi que bonne,*
> *En vertus, en beauté. Dieu du génie enfin*
> *Par surcroît la dota de son souffle divin."* *

Suzanne could scarcely be expected to see herself in the role in which Maurice cast her—a childish dream of motherhood come true, a sort of "Madonna of the Easels." It was the last character she would ever have attempted to play. But, badly as she interpreted her importance to him, her reasoning was intelligent and brave, her devotion to her own creed selfless and vehement. If she found happiness in believing that her son came to her studio in order to draw from her the full power of his talent, that he sensed that her understanding of his art was greater than his own, there was no evidence to the contrary; in fact, there was ample reason for her to have been right. For it was clear that to Maurice, whatever she said was wisdom, all that she did was perfection.

The "dreary human muddle of fabricated doom" which was the war dragged on. The united excitement—the feverish dislocation of the call to arms, the German lunge at Paris, the taxicab army—had boiled down to dismal months of inconclusive trench warfare. From the sandbags and mud of the front a mood of bitterness and misery slowly crept over

---

* "Suzanne Valadon—my mother is so called.
   A noble woman, as beautiful as she is good
   In virtue, in beauty. The God of Genius
   In addition, endowed her with his divine breath."

Maurice Utrillo, "A ma mère"; Preface to Jean Bouret, *Suzanne Valadon* (Paris, Pétridès, 1947).

the country. The dreaded telegrams from the Ministry of War arrived in ever-increasing numbers. People muttered about "useless slaughter," "false patriotism," and "criminal stupidity." "What good can come of it?" they asked.

But in 1915, when Berthe Weill staged the first one-woman show of Suzanne's paintings, civilian spirits were still high. Paris had been saved—for the time being, at any rate. Disaster had come very close, and one of the first things everybody had thought about was money. What could you do with your money? Surely you didn't buy pictures with it? Notwithstanding their unwillingness to buy, the public came to the show. "At the point of her brush," wrote the critic Clarensol, "everything comes to life, lives and breathes. This extraordinary woman is passion itself, and one seeks in vain for anyone to compare her with. . . . Madame Valadon is justly celebrated. She paints solidly." "Cézanne himself could not use a different word," wrote Gustave Coquiot.

Suzanne had reason to feel that her future was about to brighten. If anything, it became more precarious.

Before the end of the year Maurice was in another hospital at Villejuif, where he stayed from August to the beginning of November. In 1916 Suzanne put him in the hands of a Dr. Vicq at Autnay-sous-Bois, where he lived in the doctor's house as a member of the family and apparently kept in buoyant spirits for about six weeks. He had a good number of long talks with the doctor, and the fact that he roused himself from his customary taciturnity was in itself a hopeful sign. It was during these talks that Dr. Vicq attempted to probe into the sexual disturbances which he had reason to suspect lay at the root of the patient's alcoholism. Evidently Maurice responded for a while with candor and interest, but in the midst of the consultations he suddenly bolted for Montmartre and refused to return.

Meanwhile in the rue Cortot Suzanne's restless attempts to forestall old age continued. The irrepressible chatter, the parties, the myriad amusing happenings of daily life went on in the face of an ever-deepening atmosphere of restlessness. In the ground-floor flat of the building, Othon Friesz's malodorous cheese became the bone of contention among his neighbors in what soon came to be called "the Battle of the rue Cortot." In the flat directly below Suzanne's studio, the poet Pierre Reverdy, home on leave, fired his revolver into the ceiling in a vain attempt to command silence for his muse from his neighbors overhead. An old corporal, a veteran of the Crimean War, drilled three of his ancient comrades on the cobblestone street. In the garden behind No. 20 a schoolmistress from Picardy was constructing an airplane which, she said, would also "fly under water." And Frédé's donkey Aliberon, nicknamed "Lolo," made love to a pony from the Cirque Medrano in the middle of Place du Tertre.

Sometimes Suzanne would get away. While Maurice was in Dr. Vicq's hands she had a short holiday at Pontoise with Mme. Coquiot during which she painted a few landscapes. And there were rapturous weekends at Evreux and Levallois when Utter was home on short furlough.

Degas came to see her occasionally, fumbling on the narrow spiral stairs. The old man, complaining of deafness as well as blindness, now wandered aimlessly about the city he no longer understood. With him came the bittersweet aura of the past, when gaiety and high spirits were realities and there was no need to change your personality to suit the times. Occasionally a friend would bring Suzanne word of Renoir at Cagnes in the south. The lover who had brought nosegays to the door of her tenement room in the rue Poteau now painted in a wheel chair with a brush strapped to his arthritic hand and worried through sleepless nights over his two boys who were at the front.

In 1917 the Bernheim Jeune Gallery put on a joint exhibition of Valadon, Utrillo, and Utter—the wicked trinity (*"la trinité maudite"*), as some anonymous Montmartre wag had dubbed the three when first they were established in the rue Cortot. The interest in the show was lively, less so perhaps because of the paintings than because of the painters: to a war-weary, patriotism-stuffed citizenry, a woman who lived with her drunken son and a husband three years his junior was likely to prove a lurid and amusing character. A strong scent of unholiness wafted about her name among those who were "in the know." There were extravagant legends of her past: she had been the mistress of the whole Impressionist movement, with Van Gogh and Toulouse-Lautrec thrown in. She was an alcoholic and an opium smoker. She had danced naked through the streets of the Butte in a wild bacchanalia. A dozen men had killed themselves for love of her. The curious, then, were hardly to be satisfied on the opening day of the exhibition by the appearance of the elfin figure with soft, luminous eyes and tremulous, childlike movements, dressed in a long sack tunic and large flat-heeled shoes, and carrying a string bag of vegetables, who stood about peering at the pictures as though she were seeing them for the first time, and who, in departing, explained to M. Bernheim, not without a note of irony in her voice, that she had to leave because she "had some soup on the stove."

Certainly there was about this first exhibition of the three an air of scandal which attracted the sensation-seekers, and to deny that her unique ménage had no bearing on their acceptance as artists would be nonsense. The very staging of the show was a bid for sensationalism. The man who was responsible for it, Felix Fénéon, the *directeur artistique* of the gallery, had a flair for showmanship. His personal appearance alone was theatrical. With his lean gargoyle figure, his stringy goatlike beard, and his casual manner he was also to be easily recognized as "M. Fénéon, the well-known critic and *directeur artistique*" by the midget-sized round black hat on the back of his head, the patent-leather shoes, the pepper-and-salt tweed cape and tippet, and the crimson gloves he wore.

Yet in his long career there were few who could claim a better record of artistic integrity, more meticulous devotion to work, or greater clarity of perception in approaching the problems of painting. At twenty-three he had been the first to understand the meaning of the art of Georges Seurat and the Divisionists. It was he who had coined the word "Neo-impressionism," both as a gesture of respect for their illustrious predecessors, the Impressionists, and to emphasize the differences in their methods of achieving their common goal of light and color. At Volpini's show he had espoused the cause of Gauguin and his friends, noting that "It is not easy to see these canvases through the buffets, beer-faucet handles, and tables, not to mention the breasts of M. Volpini's cashier. . . ." And with the founding of *la Revue Blanche,* of which he was the first art critic and later secretary-general, he became the leading champion of the Nabi movement.

Fénéon's interest in Suzanne Valadon dated from the Impressionist and Symbolist Exhibition at Le Barc de Boutteville's in 1892, and it was only natural that it should lead him to her son and husband. Although he was concerned with the work of the three artists, not with their private lives, he was at the same time shrewd enough to know the foibles of the picture-buying public and its appetite for scandal.

However, little came of the exhibition. The war was not over. The era of sensational purchasing was still in the future. At Bernheim Jeune's in 1917 the spotlight merely picked up the first glimmer of commercial possibilities in the art of "the wicked trinity."

A glimmer was all Paul Poiret needed. By 1917 this remarkable little man with the pale myopic eyes and grizzly beard had transformed a few scraps of umbrella silk into one of the most extraordinary commercial enterprises in the world. It could not properly be called a business. True, it centered about the designing, manufacturing, and selling of women's gowns. Indisputably the name Poiret stood loftily above all others in *haute couture*. On six continents ladies of fashion awaited Poiret's dictum as to the bulge of their hips and the sweep of their chiffon drapery. At his bidding they had plucked their eyebrows into graceful Moorish arches, donned purple and pink wigs, lacquered their fingernails in gilt, and painted their sandaled toes. His influence had long since gone beyond decreeing what should go on their backs. He had made them, by his own account, "works of art." In his palatial house in the Faubourg St. Honoré he gave parties which in their sumptuousness recalled the last days of the court of the Second Empire. Indeed the Empress, now living in retirement in a small suite in the Hôtel Continental, appeared at some of them. Nijinsky and Fokine danced in his magnificent gardens before an audience which included the Grand Duke Alexander. Réjane, Mary Garden, Mistinguett, Sarah Bernhardt, and Isadora Duncan were among his most doting admirers. Claude Debussy and Maurice Ravel performed in his drawing room; and Anatole France, Alfred Savoir, D'Annunzio, and André Gide were among his guests at table. To his "Fête des Rois" he issued invitations in the name of Louis XIV. For his "Thousand and Second Night" he provided costumes of his own design and making. On his own *bateau mouche*, the *Paniche*, the cream of international society dined and danced.

In Poiret's volcanic mind all the glitter of the world was a part of his "business." The theater, the dance, sculpture, painting, and literature followed his erratic course through the heavens—the tail of his comet. Nor was Poiret insensitive to the possibilities of brilliant light in the future. At one time half the theaters in Paris bore the names of Poiret protégés (and protégées) on their programs. Aspiring actors, scenic designers, and musicians had him to thank for their jobs. Both Robert Piquet and Alfred Lenief, who eventually became famous dressmakers, sold him designs and worked for him, and it was Piquet, of all those Poiret had helped, who did the most for him when his nebulous "business" disintegrated.

Dufy received a retainer from Poiret for designing many of his fabrics. Dozens of young sculptors and ceramists were part of the "business," exhibiting their pieces in his *salon* and in his home. A young jeweler in one of the shops off the rue de la Paix had the legend "Jeweler to M. P. Poiret" in gold leaf on his window. Paul Poiret was also the founder of the Martine School of Decorative Arts.

"Each time I 'make' someone it is good for my business," Poiret used to say. But in no other field did he aspire to "make" new talent as he did in the field of painting. The walls of his house were covered with canvases by painters whom he expected to be great artists. The majority of them disappointed him in the end, but pictures by Matisse, Picasso, Derain, Vlaminck, Dufy, Friesz, and Modigliani were on his walls long before they decorated any other walls in the Faubourg St. Honoré.

If Paris was "the fashion capital of the world," Paul Poiret knew that it was also "the bourse of art," and that the customers were the same people—"the kings and princes of cattle yards and railroads," as Ambroise Vollard called them. "Yes, and they will say, 'Ah, that Poiret, he is a genius in all the arts.' And look! How happy are the artists!"

At the Valadon-Utrillo-Utter Exhibition at Bernheim, Paul Poiret bought a Valadon nude and a "Moulin de la Galette" by Utrillo.

In May, 1917, Utter was wounded in the shoulder at Champagne, and in January he was sent to convalesce at Belleville-sur-Saône, near Lyons. Suzanne joined him there almost immediately. She left Paris in a state of great excitement, having first disposed of more than a dozen canvases and about fifty drawings and etchings in order to meet the expenses of the trip. Most of these she sold to Leopold Zborowski, the ex-poet and devoted friend of Modigliani, who was struggling now to make a living as a picture dealer in a tiny gallery in the rue de Seine on the Left Bank. She left Maurice in M. Gay's charge.

The reunion was ecstatic. Except for a few weekends, Suzanne and Utter had not been together since Utter's enlistment. Shortly after Suzanne arrived at Belleville they were able to take a room in a small inn away from the town. Their days were filled with pastoral rapture. In a horse and trap hired from a farmer they went for long drives along the poplar-lined roads among the rolling hills of the countryside. It was a beautiful sun-drenched spring. As Utter's health improved they took to walking. The Lyonnais inns abounded in good food, so difficult to come by in wartime Paris. Always together now, Suzanne and Utter picnicked and painted along the low banks of the Saône—old bridges, rowboats, the wayside shrines in the vineyards. It was their first protracted period alone, a holiday—without Maurice's dark moods haunting them, undisturbed by the turmoil which had always whirled about them on the Butte; and they enjoyed it with unflagging good humor. It never grew dull. Utter filled the days with ebullient monologues about his artistic theories, his political convictions, his thoughts on science and religion, his hopes for their future. The magic of his mind fascinated Suzanne as it always had. She would listen to him endlessly. The specter of old age which had haunted her since he had enlisted vanished. His indefatigable vigor permeated her entire being. She fluttered about him like a butterfly, waiting on him, lighting his pipe, even reading to him in her halting way. She was replete with youth and happiness.

For almost three months they lived in a state of idyllic delight, and in the manner of sentimentalists, which at heart they both were, the Lyonnais countryside became for them a symbol of their happiest hours.

But when Utter returned to his regiment and she was back

again in the rue Cortot, the old fears began to assail Suzanne. On the 17th of September Degas died. In a bittersweet mood of recollection she saw him in his dreary study in the rue Victor-Massé, beside the window with the portfolio of her drawings in his hands. She heard him slam it shut and his nasal voice say, "You are indeed one of us." Somehow she could not help feeling that she was part of that generation which had all but passed away before her—Toulouse-Lautrec, Van Gogh, Puvis de Chavannes, Gauguin, Seurat, the Nouvelles-Athènes, the Assassins when Adèle had been there, Sunday afternoons at the Moulin de la Galette (and even the boisterous Monday nights)—all gone.

Suzanne was fifty-three, admitting to fifty when cornered by people who had known her since she was a child; otherwise the hint was strong that she was in her late twenties. It was impossible for her to accept any notion that her day was done. She could still outlast any party. Her stay at Belleville had convinced her of her durability. But in the last year of the war it was not easy to keep up a front of youthful indestructibility. Suddenly Montmartre's indifference to the course of the fighting irritated her. She was annoyed by the troops of friends who always seemed to be bounding into her studio. Parties were almost unbearable. She wrote to Utter rarely, and then only to complain that his biweekly letters were too infrequent. Her financial plight was increasingly precarious. The niggardly prices which she had always managed to get for her pictures slumped.

Most of all Suzanne was upset by Maurice. Outwardly he seemed no better or worse than usual. But she had seen signs which now terrified her. After his release from Villejuif she first noticed a change in his painting. Until then, barring the first canvases at Montmagny, his work had been of astonishingly consistent quality. Now the colors had suddenly begun to brighten and sharpen. The rigid lines of realism began to dominate his perception. The poetic quality began to falter.

The post cards were no longer transformed; they were being enlarged in paint.

Suzanne studied him closely at work. He painted more slowly, seemed to select his colors only after periods of perplexity. No longer did his brush move automatically from palette to canvas. Painting seemed to require an intense mental strain from him—something it had never done before.

At first she was rather hopeful. The rapidity with which he worked had always bothered her. With the slackening of this speed, she told herself, there would soon come a new phase in his painting. For a while she went so far as to expect a fresh and brilliant manifestation of his creative powers. But by the time he came back from Dr. Vicq there was a suspicion that he was actually losing them. It was something which in her wildest imagination she could not have foreseen, something she had never thought possible. Nowhere in her experience had she ever heard of this happening. The possibility of what might become of him if suddenly he should no longer be able to paint became a nightmare to her.

Bewildered and terrified, she finally persuaded Maurice to have himself committed to the mental hospital at Picpus. He went voluntarily—but not for long. He escaped. And instead of going back to the Butte, where he knew the authorities would be sure to find him, he made for Montparnasse.

He found Modigliani, who took him to a restaurant for dinner on credit and then to his studio. There Maurice painted a couple of Montmartre street scenes from memory in order to raise money for drinks. Modigliani took the wet canvases to Zborowski, and on the proceeds of the sale he and Maurice launched a three-day tour of the bars of the quarter. It was, as always, a wild binge. What money they did not drink up was folded into paper airplanes and sent gliding into the trees along the Boulevard Raspail.

Ultimately the two rolled back to Modigliani's studio to sleep. When Modigliani awakened, Maurice was gone, and

so were Modigliani's clothes. However, Maurice soon re-
appeared quite drunk and laden with bottles of wine. These,
he explained, he had bought after pawning his friend's clothes.
Now their drinking could go on! Chaim Soutine came in at
what might have been the tail end of the ensuing drinking
bout, and at Modigliani's suggestion he took Maurice's clothes
to the pawnbroker in order to buy more wine. When
Soutine informed Zborowski of what was going on, the ex-
poet managed to reclaim the pawned clothing and then succeeded in bustling Maurice off to a hotel room of his own.

The friends never saw one another again. A few weeks later,
in January, 1920, Modigliani died in the Hospital of Charity of
a combination of pulmonary meningitis and tuberculosis. His
final words were familiar to many who had known him:
"Cara, cara Italia." From Rome his brother Emmanuel, a
Socialist deputy, telegraphed, "Give him the funeral of a
prince." The evening Modigliani died, his young wife
Jeanne, the mother of his child and pregnant again, returned
to her parents' home near Père-Lachaise and threw herself to
her death from a fifth-storey window.

Through the streets of the city he had come to conquer, a
great crowd of artists, writers, musicians, and humble people
who had never been able to love him followed the remains of
the strange dark prince, carrying flowers. His sins against
them all were forgiven. Only Suzanne Valadon and André
Utter, walking behind the hearse, wept.

When Utter was released from the army only a few days
before Modigliani's death, Suzanne was already in an acute
state of nervousness. There was little domestic amenity to be
enjoyed in the studio. Maurice had moved in with her, and
the place continued to swarm with friends and sycophants.
Amid all the hullabaloo she had developed a gluttonous
stomach for admiration; it had suddenly come to be as necessary as the air she breathed. Nothing seemed to be more im-

portant to her than her ability to make an impression on other people, and she cast frantically about for any means by which she could compel attention or adulation. Like a circus performer who had outlived her star billing, she strove, with unquenchable hope, again and again to command the limelight. Through the force of her personality the studio in the rue Cortot was to become the hub of bohemianism in Montmartre. She was at once the foremost artist on the Butte, the most sprightly intelligence, the soundest critic, the gayest *bon vivant*, the best cook, the most irrepressible spirit.

To the public Suzanne presented herself as an eccentric. At one time she took to wearing a corsage of carrots on her ragged coat, at another she would carry a nosegay of lettuce and live snails. The Butte often saw her in outsized Indian moccasins with a pair of cats in her arms and a goat at her heels. On the night of the Armistice she appeared in the Place du Tertre clothed in nothing but fluttering flags of the Republic and a moth-eaten fur tippet. One night sightseers were flabbergasted to see her before Chez Ma Cousine milking a mare into a wine glass and drinking the milk with apparent pleasure.

Utter's homecoming served only to heighten her mood. With his boundless high spirits and full-blooded temperament, he was indeed actually the chief cause of it. If now she strove to focus attention upon herself, it was because she wanted above everything to be more desirable to him, to dazzle him. Unfortunately she allowed the role to run away with her, and expected Utter to sit enraptured at her feet. He might have done so had she given him time. At the moment he was in love with everything, for he was home after four years in the army. But in her state of excitement all responses had to be immediate, and when they failed to be she was piqued and cantankerous. She accused Utter of lack of feeling, of egotism, of having grown tired of her. Sensitive always to his appeal to other women, she began to harbor the notion that he was unfaithful. Then, devastated by her own accusations, she sought his forgiveness by bringing into play all her coquetry—acknowledging his mental superiority, extolling his artistic taste, his generosity, his sincerity, and his masculine beauty. He responded with grace but also with bewilderment. After four years away from her he was mature enough not to expect the ardor of their first passion to have remained intact. Belleville had made him very happy, but it had not deluded him.

Their relationship had always been stormy, but they had so much delighted in each other that they were always able to make up. A considerable part of the excitement they generated for each other lay in these scraps and fervent reconciliations. Somehow, Utter noted now, there was little disposition any longer on Suzanne's part to patch up their quarrels. At first he tried to make them up in the old way, but his efforts seemed only to heighten her vindictiveness. Then, rather than carry the fight to the point of bitterness, he retreated, allowing her anger to peter out as it would. Occasionally he was unable to control himself; once he struck back, it was with animal ferocity and no holds barred. The wild fires that made Utter the man she loved were still there. At such times, in the intensity of his rage he did not even notice that she cowed before him and sued for peace. He hated such exhibitions; in his eyes they indicated a lack of mental maturity. He did his best to regard the present turn of events with impish good humor and bide his time. Optimistically, he was certain that they would run their course shortly, and that once again Suzanne and he would be able to forge together the life he was sure they both wanted.

Even so, Utter could not play to order the ludicrous part Suzanne expected him to play in public and among their friends. He felt a fool—a dangerous feeling indeed for a young man charged as he was with a sense of his own high purpose. At the same time Suzanne was to him, as she had always been, the most beguiling of all feminine creatures; and it was for this reason that he was willing to put up with what he really believed at first was nothing more than another facet of her enchanting temperament.

Besides, being back on the Butte was glorious fun. "Dédé is back! Dédé is back!" the laundresses in the rue Lepic squealed on the first day, and immediately he was besieged in the street by dozens of people he had known all his life. It was what all the men in the trenches who came from little towns had been dreaming it would be. In the cafés he was hugged and kissed by men and girls alike. A score of genial *patrons* proffered toasts until he was quite drunk. Pastries were stuffed in his mouth and chocolates in his pockets. The girls of the *maisons closes* offered him their services gratis. Flowers and cases of champagne followed him up the stairs to the studio. Necklaces of onions hung about his neck. There were charming formal calls—from the priest who had baptized him, a couple of old professors from the Lycée, the police sergeant, an old lady who had been in love with his father. A barman and a butcher came to tell him that they had wiped off their ledgers "little outstanding matters" dating from five years ago.

Then there were the old friends—the engraver Galanis and his wife, who lived across the courtyard; Othon Friesz on the ground floor below; his former schoolmate Edmond Heuzé; the writers André Salmon, André Warnod, Jean Vertex, and Francis Carco; Jean d'Esparbès and Robert Nalcy, two old drinking companions, and Georges Braque, their neighbor at the Impasse de Guelma. And Suzanne's new friends—Derain, "the intellectual Fauve," and his beautiful wife; Maurice Vlaminck; Pascin ("the Little League of Nations" Utter was to dub him*) and his painter wife Hermine

* He was born in Bulgaria, the son of a Spanish-Jewish father and an Italian-Serbian mother. He became a naturalized Frenchman.

David; and the Czech painter Georges Kars and his expansive wife Nora.

Around these hovered a miscellaneous collection of cliques and isolated personalities. All the groups argued interminably with one another and among themselves. Loyalties were always crumbling and reshaping themselves; erratic disciples continually flitted from one group to another as each new theory or idea bubbled. This artistic turmoil was set against a background of parties, pranks, antics, love-making, and alcohol in an atmosphere of picturesqueness, poverty and decay. Busloads of tourists and curiosity seekers had finally conquered the Butte. A rash of night clubs crept up the hill, accompanied by the syncopated palsy of *"le jazz hot."* Soon its rising tide would reach the crest. But meanwhile the little band of true Bohemians, the tradition-destroyers who had found at last a tradition they would have liked to be able to save, awaited the flood with light hearts. And after four years of intellectual and artistic suffocation in the trenches there was none lighter in heart than André Utter.

Shortly after the Armistice, Berthe Weill staged a Valadon-Utter Exhibition, and the dealer Lepoutre staged one of the work of Utrillo. Money was free again, and all over the world the war-weary cashed their war savings and converged on beautiful, wonderful Paris. In wave after wave they came —from America, Britain, the Orient, South America, Africa. Trainloads and busloads from Germany and the Balkans, too, whisked by the devastated villages of the eastern *départe-ments* with their newly erected memorials to "the glorious dead," athirst for the wine, the delicious food, the daring fashions, the cosmetics, and the art treasure of fabulous Paris.

The international millionaires arrived once again, to discover that most of the Impressionist paintings had been sold to their competitors and that those which were left were tagged at astronomical prices in the Faubourg St. Honoré. Not that the prices daunted them. They loved everything with a high price on it; it gave them an opportunity to spend big money. They had come to spend. Europe could be saved by their spendings. A bullish mood dominated "the bourse of art," as it did all other markets.

But bargain hunters who could not afford Faubourg St. Honoré prices heard of "modern art," and taxicab drivers knew addresses in little side streets, like the rue Lafitte, the rue de Seine, and the rue Chevalier-de-la-Barre, where "comers" could be bought for a song. If one bought in a hurry, one could perhaps sell at a profit. Yet even at Berthe Weill's and Lepoutre's there was a sharp difference between present-day prices and those of the prewar level. The Utrillo which Francis Jourdain had persuaded Octave Mirbeau to buy for 100 francs now went for 1,000. Less than a year later, at Libaude's sale, another was bought for 2,700 francs. "Now," said Maurice, "Libaude should be able to bring me a box of cigars." The dealer had paid Suzanne his usual fifty francs for the canvas.

One day shortly after the Libaude sale Suzanne was to answer a knock on the studio door to discover on the threshold, as she said later, "a long, tall man with a gold-headed stick and his wife decorated in ostrich plumes." The man introduced himself as M. Pauwels, a Belgian banker. He was interested in buying some paintings of hers and her son's. M. Pauwels, his wife explained, was interested in everything —blooded horses, flowers, and birds, and was an art collector to boot. A tip from a taxi driver had brought them to the rue Cortot.

Suzanne claimed afterward that her first impulse was to shut the door in their faces, and as an old woman she often bemoaned the fact that she had not done so. But she let them into the studio, and they bought a couple of pictures. From that time forward the name Pauwels was destined to weigh heavily upon the heart and mind of Suzanne Valadon.

Almost immediately Suzanne recognized in Lucie Pauwels her match in will power. A former actress in a small provincial touring company, Lucie had deserted the stage for a marriage of "real distinction." "I have always been extremely gifted," she reported to Maurice's biographer Robert Coughlan. "I came from a wonderful family, the de Veaus of Angoulême, and as a child I recited poetry so beautifully that it was decided I should be an actress. I was always called in when great artists came to play in the city. The great Coquelin heard me one day and said immediately, 'There is a girl who should be on the stage.' Of course he was very, very old then and I was very young. If I had stayed on the stage, there is absolutely no question that I would have been the greatest actress in France." *

Lucie immediately offered Suzanne her intimate friendship, which Suzanne was uneager to accept. But from the time when she first appeared in the studio Lucie seemed determined that her fate was to be bound to the ménage in the rue Cortot. She became a frequent visitor. She bought pictures. She offered her heart in undying devotion to her "dearest friend, the great artist Suzanne Valadon." Suzanne and Utter were often amused and somewhat charmed by Lucie's airy assurance during her visits. Maurice seems to have taken at first no very active part in Lucie's friendship with the family. It was twelve years before Lucie would embark on a new role that would dramatically alter all their lives.

The sales at Berthe Weill's and Lepoutre's gallery were gratifying indeed, so far as Suzanne's and Maurice's canvases were concerned. At the exhibition at Lepoutre's they were

---

* From *Wine of Genius,* by Robert Coughlan (New York: Harper & Brothers, © 1951).

considerably stimulated by the appearance in *L'Oeuvre* of the first serious critique of the artists by Adolphe Tabarant, one of the leading critics and Maurice's future biographer. Albert Flamant contributed a sensitive commentary to the catalogue of the Valadon-Utter show at Weill's. Writing in *L'Information*, Robert Fels spoke of the work of Valadon: "The material is rich and clear, the color sober and vibrant, the touch forceful and ardent. There is in the painting a faith and certainty which can be acquired only by those who have learned to use their fists. This is what one recognizes in Valadon, the artist who one day will be among the glories of feminine French painting."

Of Utter's work in the same show Gustave Coquiot wrote: "When I look at his work I think of Vincent Van Gogh— obviously a stabilized and wise Van Gogh, but André Utter has the constitution, the same aggressive air of that rare Dutchman. . . ." But Utter's paintings did not sell. To Utter, had it not been for the success of his wife and stepson, Coquiot's words might have been consoling. Yet try as he would, he could not help but be bitter. The war had put him in a back seat.

Suzanne hardly improved matters. The Weill exhibition, her first concrete success, became in her eyes proof of her superior powers as an artist. Superior to whom? In the first flush of excitement she may have cried triumphantly "superior to all"; later she may have been more pointed: "To Dédé, of course." In her own eyes she was now clearly the center of the universe. She did not admit, she seemed not even to be aware of any authority but her own. What she approved of was right, what she disliked wrong. One moment she was the munificent and kindly queen of the art world; the next she was a barbarous shrew. In either mood she thought herself beyond criticism, and other people had to think so as well. She was capable of the most extravagant remarks: "I do not seek to be known but to be renowned. For I shall go

Woman with Cat. Oil painting by Suzanne Valadon. *In the collection of Mr. and Mrs. J. Garfunkel, New York.*

Vive la Jeunesse. One of the last paintings by Suzanne Valadon. *Courtesy of Paul Pétridès, Paris.*

Self-Portrait. The artist at 62. Oil painting by Suzanne Valadon.
Courtesy of the Lefevre Gallery, London.

to the Louvre. That will be my glory." And when in 1920, through the influence of her friends, she was elected an associate of the Société des Artistes Indépendants, an impressive honor, she proceeded to issue her dicta to the Salon on the spot, apparently oblivious of the fact that practically all her proposed rules had been in effect for thirty-six years: "No jury. No awards. No board of admission. No *hanging committee*. To no one the place of honor. And the hanging committee [which she had scarcely finished saying must not exist] to be drawn by lot." She could not face the fact that her inflated vanity made her extremely vulnerable; and her egotism was so unbounded that she was incapable of reforming herself. Instead, bewildered, terrified, and resentful, she rushed blindly about seeking, she hardly knew how, to hold her quaking dream together.

The brunt of her tyranny fell on Utter. Suzanne insisted now that he must love her not only because she was a superior being but also because she was the cynosure of all eyes. She demanded sycophancy as well as adoration. In the company of their friends she ordered him to fetch the groceries. His pipe annoyed her. When he spoke in a discussion she found a pretense to leave the room, or started a raucous conversation of her own. The family money she kept in a cloth bag under her skirt and doled it out to him as though he were a child. And when she could needle him no further, she flew into wild, screaming rages, in which she accused him of stealing "her" money, of plotting to kill her, of smearing her paintings, of turning the whole world against her.

One thing only seemed to bring her to her senses—Maurice's crises. For the most part Maurice lived in the rue Cortot now, shambling about the four rooms muttering incoherently to himself while Suzanne raged on. Sometimes he would sit in the corner of his room biting his nails and weeping. During a breathing space in a tirade he might venture, "It is much nicer here when everyone is friendly," or "Dédé is my friend," or yet again, "Suzanne is very beautiful." Or suddenly fury would possess him, and he would kick out the windowpanes or send a flatiron hurtling into Galanis' studio across the courtyard.

With the outburst all the air would rush from Suzanne's sails, and she would suddenly become a courageous woman whose entire purpose in life was to protect the pitiful sick one in her charge. But even here her response was hysterical. When in April, 1920, Maurice was ordered by the chief alienist of the Department of the Seine, Dr. Briand, to be confined at Picpus as a mental patient, she was panic-stricken by the notion that he was being taken away from her for good. She went from one to another of her friends with a stack of his canvases. "Crazy?" she cried to Francis Carco. "Is a boy capable of producing masterpieces like these crazy? We must protest. Go to the newspapers and tell them. They'll believe you because you know him. You must do it." As a matter of fact, she was very much in doubt herself as to whether Maurice was sane or not. What she had recognized as the beginning of deterioration in his painting might well have been the portent of a final mental crack-up. It was that fear, as much as her relationship with Utter, which was responsible for her perturbation. Yet she dared not acknowledge its existence. But when for the second time Maurice escaped from Picpus, she went wild with terror at the thought that he might harm someone. For five nights she did not sleep. Ghostly pale, bone-thin, and with eyes starting from her head, she looked insane herself as she hurried along the alleys and streets of the Butte inquiring after the whereabouts of her son and warning the people she knew to keep their doors locked against him.

Fortunately he had gone to Montparnasse again, and Zborowski had found him. He had installed him in a little hotel and pawned a suit in order to keep him supplied with painting materials and food. By the time Suzanne arrived

Maurice was in excellent spirits, sitting at the window looking down into the trees on the Boulevard Raspail and painting "A Country Church." Suzanne collapsed in a heap on the threshold.

There were bright spots, however. It was not always, as Utter referred to it later, "the House of Usher," "The Heights of Hurlevent," and the "Voyage to the End of Night." The arrival of a tipsy friend, a birthday or an anniversary, the sale of a picture, or perhaps the appearance of a laudatory criticism in a journal would be the signal, as it always was in Bohemia, for revelry. For a few hours the air would clear. Amicability and affection would be the order. There would be wine and food, and the company might be treated to the sight of Suzanne squealing with delight in her husband's arms and smothering him with kisses. On the occasion of her election as an associate of the Société des Artistes Indépendants the party which began in the Maison Rose lasted for three days. Called upon at one stage of the revels to make a speech, Suzanne laid the reason for her success in Utter's lap: "Without my darling Dédé there would be no love; and it is from love that I paint."

Happily for "the trinity," André Utter was not a man to let personal disappointments or his wife's delusions depress him. Frustrated by the hysterical atmosphere in which he found himself, he nevertheless began to concentrate his abundant energies on the development of his own resources. He continued to paint, but less with an eye to achieving recognition than for the sheer love of having a brush in his hand. Strangely enough, it was at the beginning of these chaotic years that he threw aside the emotional control which had always characterized his work, and painted like Suzanne. "His robust temperament banished cerebral speculations," wrote André Warnod. "He was too much a sensualist not to prefer to confront nature face to face, brutally." Painting was where his heart would always be; his mind he turned to less aesthetic matters. And so he became a businessman.

"Maurice Utrillo is the prettiest piece of business to appear in half a century," Utter later told his friends Heuzé and Carco. He was no admirer of Maurice's talents as a painter, but he had no doubts as to their commercial possibilities. Hardly less quick than Suzanne, he was aware of the deterioration which had begun to set in. It did not bother him much. "Once an artist begins to sell, the public will buy anything," he told Heuzé. The signs were in the wind—the prices paid at the Octave Mirbeau and Libaude sales, the results at the Lepoutre Gallery. It was a time for bold action. Utter's plan was simple. He proceeded to sell one Utrillo in the Faubourg St. Honoré in order to buy up several Utrillos in the bistros and byways of the Butte, where once they had been exchanged for drinks, food, or a few nights' lodging. Taking his cue from the canny Libaude, he set himself to build up a large collection. Nor did he exclude the possibilities of Valadon. His own experience at Berthe Weill's had indicated the public taste for his wife's work. He began to scour Paris for everything by these two artists which he could lay his hands on. When he ran out of money he exchanged his own paintings in order to reclaim theirs: he gave as many as ten of his own for one Utrillo.

In 1921 Utter arranged with Berthe Weill for another exhibition—this time Valadon and Utrillo. The success of this show made it clear that he was on the right track. Francis Carco contributed considerably by writing his short book, *Maurice Utrillo*. And in the following year, carefully eying the collection he had on hand, Utter allowed the Paul Guillaume Gallery to buy ten Utrillo paintings from his stock for a reputed 30,000 francs. "Unbelievable!" Derain exclaimed when Utter told him of the deal. "Ah, my friend," the painter-turned-businessman replied, "it is only the beginning of the story."

VIII   Fruits of Success

UTTER WAS RIGHT. IN MAY, 1923, PAUL POIRET INTIMATED
to the world of fashion that it was chic to own the paintings
of Maurice Utrillo and Suzanne Valadon. In his *salon* on the
Champs Élysées he presented an exhibition of their work, the
success of which was reflected immediately in demands for
their paintings from the dealers in the Faubourg St. Honoré.

Following it, Bernheim Jeune suggested another exhibition.
They would have liked to make it a one-man show of Utrillo.
However, Utter explained tactfully that if they wanted
Utrillo, they would have to take Valadon too. This was no
heroic gesture to ensure peace at home. Suzanne's pride in
Maurice's work was untainted by jealousy, and this Utter
knew. But whereas he was completely cynical in his attitude
to Maurice's painting, he believed profoundly, as he had from
the first, in the "divine magic" of Suzanne Valadon. "The
Valadon drama" was in his hands and, irrespective of his personal relationship with its author, he was its consecrated
custodian. There remained always in André Utter an in-
genious enthusiasm, a boyish passion for the ideal, for the
good things in life around him. The battles might be vicious;
somehow they were never real. As time was to prove, he was
not a saint. Once his temper was aroused (and it took a very
long time to rouse it), he was capable of the crudest brutality
and unspeakable meanness. But these manifestations were

213

only flashes of lightning in the storm he could never quite believe existed. His amiability and cheerfulness were his armor against the merciless needling of the woman he loved and the indifference of the world which did not want the beautiful pictures he painted. They were also his stock in trade in business. A playful naïveté pervaded his commercial operations and was, indeed, the reason for his singular success.

"All the time we were talking business we laughed," the dealer Pétridès said of him. Often Utter's demands struck a disarming note of innocence and candor. "Let us look at this picture post card," he would say as he showed a prospective customer an Utrillo canvas. "It will take a lot of postage stamps to move it from here, eh?" What might have sounded absurd, under cover of his infectious humor often became daring and reasonable. "Why should big, important fellows like us talk about fives and tens when we can quite easily talk of hundreds of thousands?" "A small exhibition is a fine thing—for small profits." And in arranging for one of the first German exhibitions of Valadon, he advised his customer, "In your country a few words to the press and Valadon will go right to the sentimental hearts of the Germans—Trilby, Mimi, and Marguerite Gautier all in one."

Utter would also be tantalizingly casual, arriving two hours late for an appointment, or breaking up a conference because he had "to take the dog for a walk." "On the Butte we never know when we are going to do anything, and mostly it is all right when we do it. Earlier would be too soon," he remarked to an American collector who had come to the studio to buy an Utrillo. The first Swiss exhibition of Utrillo was arranged while Utter was running to catch a train. He made his contract with Paul Pétridès while having his trousers fitted. And when, at the conclusion of the enormously successful Valadon-Utrillo show at Bernheim Jeune in 1923, Fénéon and Bernheim tried to speak to him about the possibilities of drawing up a contract with Suzanne and Maurice for their future work, he sent back word that he thought they would all come to the point more quickly after he had had a holiday.

With Suzanne and Maurice, their friends Georges and Nora Kars, and an amazon who was known simply as Paulette, he left in a hired car headed for Orthez in the Basses-Pyrénées. None of the party had bothered to consider that Kars, who made the arrangements for the car and proposed to drive it, had never before sat in a driver's seat. The trip south was a succession of hilarious mishaps which included being unable to put up the top in a hailstorm, the loss of a wheel on a mountain grade, and a collision with a cow.

Paulette had been attached to the household for some months as a cook, cleaning woman, and bodyguard for Maurice, and only lastly as a model. A large, lusty fisher-woman with a fondness for tight-fitting cerise satin clothes, she had come to Paris to seek wider opportunities and had ended up selling fish in the market of Les Batignolles and taking on odd modeling jobs in her spare time. The turbulent atmosphere in the rue Cortot somehow appealed to her, and on her first visit she announced her intention of remaining as a member of the ménage. A few days later her effects arrived, and she moved into the kitchen.

At Orthez, Suzanne was suddenly seized with the notion that Paulette should marry Maurice. The idea that Maurice ought to be married was not a new one with her. That he was still unmarried bothered her considerably. It set him apart from other young men, made him appear abnormal. And remembering always the doctors' hints that some sexual disturbance might well be at the seat of his alcoholism, she was sure that a normal sex outlet would go a long way toward curing him. She had always encouraged his association with women. For a while she had thought that something might develop between him and Marie Vizier, the proprietress of the Belle Gabrielle.

Marie was a lively, generous woman about Suzanne's age who had assumed a proprietary interest in Maurice. He had decorated the premises with murals, including the water closet, which in a fit of anger she scrubbed clean upon discovering, when she went into it in the dark, that the wet paint had come off on her new frock. Something of a nymphomaniac, she made no secret of the fact that she was initiating Maurice into the mysteries of love. People twitted him about his "whore Marie," but he only gave them a sly smile. In one of his pictures of the rue Norvins which included the Belle Gabrielle he painted a small boy writing on the wall of a building across the street, "On the other side of this street are the best memories of my life." Marie tried to reform his drinking habits by refusing to give him wine and by insisting that he eat the gargantuan portions of food which she put before him. He stuffed the food into his pockets when she was not looking, and went for his drink elsewhere. If she had matrimonial ambitions as far as he was concerned, his perpetual drunkenness eventually dampened them, and after a while she even lost interest in continuing his sex education.

As the *affaire* Marie Vizier petered out, Suzanne prodded Maurice to go to prostitutes. At first she gave him the money; then, aware that he was spending it on drink instead, she took him to the *maison close* herself, made the necessary financial arrangements with the management, and waited in the street until he came out. On occasion she also brought girls home and locked Maurice in with them, in which situation he was just as likely to sit in a corner and read a book as to do anything else. If the girl grew too aggressive, or if he felt otherwise harassed, he would fly into one of his diabolic rages until she screamed for help and was set free.

During the war Suzanne had tried to arrange a marriage with a laundress named Gaby. It was of this affair that Maurice spoke wistfully to Francis Carco many years later.

"You know," he mused, "it wouldn't have been bad with her, but how the bitch drank!"

When Suzanne decided that Maurice ought to marry Paulette, she was hardly less direct in her maneuvers. She gave a large party to announce the engagement, which was something of a shock to both the persons involved. Maurice seemed pleased; he painted a colorful view of Orthez which he presented to his betrothed. For a few days Paulette appeared to be rather gay about the sudden turn of events: she combed the Orthez shops looking for cerise satin. It was not until Suzanne had gone to the *mairie* to make arrangements for the wedding that Paulette showed signs of nervousness. And then, in the middle of the night, she packed her things and disappeared, leaving the view of Orthez behind her. Maurice was not disappointed, so Suzanne gave another party to celebrate her son's freedom. Back in Paris, she reported, "It was the best party in the Basses-Pyrénées in a hundred years."

The holiday over, Utter returned to Bernheim Jeune, and the results were spectacular indeed. To the consternation of the Faubourg St. Honoré, Bernheim Jeune agreed to guarantee a million francs a year minimum (then approximately $60,000) to Utrillo and Valadon in exchange for their future production.

For the moment all the bitterness of the past five years was washed away by the tidal wave of jubilation. Long-outstanding bills were paid. At Utter's insistence, Suzanne appeared at Patou's for a new tailored suit, which in another six months she would be painting in. All the customers at the Lapin Agile drank champagne for a week in honor of the new contract and at the expense of the two artists who were parties to it. Montmartre urchins ran about the streets of the Butte delightedly waving hundred-franc notes tossed to them from the studio window at No. 12 rue Cortot. And with an uncharacteristic eye to the future Suzanne had Madeleine's coffin surmounted by a splendid granite tomb bearing the legend "Valadon-Utter-Utrillo" in gold letters.

Before the year was out Suzanne and Utter, caught up in a billow of sentimentality, journeyed back to the Lyonnais countryside bent upon recapturing the ecstatic days of their wartime stay at Belleville. By the time the train reached Lyons the resolution was in tatters. Suzanne was the most trying travel companion imaginable. The excitement of the past few weeks had heightened her nervous instability as never before; her moods changed not every day but every quarter of an hour. A taxicab was too slow; the hotel room was "filthy," the food garbage. She flirted outrageously with every young man she saw, abused waiters and porters, and dispensed munificent tips to chambermaids. She was not above introducing herself anywhere as "the famous artist." At Belleville she wept for a day and refused to eat because the horse they had driven about the countryside five years before had died. All her memories of the idyl were garbled. What she remembered as being on the right side of the road was now on the left. Where there had been a sweep of the Saône there was now a cornfield. And apparently Utter was responsible. When he went off to find tobacco for his pipe, she accused him of infidelity. A few glasses of wine made him a drunkard. When he showed interest in the architecture of a church, he was tiring of her. If she could not sleep, she woke him up. When he suggested going off by himself in order to paint, she swore that if he did, he would never see her again. Word went about that he was a desperate dope addict whom she had undertaken to cure.

Unexpectedly, however, the trip ended on a high note of hilarity: they bought a château. In a village café at lunch one day they overheard the proprietor mention that the nearby Château St. Bernard was for sale. For the first time in a long while they had the same inspiration: buy it. And within the hour they owned a large, square patchwork of three hundred years' assorted architecture, crumbling staircases, flaking plaster walls, and feathery acacia trees. It was the sort of madness which they might have dreamed of in the first flush of their love. Coming as it did now in their days of perturbation, it was, if anything, more delicious. No celebration could be too preposterous. They sent money to their friends on the Butte to come and witness their delirium. The Karses arrived with Maurice and Utter's young sister Gabrielle. Gustave Coquiot and his wife came. So did the sculptor Leonardi and Max Jacob. A score of "old friends" from Belleville and half the surrounding countryside managed to find their way through one of the many doors of the Château St. Bernard. A winegrower from Macon delivered an entire *cru*. In the middle of the week's festivities Suzanne dispatched a telegram to Édouard Herriot, the mayor of Lyons, who happened to be at the moment premier of France, inviting him to come and see her paintings. He claimed later (when, indeed, he was often a guest at St. Bernard) that he had never received the telegram. In any event the party did not stop to wait for him. It finally tapered off with some groaning hangovers, a few skinned knuckles, and a black eye or two. But the host and hostess were radiantly happy. In a single stroke they had swept aside the frustrating years and gained the enchantment of their early rapture.

Nevertheless it did not last long. Once they were back in Paris, a rift began to show itself again in their relationship which was to bring down their married life in irreparable ruin. Strangely, the more destructive tools of demolition were in Utter's hands. In spite of his careful good humor and his efforts to treat Suzanne's caviling with a light touch, there remained in him the eager appetites of the sensualist which he was less able to control than his temper. In their prewar life together Suzanne had altogether satisfied these demands of his character. A beautiful woman, considerably older than himself, she had been at once challenge and fulfillment of his passionate cravings. In the intoxication of their daily existence all desires were satisfied. Other women meant nothing to him. Thirst for alcohol, which had been very much a part of his early youth, had abated. Experimental ventures into the drug addict's feverish world were no longer necessary. To him Suzanne had been an amalgam of worldly pleasures, of all good things.

But now her beauty was fading rapidly. She was an old woman, a hysterical shrew, except for the infrequent bursts of animal sexuality which would still seize her. At such times they would both be transported, and all the magic of their former days of love would envelop them. The years would drop away. The tensions of the past would be forgotten. But such occasions were naturally rare.

In the meantime the world about Utter offered many compensating temptations. Still, Utter might not have allowed himself to drift into them had he been able to turn to his work for consolation. As it was, work offered him little but frustration. He garnered small pleasure from the fact that he was a success as a businessman and a failure as an artist. Although his original accomplishments in the commercial field amused him, he was miserable in the face of spending his future "haggling with the cardinals." He felt trapped. Each "deal" somehow led him into the next. Nowhere was there a breakaway point from which he could escape to pursue his life as he wanted it. Money added to his frustration. He wore elegant clothes and rosebuds in his lapel. He drove a car. His free spending in the bars and restaurants of the Butte, where he had passed his life with only a few francs in his pocket (and sometimes none), gave him a feeling of importance he had never known before. But he always had the Bohemian's scorn of money, and to discover himself now in thrall to it like the despised bourgeois was to acknowledge that his lofty principles had deserted him.

Nor was the situation more tolerable because the money he made was, in large part, the fruit of Maurice's success as a painter. Utter was neither charmed nor interested by the endless succession of street scenes, walls, and architectural masses which had become the objects of adulation and commercial competition in the Faubourg St. Honoré. To him, Maurice as an artist was a cheap trick, a phoney, a drunken "character" who had nothing to say and had somehow stumbled upon popular acclaim, while a thousand serious, dedicated artists (including himself) with imagination and intelligence, struggled to find recognition in a morass of apathy. His bitterness toward Maurice did not, of course, stop with the artist. He took umbrage at the monopoly which Maurice seemed to hold on Suzanne's attention. At the beginning of their life together he had accepted Suzanne's concern for her son's welfare with pride as a superb exhibition of maternal devotion. It was another one of her fascinating virtues. Besides, he felt sympathy for the poor wretch who was unable to free himself from his passion for drink. However, a reformed drunkard of sorts himself, he was not sympathetic for long. As time went on and his own life became complicated by another's moods and crises he grew increasingly resentful. Eventually his rancor found expression in a thousand childish taunts and mockeries which he heaped upon the unfortunate Maurice, who either failed to comprehend them or, if he did, transcended them, sublimely certain that in André Utter he had a friend.

It was behavior which Suzanne could not be expected to take as passively as did her son. Appalled by its meanness, she soon fiercely counterattacked. The little street echoed with scene after scene. Abuse and curses, hurtling crockery, scissors jabbed into the breast of a nude on his easel, doors bolted against him, his clothes ripped and thrown into the courtyard, threats of murder and suicide, public denunciations in restaurants and pavement cafés—these were the measure of the intermittent fury that came upon her as she protected her son. Nor did she revile Utter solely in defense of Maurice. What she most feared had come to pass: Utter had gone to other women. Like the majority of wives, Suzanne learned it last, even though recent years had been a maze of suspicions, accusations, doubts, and fears. This, she had told herself repeatedly, would be the end of her life, a shame she could never bear. But even as she strove frantically to prevent its happening, she had begun to prepare for its eventuality. Utter now had free rein to come and go as he pleased. No longer did Suzanne pass from café to café looking for him. When he came home she was often not there. As early as 1923 she had faced the deterioration of her beauty by painting an extraordinary self-portrait, a picture no other woman would have painted of herself—flat-faced, the sensuous lips drawn to an absurd rosebud mouth obviously holding in badly fitting false teeth, the pendulous breasts of a dissolute savage. There she was—naked, completely immodest and old, and considerably more durable than the fitful humors of love.

Her reaction to Utter's infidelities surprised even herself. Despite the rage which his faithlessness generated, and which she lost no opportunity of unleashing in his direction, she saw something ironically amusing in it. The spectacle of his involvement with other women had, indeed, a touch of the comic about it. For all his indolent, worldly manners, the smart cut of his clothes, the eager light in his bright blue eyes, Utter was forty years old—rather more than double the age he imagined himself to be. And although apparently his sexual prowess was untouched by the years, he was unable to muster the gay imperturbability which had characterized the amatory exploits of his youth. Each adventure became an infatuation, each flirtation a transport of love. In either case he suffered. The emotional demands which women made on him were inexhaustible—and they were also very costly. He was continually beset by the claims, protests, and abuse not only of his present inamorata but of former loves, as well as by the wiles of those who aspired to his favors in the future. Often there were noisy, embarrassing scenes in public places when past and present—and sometimes future—converged on him simultaneously. Bills arrived from everywhere. When he failed to indulge one of his mistresses, a model called Eveline, in the presents which she thought her due, she bought what she fancied on the Champs-Élysées and had the bills sent to him. Another mistress always needed money—for doctor bills, for her landlord (who later turned out to be her husband), for sick relatives in the country. Many other demands were made on him. Models wanted him to arrange sittings for them with his artist friends. Artists wanted him to show their work to the dealers he did business with. Aspiring actresses, musicians, and dancers wanted him to press their talents upon his theatrical impresario friends. All of them consulted him about their endless family problems.

Utter played his part with all the spirit he could mobilize, but it was never enough to prevent him from being slightly absurd. Everyone knew his troubles; often people knew more about the object of his devotion than he did himself. When he appeared at a familiar haunt with a new love, he was cheered like a victorious football player. The entire Butte was entertained by the love life of "the Pope" of Montmartre.

He was too sensitive not to know that he was making a fool of himself, too entangled to be able to cut himself free. When momentary release came he was at Suzanne's feet, full of remorse, begging her to forgive him, telling her again of his love for her. And she, no longer haunted by fear, and rather pleased to see him the harassed victim of his own folly, could be magnanimous. It would be mistaking her character not to recognize that part of her magnanimity was prompted by her knowledge that the eyes of the Butte were upon her, that she was being called upon to enact the role of the injured but forgiving wife. She played it to the hilt. Her clemency was on view at the greengrocer's and the baker's, in the bars and restaurants, and in their studio in the rue Cortot, where they again painted together, if anything more harmoniously than of old. Such public displays of generosity, however, were only pale reflections of the unbounded joy she felt at having him with her once again, of knowing that, for the moment at least, she had triumphed over some youthful rival, that it was *she* who was the pivotal point of his life. But most of all she was charitable because she loved him, because for all their differences and battles, the bitterness, the recriminations, even the hatred which sometimes flashed across the drama of the life they shared, loving him had been the greatest joy she had ever known.

When Utter could not bring himself to plead for his wife's grace, he drank. Drunkenness was much the easier escape from his misbehavior, for even when he and Suzanne had been reconciled, the old recriminations were bound to follow. In alcoholic befuddlement he could escape all women; men, too, if he chose. He could vent his resentment against the world for its failure to appreciate his painting. He could curse the commercial stratum of society in which he was compelled to sully himself. He could fulminate against critics, dealers, and collectors. And he could heap scorn upon Maurice Utrillo. At such times he became repulsive and malevolent, debasing every endearing facet of his character, a spectacle far more painful to a woman who loved him than his philandering.

That so despicable a creature should be the object of the great passion of her life was a searing blow to Suzanne's self-esteem. But years of experience with Maurice had instilled in her compassion toward a drunkard that no blow to her pride or wounding of her sentiments could overcome. When she was put to an actual test her vanity crumbled completely before what she recognized as her duty toward another human being. To desert Utter in his misery would be against the very core of her character. Still, she began to feel that the less she saw or knew about the sordid side of his life the better off both of them would be, the better she would be able to work, the more securely she would keep her love for him. For the most part they still slept under the same roof; occasionally they dined together in public in comparative calm; and nearly every day they painted together. But they went their separate ways. In spite of their love—or in order to keep it a living thing—they no longer sought their destiny in one another.

As a matter of fact, Suzanne was already in a hurly-burly of fresh excitement. It was only natural that fame and money so suddenly come by should alter the tenor of her life. The long struggle to attract attention to herself and her work had ended in a burst of glory. It mattered little that the lion's share of the fruits belonged to Maurice, that his pictures now sold for four and five times as much as hers. To be his mother was alone something to be proud of; and everyone knew that she had been his only teacher.

Not that she was content to bask in his kudos. She worked very hard indeed, once again with all the heart and vigor which had characterized the first paintings of the Impasse de Guelma and the rue Cortot. But now her canvases were, in the main, smaller, her compositions more compact. There were fewer nudes, more of the vibrant details of daily life in casual, indeed offhand arrangement—still lifes of fish and wine bottles, plates, baskets, napkins, onions, apples, dead pheasants and hares, and especially flowers, in all the crude colors for which she had such a passion. Her pictures were vigorous and incisive, their inner structure sound and certain. They reminded one of Cézanne and his solids. "Does an apple move?" he asked disgustedly as his sitter Vollard shifted his weight in his chair. Everything else in Suzanne's life was moving; only in her painting could she feel that her feet were on the ground. But she was far from disgusted with the state of things about her.

Her Russian-style clothes were designed by Yteb in the rue Royale and modeled by lovely mannequins of the Russian nobility. Her suits were by Paquin and Alex Maguy, and she wore tea gowns by Lucille, Lady Duff-Gordon. At a private showing at Vionnet's she sat alone with Queen Marie of Romania. Not that she cared a fig for fashion. In a few weeks she would be wearing her "creation" besmeared with paint at her easel. "One has one's caprices, and when one has money one buys them," she said airily. The Persian-lamb coat she had often dreamed of owning served as a bed for her dogs more often than it appeared on her back. The dogs lived very well indeed, dining on *faux-filets* specially prepared for them to their mistress's order at the restaurant Moulin Joyeux. Her cats had beluga caviar on Fridays.

Suzanne now cruised about Paris in a gleaming Panhard driven by a chauffeur in white livery which he was obliged to change twice a day. When the Panhard was in the repair shop she rode in a taxi. Once she took a taxi to St. Bernard, a distance of 350 miles, in order to pick strawberries out of the garden. At the château she caught from the window a view which she thought she would like to paint, and sent the taxi driver back to Paris to fetch her paints. When he returned a couple of days later, naturally the light had changed. In the meantime she had decided that she would not paint the view anyway, and had taken the train back to Paris. Another time she drove to St. Bernard, again in a taxi, and asked the driver to wait for her at the gate. It was two days before she remembered she had left him waiting, and she was indignant that meanwhile he had taken a room in the village inn and supplied himself with food and wine.

Always one who loved to entertain, she could do so now with a princely flourish. At St. Bernard there were elaborate wine-tastings and luncheons alfresco, and the guests now often included Premier Édouard Herriot. At sumptuous buffets in the rue Cortot prepared by Escoffier, the great names of the theater—Lugné-Poë, Copeau, Mistinguett, and Diaghilev—mingled with the foremost names in the world of art. There were dinners in the great restaurants—Le Tour d'Argent, Prunier's, Laperousse; thés dansants at the famous Café de la Cascade in the Bois de Boulogne. The originality of Suzanne's parties was often not without a touch of madness—a picnic in the Metro catered for by Maxim's, a midnight supper among the tombstones of the cemetery St. Vincent, and a soiree at the celebrated maison close La Belle Poule.

Entering a flower shop to pick up a bouquet or table decoration, Suzanne would be unable to make up her mind what she wanted, and to save time would buy everything in the store. Or, picking out a single bloom, she might order the rest of the stock to be sent to a sick friend.

Nature, having endowed her with pride, rage, and fearlessness, had not failed to add compassion and generosity to her character. Believing, as she always had, in the infallibility of her own powers, she aspired far more passionately than most people to live a noble life; if her heart was touched, she responded with a sincere urge to show kindness to her fellow men. Thousand-franc notes squeezed into a lavatory attendant's fist, left under a plate in a bistro, could bring to the lives of less fortunate people radiant moments which, as she knew from her own experience with poverty, were the substance of poor men's dreams. The pleasure of giving was enough: she wanted no thanks. When a waiter rushed to the street to thank her for a fantastic tip, she assured him that she had been sitting at another table.

Suzanne knew that many of the people whom she helped thought her an irresponsible fool. Jokes went around the Butte and even appeared in the press about her wild extravagance. She was hurt but undaunted. Most of what was said of her was exaggerated anyway. The unpredictable, the whimsical gesture had been a part of her make-up all her life. Now that money had suddenly thrown open fresh fields she was not likely to change her nature. To be able to collect fifty children from the streets on the spur of the moment and take them to the Cirque Medrano; to overhear the butcher's wife complain of lumbago and be able to send her to the Riviera for a month; to see a young artist at his easel in the street painting on cheap cotton canvas and be able to present him with a dozen good frames and a bolt of the best-grade linen; to notice a cigarette burn on a friend's sofa and be able to send him a new sofa; to buy a violin for a street musician or a piano for a new cabaret; to remember a laundress's birthday or the postman's wedding anniversary and be able to send a beautiful gift—this was what money was for. If people thought she was ostentatious, ridiculous, or mad, she cared little. She was convinced that her motives were sincere, and followed her course with princely insouciance. It was not always easy, for she was also engaged in the grimmest battle of her life.

In the spring of 1924 Maurice had agreed to undergo treatment for several months in a sanatorium at Ivry. The succession of accolades of the past two years, the vast sums of money now at his disposal, the fact that he was a respected celebrity of the Paris scene, with people bowing to him in the street and writing articles about him in the newspapers, filled him with nothing but an overpowering desire to lose himself. The notion that people were hostile to him was superseded by the fear that he was crazy and that people wanted to see him put permanently in an asylum. Ten years before, he had written in the fanciful autobiographical sketch composed at M. Gay's: "People said I was mad, the fools. But when they put me in Villejuif they called me not a 'lunatic' but a highly strung person who has been overstimulated." Nevertheless, the thought that the "fools" might have been right and the doctors wrong haunted him. "I'm not crazy! I'm not crazy!" he would shout when he caught a stranger looking at him. Passing a group of people with a friend or his mother, he would begin to shiver in fright. "Look at them! They think I'm crazy. They're going to put me in Picpus again." His new-found fame, of course, only heightened public curiosity. He was pointed out wherever he went, drunk or sober; and the more attention he attracted, the more desperate he grew, the harder he drank to escape notice, and the wilder became his fears that he was losing his mind. Finally in a police station he attempted to commit suicide by smashing his head against the wall.

Suzanne saw his attempt to destroy himself as the fulfillment of her direst fears. In the very hour of his success Maurice was struck down by the lunacy which had dogged him all his life. Now, when it was too late, she could see the long chain of symptoms which she had obstinately refused to recognize—his odd behavior as a little boy, his desperate, unfathomable moods, his alcoholism, and his strange sexual behavior. Even the curious development of his art should have forewarned her of the tragedy which now confronted her. In the end his art, on which she had pinned her hope, had failed to save him: it was gone, and nothing but the wreckage was left.

For several weeks Maurice lay semiconscious in the studio, his head swathed in bandages while the doctors tried to assure her that he would recover. She was inconsolable, certain that she knew more than the medical profession, afraid to hope. Her own health began to deteriorate. She had violent headaches and ate nothing. Friends who came to see her reported that her skin was jaundiced and shriveled, and that she seemed to have grown old overnight.

Gradually hope rekindled. Maurice began to talk. Most of what he said was garbled, but there were flashes of intelligence. He asked for an orange, and that the statuette of Joan of Arc be put beside his bed. He noted each day's change of weather. Sometimes he talked about painting problems which he had faced in the past.

As soon as the doctors would allow it Suzanne whisked Maurice off to the sunshine at St. Bernard. Recovery was slow and by no means steady. For months he meandered aimlessly round the house and grounds in an apparent daze broken by odd bits of conversation, a sudden fit of inexplicable rage, or a wild, maniacal seizure of laughter. In his small whitewashed room he sat on the edge of his bed staring at the rolling cornfields. Often he seemed incapable of understanding what was said to him. For the most part his speech was incoherent.

Suzanne hired a male nurse, an ex-keeper from Picpus, to take care of him, but she insisted upon dressing and feeding him herself. If the nurse took him for a walk, she followed. At night she sat beside his bed until he fell asleep. When she managed to exchange a few intelligent sentences with him her spirit soared: everything was going to be all right. But most of the time she was sunk in black depression; or else she was in a state of nervous irascibility which set her darting about the house, pacing the garden, nettling the servants, unleashing a gust of temper on Utter, or even storming off to Paris for two or three days. Her nerves were raw despite all the effort she made to maintain an atmosphere of tranquillity for the patient. A sudden noise—a door slamming or a bell ringing—sent her rushing to Maurice's side in a panic. The sight of the unused easel in his room caused her to burst into tears.

Strangely, as Maurice improved she became more irritable, and when he finally took up his materials and started painting again she fled to the room in the tower which was her studio.

In a few weeks Maurice had recovered sufficiently to work on a commission from the great Russian impresario Diaghilev, who had asked him to do the sets and costumes for a new ballet, *Barabau,* with choreography by Balanchine and music by Rieti. Within two weeks he had read the libretto and submitted finished designs. They were fresh, colorful, and superficial: the backgrounds were white. But once Maurice was back at his easel it was clear that he no longer had anything to say. He was resorting to cheap devices and easy effects: flat, meaningless white was everywhere. When Utter pointed this out Suzanne flew at him in a defensive rage, accusing him of jealousy. Maurice was the greatest painter in the world—a great genius. But the same evening at dinner she was heard murmuring to herself, "I should not want to be able to draw even a sugar bowl from memory."

Her inquietude was hardly lessened by Utter's comings and goings. "This Eden was transformed into a real hell," Utter wrote later. "I thought we had bought the place for peace. But Maurice was able to scream and shout about to his heart's content. Suzanne replied in kind. And only the walls and the fish in the Saône listened to them."

Utter and Suzanne were living apart now. In 1925, alarmed by Suzanne's lavish spending, Bernheim Jeune had bought a modern house in the Avenue Junot in Maurice's name. It was only a short walk down the hill from the rue Cortot, sitting rather prettily in a small private courtyard called "the Hamlet." There was a large studio: Maurice's room on the first floor had heavy iron grilles at the windows and contained an old harmonium, which he loved to play by ear. Behind the house was a small garden which Suzanne tended herself. It was probably the only material thing in the world that she ever really treasured. She gardened with burning passion and with the haphazard lavishness which she brought to everything she did. She was always buying flower seeds, and she accumulated barrels of unlabeled bulbs in the basement. The names of flowers meant nothing to her. When she painted an arrangement of flowers she usually called in her neighbor, Mme. Poulbot, to give the picture a title. She bought flowers by color alone, and this often led her to put fall plants at the edges of the borders and the pansies or violets behind them against the wall. The appearance of each new shoot was an occasion for jubilation. Many were the times she rushed up to Paris from St. Bernard in order to catch the blossoming of a favorite shrub, to fertilize one of the flower beds, to spray a rosebush, or even to pick some blooms for an arrangement which she wanted to paint.

Utter did not move into the house on the Avenue Junot. The old studio in the rue Cortot was the scene of his happiest memories—of those years before the war. There he had loved in joy the beautiful little woman who to him meant more than any other creature in the world. There he had painted with the exhilaration born of love and with undimmed hope of being one of the important artists of his day. There he would stay. Even so, he was at the Avenue Junot daily whenever Suzanne was there—to boast, to quarrel, to curse his lot, to mock Maurice, or to make love. Years later, when Suzanne was dead, Utter wrote to a friend: "Always I dream of the rue Cortot and the beloved Suzanne. When we first moved there, how beautiful everything was—except for the gossips! And I knew then that it was the place I should always keep in my heart. Every man has a home. He is lost if he does not treasure it."

Now, while Suzanne and Maurice were living at St. Bernard, Utter would arrive without warning and leave equally abruptly, often in a fury. He was full of irritating chatter about his "deals," and usually before his visit was over he was too full of wine. He painted a great deal—exciting, beautifully thoughtful pictures which he carried back to Paris to sell for a few francs. He came because he loved the countryside—the white sky, the slashing sunlight, the swaying columns of the poplars—and because he knew there was genuine sympathy with his lot. For when it came to his failure to win recognition as an artist, Suzanne was deeply touched. He was a fine painter, far better, indeed, than many who were enjoying current popularity. It was painful to see him frustrated and embittered by the public taste. And yet there was nothing she could do to change matters. If he would only be patient and sanguine, she told him, his success would come in due course as it had to others—to Renoir, to Monet, to Lautrec. "Or poor Modi, or perhaps Van Gogh," he fired back; he saw small comfort in posthumous recognition.

When Utter was at St. Bernard the tension was almost unbearable. Suzanne tried to avoid it by having large house parties and troops of friends from Paris: Max Jacob, the Coquiots, Roland Dorgèles, Derain and his wife—but more often than not the guests eventually witnessed a battle. And yet Suzanne dreaded his departure. Whatever his excuse, she knew that he was leaving her to go to another woman. By turns she was indifferent, mocking, or furiously jealous—all to no avail. She went so far as to hint that she herself had a lover, possibly "a high official in Lyons." When that failed to bring the hoped-for response, it was her turn to flee to Paris. Sometimes she took Maurice with her; more often she went alone. For a few days she would dispense quixotic bounty on the Butte, attend a round of parties, perhaps give one herself. But if she did not have her eye on Maurice, she could not stay away for long.

Fate did not see fit to release Suzanne from this thwarted and stagnant situation for twelve years. Maurice made no further suicide attempts, and that was about the measure of her victory. For the rest, it was one tedious battle against the deterioration of a man's mind, and another to hang onto some part of what had been the love of her life. In neither engagement was she ever to feel that she had won.

She continued to paint, and there were important exhibitions. She was invited to show in the Exhibition of Contemporary Art—Women and Flowers, in 1929, and again in the same year in the Painters, Self-Portraits exhibition. She showed the extraordinary nude of 1923 and a poignant reflection of an aging woman in a mirror done in 1927. In 1932 Utter arranged with the Galerie Moos in Geneva for the first *trinité maudite* exhibition outside France, and to Suzanne's and Utter's delight his sales were very good. Suzanne had a one-woman show of paintings, drawings, and etchings at the Galeries Georges Petit that same year. It was of this exhibition that Édouard Herriot was to write:

"Alive as springtime itself and, like spring, clear and ordered without interpretation, Suzanne Valadon pursues her magnificent and silent work of painting. . . . I think of the words of Théophile Gautier, 'Summer is a colorist, winter a draftsman.' To us who admire and love her art, Suzanne Valadon is springtime—a creature in whose sharp, incisive forms we find the fountains of life, the spontaneity of renewed day-to-day living. And before this very great and dedicated artist, the heir of those masters of the nineteenth century whose names we now revere, I marvel that so scrupulous a respect for the truth of form is able to achieve such a fete of color and movement."

Indirectly, Maurice himself provided some deliverance. The possibility of his marrying arose once again. This time the would-be bride was Utter's younger sister Gabrielle, a solid, devout young woman who was often a welcome guest at St. Bernard.

Suzanne always had in her heart a deep sympathy toward humble, simple people. Surrounded, as she had been since girlhood, by egoists and eccentrics possessed of fiery temperaments and flaming ambitions, who were nevertheless the breath of life to her, she was truly at ease only among the common people. The compassion she had for the thwarted, the outcasts of fortune, the drunkards, the derelicts, and the prostitutes was actually a dramatization of the genuine warmth and friendliness which she felt toward the people who worked as waiters, sold groceries and vegetables, tilled the fields, delivered laundry, or swept the streets. From earliest childhood this feeling of kinship had been strongly with her, sharpened greatly by her mother's neglect. People who went about performing their dull tasks without complaint had in her eyes a special glamour, and commanded both her loyalty and her affection. Her most intimate friends were women of this cut—seamstresses, the café *patronnes*, laundresses, village women, the Paulettes of this world, with whom it was possible to talk on an easy, amicable basis. Gabrielle Utter, the plumber's daughter, was one of these, so different from her mercurial, intellectual brother with his brooding resentments and unpredicable moods. Gabrielle was forthright and dependable. With her simplicity, her quiet affectionate manner, and her piety Suzanne was sure she would make an admirable wife for Maurice.

Gabrielle was willing. By no means was she an unattractive woman, and it was probably because of the qualities Suzanne saw in her that she had withstood, into her thirties, the marriage proposals of other Montmartre blades. Her pity for

Maurice tended to inspire love—of a maternal or sisterly sort. She was sympathetic and kind; and only when he was with Gabrielle did Maurice seem to shed the pitiable child-like dependence on his mother. For four years Gabrielle came to St. Bernard. Together they sat talking for hours, or rather she listened as he talked about his miserable past ("I was never hungry. Never. But I was often thirsty"), and about his religion which ever since he had come by the statuette at St. Sulpice had occupied a great part of his sober thinking hours. They played cards. He read to her—again something religious: the psalms or lives of the saints. Often they walked the country roads hand in hand. Whenever he was in Paris he went to see her. They dined out frequently; a single glass of wine was all he would drink, but he asked her to pay the bill for him because he did not like to touch money. It was with Gabrielle that he saw the first performance of the ballet *Barabau* in 1925.

Some sixth sense must have stayed Suzanne's unsubtle hand: she failed to charge in with a suggestion of marriage—for four years, at any rate. Instead she waited and watched with airy hope. From time to time she was disconcerted by the rudderless course which the lovers, as she came quickly to think of them, steered. Sometimes a shadow of apprehension flickered across her mind when Maurice did something especially juvenile, like hiding Utter's painting materials or insisting upon holding his mother's hand when they walked in a crowd; or when he managed to get hold of the household wine and got drunk again; or when he suddenly broke into a fit of laughter or into one of his terrible rages. Such moments of doubt were soon dispelled by the confidence Suzanne had in Gabrielle as a potential wife. But she would not have been Suzanne if she had kept her self-control indefinitely. After four years of waiting and hoping, she could remain silent no longer. She spoke to Maurice; he balked. Then on the first available train he fled to Montmartre and a terrific bout of drinking. A few days later a deflated Suzanne received a note from him. She handed it to Utter. It read: "I've had enough tragedy in my family with one of that family. That is quite enough."

Apart from the fact that she herself was sympathetically drawn to Gabrielle and that Maurice seemed to get on happily enough with her, Suzanne had counted on Gabrielle's piety to seal the alliance, for Maurice had entered a new phase. In the first months of his convalescence at St. Bernard he had come upon a Catechism belonging to his nurse's small daughter. At a time when he seemed only dimly able to communicate with the world around him, the book had a strange fascination. He carried it with him always, as he continued to carry the statuette of Joan of Arc, and for long hours he sat reading it and memorizing questions and answers that struck his fancy. From his reading he began to fabricate the framework of a religious belief—mystical, confused, and disjointed, an eccentric tangent to the teachings of the Church. Not that he dissented. In truth, his trouble was that he tried to accept Christianity as avidly as he had consumed his bottles of wine, and with the same motive—to lose himself where he would be able to avoid humanity. The result was that once again he was floundering in something he did not understand. With the slyness of the alcoholic, when he did not understand he improvised. Around him swirled the great issues of faith and ethics, which to his already confused brain were incomprehensible. If he failed to find in them the assurance his spirit craved, he supplied his own. In the same way he created from his personal yearning the acts of supplication, confession, and adoration which he could not discover in the Catechism. On the other hand, if he found the answers he was seeking, he accepted them without question, with humility and ineffable relief. The miscellaneous collection of dogma, mysticism, liturgy, and invention in his mind never quite coalesced into firm belief. Like his drinking, it was accompanied by insecurity and fear. Even if it had been less shadowy, he would still have found no solace, for he lived in a dim world of half tones. All his life the real, the meaningful, the definite were the things he feared, and the struggle to be free of them was never won; if it had been, it would have meant that he was mad. As it was, in the end he was to live out his days in the peace of a gray world.

Ultimately he was led by another to the sacraments of the Church, and he accepted them happily and without understanding. He would not have ventured toward them on his own, for in more than ten years of meditation he could never bring himself to consult a priest.

Nor could Maurice have turned to his mother, for, apart from the short time she had been in the care of the Sisters of St. Vincent de Paul, Suzanne's life had been lived without religious instruction and with no thought of it. Madeleine had gone to church when she wanted to make a bargain with God, and when she was dying she had sent for a priest. Bohemian Montmartre was hardly an atmosphere in which religious yearnings were likely to flourish. Religion was perhaps the most despised of bourgeois conventions. When artists like Renoir or Cézanne or a poet like Max Jacob professed religious faith, they were looked upon by their comrades and associates as eccentric characters. Still, it was her temperament more than her environment which induced Suzanne to give religion a wide berth. She was too much a creature of her own instincts to be swept up by any mysterious sense of an august and unearthly power behind the show of things or governing her destiny. Her solid belief in her own powers left no room to probe their possible origin: that they were in her was quite enough. The world as she saw it was a pretty literal place. As for the idealistic intentions by which people who were religious professed to be driven, she accepted them with ingenuous faith. In fact, she rejected very little that her senses encountered. If something existed and there was firsthand evidence of it, she believed it. That it was not passive acceptance is the clue to her glory as an artist. Once believed, whatever she experienced became a passion which she had to set down in her own medium of expression—the drawing, the etching, the lithograph, or the painting. The lyrical result was a statement at once of her savage responses and of her childlike literalism.

Suzanne might be scornful of religious ideas because they were not within her experience, and she might be contemptuous of religion in so far as it was a trait of the Philistine; but when such belief was a part of an individual, she stood to one side respectfully. In the lives of many of the humble people who were her friends religion played an important part, and she was not beyond attributing their essential goodness to it. So, although religion was not for her, she welcomed its arrival in Maurice's life. At first she was worried by the extraordinary figments of fancy which it seemed to create. His brooding silences troubled her, and she was suspicious of the hours he spent in meditation. Yet after a few months she could relax and take stock of the changes which religion had wrought. Compared with the past, how few were the terrible eruptions of temper! How much less nervous he was! How much less subject to fits of depression! There could be no doubt that religion was bringing Maurice the long-hoped-for release.

Always these changes had to be considered in relation to the past, for progress was by no means steady. Nor was improvement ever to be complete. Nevertheless, long hours given to Bible or Catechism were not being spent trying to steal alcohol from a locked cabinet or wine cellar. When Maurice knelt in supplication before his statuette of Joan of Arc he was not unleashing torrents of fury. When he held lengthy conversations with God he was not in a black abyss of despair. Between his ever-increasing religious devotions and his persistent production of oil paintings for the insatiable art dealers, he was less prone to drink. At St. Bernard he was not plagued by hostile forces staring at him; the people who were there were almost all people he knew well. There was less fear. All the same, when the outbursts did occur they were as violent, as devastating as ever. Bric-a-brac flew, furniture was smashed; servants left, and the whole household was thrown into a turmoil from which it might take days to recover.

As he grew older Maurice began to be impressed with fame. He decided quite coolly to develop a stock of eccentricities which he thought commensurate with it. People who called on him were instructed to ascertain beforehand what color he wished to see them in. For weeks he refused to shave, and when he did shave, it was only with water which he had not seen come from the tap. Playing simple tunes on his harmonium, he would let it be known that he was in the throes of composing a "great symphony" and was not to be disturbed for a week. For a time he made a collection of fish eyes which he kept in his coat pocket.

But such self-conscious efforts to lend some sort of charming color to his personality were pitiable rather than amusing. Too close, indeed, stood the pathetic figure in his gray world —never quite sane, never wholly man or boy. At the Avenue Junot he spent countless hours playing with the toy electric railway which Suzanne had bought for him, or dropping little pieces of colored chalk from the barred window of his room onto the ground below. He might stroll about the house, his bodyguard behind him, clapping his hands and repeating aloud to himself, "I'm very happy today," or "Suzanne is going to let me have wine with my dinner tonight." The sight of a car in the driveway might send him to bed. He might be in a daze, mumbling gibberish and bumping into furniture. Or he might sit quietly for several days, the long wrinkles of his face caught up in an ironic sneer, his blue eyes weary and baffled, saying nothing.

It was thus that the official delegation of government representatives and young Lyonnais artists found Maurice at St. Bernard on the morning in 1927 when they came to decorate him with the ribbon of the Legion of Honor. He sat on a low bench under an acacia tree in the little courtyard, Suzanne beside him, her hand gently on his knee. Throughout the short presentation ceremony he gave no indication that he understood what was going on. "Suzanne's eyes were shut, and two sad little pearls of tears slithered down her drawn cheeks," reported one of the young artists. "Everyone knew it was the time of her bitter victory."

Once the little ceremony was over, Maurice seemed to brighten, and by the time luncheon was served he was quite gay. During the meal he kept stroking the ribbon. And when the toast "To the artist of the Legion of Honor" was proposed, he lifted his glass solemnly. "A word of warning, gentlemen," he said; "mine is watered." With that the glass was drained in a single draught. "What a glorious day!" he sighed after the festivities were over. Then he added archly, "And not even a real glass of *rouge* for the artist of the Legion of Honor."

IX   The Wasp

ONE EVENING IN THE WARM SPRING AIR OF 1937 A COUPLE OF young Americans strolling along the rue Norvins were stopped by the sound of a woman's voice. Turning, they saw at one of the little tables before Chez Ma Cousine the grinning face of a tiny gnome of a woman, with square-cut straight hair and large horn-rimmed spectacles. A big square hand fluttered at the end of a diminutive, childlike wrist, beckoning to them: "Come. Come and sit with me." She might have been drunk or a little "touched," but one came to Montmartre these days as much to see "characters" as anything else.

"It has all changed so much," Suzanne said wistfully, squinting at the crowds milling along the pavements of the little square. Under the lines of young chestnut trees people were dining in the flickering glow of Chinese lanterns beneath bright-colored umbrellas. Waiters from the cafés lining the square were juggling trays of food high over their heads as they wormed their way from the kitchens on one side of the street, through the ambling tide of sightseers, to tables on the other. At the corners of the square, artists painted picturesque café fronts and the marble domes and minarets of the basilica of Sacré-Coeur, their pictures strongly reminiscent of the poorest canvases of Maurice Utrillo; or they sketched likenesses of tourists, while around them watched the curious

242

and the amateur art critics. Everyone was pleased with how "charming" and how "quaint" the Place du Tertre was. "I Can't Give You Anything but Love, Baby" blared in French from the bar of Au Pichet du Tertre two doors away.

"Dear Monsieur Toulouse! He did not like the Butte. It was not gay enough for him. But he loved the boulevards —the Place Blanche, Place Pigalle, Place de Clichy. Oh, they were for him. All the gay places. He was always gay. . . .

"The old chestnut trees with the sun coming through them —they were what Renoir liked. It was different then. The young people used to stroll under the trees. And when there was a fete, how gay it was, with the students and the grisettes and the dancing. . . .

"That long building over there with the shutters—it was the *mairie* of Montmartre before '70. The great Clemenceau was the mayor of Montmartre once, but that was later. My mother used to clean his office. Everybody was poor then, or so it seemed. Now everything is prosperous. Everybody makes lots of money—except the artists. . . .

"And there where they sell *glaces*—that was Sergeant Gay's place—the Casse-Croute. He is dead now, poor fellow." She started to cross herself, stopped in midair, and slowly brought her hand down to the half-filled glass of wine before her. "I have just been with my son," she explained. "He is married now. He lives in a great house at Le Vésinet. Very chic. He does that"—she made the sign of the cross—"whenever he speaks of somebody that is dead. He is very religious, my son. . . .

"You know that in 1920 Montmartre seceded from the French nation? Ah! That was the day, I tell you. Jules Dépaquit—he was my son's good friend and my husband's too. They used to say he was 'the quick drinker,' but they made him 'mayor of Free Montmartre.' There was a big parade and much to drink and dancing. . . .

"Then there was the time when Frédé's donkey Lolo

painted a picture with his tail and it went to the Salon des Indépendants. And everyone said Matisse could have done as well." Her large hand slapped the table, and her high-pitched voice trailed off in a cascade of laughter.

"And Puvis"—she pronounced it 'Bou-vee'—"what a fine aristocrat he was! Wonderful great beard, and a very loving man, I can tell you. . . .

"Then there was Degas—the Master. He was the greatest of them all. . . ."

Finally she was weary. She wrapped her grimy tweed coat tightly to her bosom and leaned back in her chair. "We must have another glass," she sighed. Her eyes behind the large horn rims brightened sharply. When the waiter set the drinks on the table, she lifted hers high. "Now we must not think of the old days any more. We must drink to the present. Come, let us drink to love. *Vive l'amour!*"

But it was impossible for Suzanne not to dwell on the past. Around her the present was fast crumbling into ruin, and at the age of seventy a toast to love was a brave though hollow gesture. The fact was that the mainspring of her amazing vitality had been broken finally by the events of the past two years.

In January, 1935, she, who had never known illness before, was rushed to the American Hospital at Neuilly dangerously ill with uremic poisoning. "I was never afraid of death. Only the doctors terrified me," she said afterward. She was a trying patient, making scenes, overturning her trays of food on the floor, refusing to take the medicines prescribed for her. But when she was well enough to leave the hospital, there could be no doubt that she had come through a devastating experience and that a gray sense of the fleetingness of things possessed her spirit. Was this the acceptance of defeat? At times it seemed so. She puttered about the house, moving pieces of bric-a-brac without any definite idea why she wanted them moved or where she put them. For weeks, weeds flourished in her little garden; a canvas stood unfinished on her easel. Uncertainty dogged her movements and her speech. Seeing her shuffle unsteadily about the streets or hearing her disjointed staccato speech, people thought she was drunk. The legend grew that she was an alcoholic, a legend which those who knew her best furiously denied.

It was now when she was weakest and most uncertain of herself that she had been called upon to pass through one of the most trying periods of her life. In 1933 M. Pauwels, the Belgian banker, had died. "You have no idea," said his widow, delivering a biographical sketch of herself to Robert Coughlan, "what it is like to have been held up and supported by such a wonderful man and then, suddenly, to have him no more. . . . I didn't know what to do with myself. I was not old, but I wasn't young, and although I wasn't thinking about another husband, I wondered what the future would bring. M. Pauwels left me quite well off, even though he had suffered reverses a few years before, but I certainly didn't have enough to live in great comfort for the rest of my life." * Following her husband's death Lucie Pauwels resumed her stage name, Lucie Valore, and became an even more frequent visitor to Suzanne's studio, where she continued to offer Suzanne her intimate friendship. Few people now sought Suzanne's friendship, and in her loneliness, she craved friendship.

According to Suzanne's account, Lucie had come to visit her at the hospital and had told her, "I have decided to take care of your son since you are obviously not going to be able to." Lucie's account is considerably different. According to Lucie, Suzanne asked her from her hospital bed, "What will happen to my poor Maurice? Who will take care of him?" It was then that Lucie volunteered to assume the burden Su-

* From Robert Coughlan, *Wine of Genius* (New York: Harper & Brothers; © 1951).

zanne had carried so long. Whichever version is true, it was clear to both women and to everyone who knew them that the contest for the protection of Maurice was on. Few doubted what the outcome would be.

In none of her efforts to get Maurice married had Suzanne seriously contemplated the possibility of losing him. Had he married Marie Vizier, Gabrielle Utter, or the statuesque Paulette, she, Suzanne, would have remained in charge of his destiny. He would still primarily have been hers. But if he were to marry the capable Lucie Valore, Suzanne felt certain her boy would be lost to her forever.

Would it help save Maurice if she piled insults on Lucie? If she ridiculed her? If she evinced contempt of the erstwhile affluence of Mme. Pauwels? Would Maurice decide to cut himself off from his beloved Montmartre, from their free, undisciplined, creative world, to try to replace the late respectable and prosperous banker at Mme. Pauwels' side?

Although Suzanne employed every trick she was capable of using, Maurice gradually made his decision. He was baptized, confirmed, and received his first communion under Lucie's watchful eye. And when all was thus in order, she married him in a civil ceremony at the Montmartre *mairie* and after that at Angoulême, in a church ceremony. Suzanne witnessed all but the religious marriage ceremony. When it came time to proceed to Angoulême, Suzanne was well aware that she had lost the contest. She refused to go on with the show.

Maurice and Lucie stayed in Angoulême for a year while Lucie launched herself in the dual role of bodyguard and business manager to "the greatest man living in France." In both roles she was successful from the start. On watered-down wine given him in doses carefully apportioned by Lucie, Maurice continued to paint pictures with lots of white in them for the greedy appetites of the "bourse of art" and for the free-flowing purses of millionaire collectors. She dismissed Utter summarily. For a while she stopped all sale of Maurice's canvases, and during this period the word spread abroad that he was no longer able to paint. Because of this, prices for his work rose substantially. Presently Lucie began to release the pictures she had on hand. She received such good prices that about a year after their marriage, the couple were able to buy a house and extensive grounds in fashionable Le Vésinet, outside Paris. They called the villa "La Bonne Lucie." In the garden a show of nineteenth-century pieces of sculpture and artificial frogs, ducks, and turtles brightened the lawns. They had a big car and a chauffeur, a secretary, a Polish bodyguard and his wife, a cook, Pekingese dogs, a houseful of rococo furniture and *objets d'art*, and an Aubusson carpet of which Maurice was inordinately proud. Lucie wore clothes by the leading Parisian couturiers, and she gradually acquired an impressive collection of diamond jewelry.

Amid this splendor lived the little man whose only concern with money was how much red wine it would buy, his gray, misty world illuminated by an occasional mystic transport during one of his long daily bouts of religious devotion, by a gentle joke which he might rouse himself to make, by one of his old flashes of rage. Toward Lucie he maintained a curiously distant and baffled attitude, as though he never quite believed that she was a figure in his life. When he said, as he often did, "I love Joan of Arc, my mother, and my wife," he suggested a small boy reciting a piece. Despite his pitiable dependence on his wife, when she was out of his hearing he would sometimes toss a caustic barb or two in her direction. He referred to her as one of "them"—the police, the medical authorities, the jailors at Picpus and Villejuif all rolled into one. His manner seemed by turns listless, surly, derisive, or amused. His thoughts dwelled much in the past, upon the people he had known, upon Suzanne, upon the souls of the departed: the Sergeant Gays and Zborowskis, the Modiglianis and Marie Viziers of his life. He never really knew Lucie.

All the same, Suzanne's life was hardly the happier for knowing that Maurice was in Lucie's doughty hands. From time to time she saw him. For a while she made frequent visits to Le Vésinet, and Lucie brought him to the Avenue Junot. Willing to be magnanimous, Lucie made an earnest effort to be friendly. It was lost on Suzanne.

Nor were Suzanne's feelings by any means pent up. That Lucie had taken Maurice off was bad enough, as she saw it, but that she had set him up in loathsome bourgeois splendor and kept him at work turning out bad pictures was insupportable. Forgotten entirely was her own willingness to let him do much the same thing; what with her had been therapy, in Lucie's case was crass commercialism and greed. On Lucie rained the full flood of her mother-in-law savagery—mockery, malice, contempt, fits of rage, torrents of tears. Each meeting saw a fresh eruption of acrimony. At first deeply hurt, Lucie soon began to think of herself as the harried heroine of these occasions. She recited with composed nobility and measured statements eloquent of filial affection, extravagant admiration for the sublime art of "France's greatest woman artist"—"As a painter I kneel before Suzanne Valadon"—and concern for the older woman's health.

Release of her resentment, however, did not compensate Suzanne for the loss of her son. If we discount the protestations of mother love and sacrifice which, under the circumstances, she magnified to gargantuan proportions, it nevertheless remains that worrying about Maurice's physical well-being had become a driving force in her life. Lucie's masterful control of every moment of his day left her without apprehension on that score; even Suzanne's rabidly prejudiced eye was obliged to recognize that the "asylum at Le Vésinet" kept its patient in better health than he had ever known before. But the years of anxiety had continually renewed Suzanne's strength. Now this spur was gone and her strength was waning. The very nervousness which Maurice's moods and outbursts had generated for so long was dissolving. The ferocious guardian no longer had anything to protect. These things were the fibers of her being, and to be without them was to walk closer to death.

But for one memory that remained painfully in her heart, she might not have cared: Utter. Friends noticed that mention of his name alone jarred her free of a prevailing mood. If she was particularly weary or apathetic, it could even produce tears. Now at last separation from him had poignant meaning. He came to the Avenue Junot almost every day, and, forgetting all her resentments against him, she made pathetic efforts to keep him from leaving. Practically without money again, she traded paintings and drawings with butchers and wine merchants in order to provide Utter with the beefsteaks and fine Burgundies he loved. She bought him books and gave him money, often the last she had. Lucie had offered to put her on an allowance, but had added, "And you may stay in *my* house* until you die." In the explosion which followed, the allowance was lost sight of.

Utter tried to respond by occasionally bringing Suzanne flowers, by listening kindly as she recalled the pleasant memories of the eighties and nineties, and of their first galvanic years together in the Impasse de Guelma and the rue Cortot. It was as though his mother were talking to him now. Even his own part was being played by some historical wraith who had no connection with the misery of the present. In the gathering dusk it was impossible for him to feel that between the tiny aged figure, fluttering and timorous, and himself there had once raged the wild, passionate fires of love. And yet, as he told his friends Marie and Louis Chervin, he never turned the key in the latch, or stepped into a room in which she was present, or saw her pass uneasily across a street with-

* The house in rue Junot. It was in Maurice's name.

out feeling a flutter of happiness. Whatever had happened to the flesh, for him she was the only real joy he had ever known.

Bitterness against Maurice and Lucie was almost a mania with Utter now. As long as he had managed Maurice's business affairs he could claim a large measure of respect—at least in the business world. It was some compensation for his failure to achieve success as an artist, distasteful as the compromise was to him. Lucie had put an end to that: she had removed the ground under his feet. In bygone days it would not have bothered Utter at all. The exuberant spirit would have leaped on to something more daring, more dazzling, and conceivably more remunerative. But he was too intelligent not to know that he was slipping and had neither the will nor the energy to stop himself. If he was an amatory buffoon and a drunk, it was because women and drink were the only salves he could find to soothe the sore wounds of his pride. He painted furiously. At times he went without food in order to buy paints. At St. Bernard a caretaker found him unconscious on the floor before his easel.

Suzanne came finally to understand his terrible frustration. Pitying him and hungering to care for him, she wanted desperately to have him back. But the time they spent together was spoiled by his sense of failure, his defensive egotism, and his resentment against Maurice and Lucie. Sooner or later the atmosphere of peace and solace which she sought to create for him would be shattered by boasting, self-pity, or acrimony. Only rarely would she respond in kind, and then only with a quick show of temper which was rather a memorial to the rages of their younger days than a passion of itself. Her physical weakness, for one thing, prevented her from loosing the explosions she had so easily fired in the past. In an old-womanish way she hoarded them for Lucie. The fact was that Utter had grown to be the only one in the world who made life worth living for her, and she was not going to lose him again if the only sacrifice was that she had to hold her tongue.

In his paunchy middle-aged figure and even in the cynical turn of his lip she still saw the glow of the happiest days of her life. More and more her mind tended to dwell on the past, anyway; and in the long stretch of it only the bright moments were still clear. Of these, the moments with young André Utter were luminous as no others were. Still, for all her yearning to have him to herself, she could not muster strength to fight for him. Living alone in a house which had been bought to be shared with one she loved, who was now gone from her finally, she waited for one from whom not even the wreckage of their marriage could ever separate her completely. She would sit gazing into her little garden or the tiny square before the house with its lonely young locust tree, sunk in melancholy, waiting to see him, the familiar pipe in the corner of his mouth, come puffing up the hill. When he did not come, there was nothing she could do but tell her troubles to her cats, "dear Djoubouti" and "darling Ratminou," and plead with them not to desert her too. In the quiet which she had always hated, she gradually came to accept the fact that she was old and infirm and alone.

Actually the onset of such melancholy moods was slow. Now and again the cloud lifted to disclose a glimpse of the old Suzanne: with a group of friends about her, serving them champagne and a buffet supper which she had taken days and her last francs to prepare; or at a friend's studio party, giving a waspish imitation of Renoir dancing at the Moulin de la Galette or of Louis Libaude appraising a picture. On other occasions she might shuffle up the hill to the Place du Tertre in her bundle of soiled and frayed tweeds and outsize moccasins to sit away an afternoon or evening in a familiar café. Members of the old guard of the Butte would spot her and perhaps buy her drinks, and the hours would fly by while they laughed and talked about the days that were past. When she was unnoticed she often sat down at someone else's table, or called to a stranger to sit with her while she launched into an autobiographical monologue quite different in content from the last one she had delivered.

But it was when she approached her easel that the old spirit found itself and took wing. There is no mistaking the bitter-sweet sadness which pervades these last paintings—her cats and her flowers which alone shared the intimacy of her declining years. Her golds are those of the setting sun, her browns and ochers those of the plow-worn earth. Brooding magentas and purples linger among the fresh full colors of spring. On a workaday crockery vase stand the words "*Vive la jeunesse*"; on another "*Joie de vivre.*" The poignant love of life is still there, sharpened, if anything, by the maturity of her talent. No surface is flat or inert, no color smooth. The calm of age cannot smother the passionate vibrations. Each canvas is invested with a secret of life of sweetness and compassion—the embers of a blaze which still smolders with a fierce heat.

In May, 1937, Suzanne attended the Women Painters Exhibition at the Petit Palais, in which several of these last paintings hung, together with a small representative collection of her earlier work. Around hers hung canvases by Vigée-Lebrun, Berthe Morisot, Séraphine Louis, Marie Laurencin, Marie Blanchard, Eva Gonzalès, Sonia Turk, and others whose creative artistic powers had brought a not-inconsiderable measure of glory to the history of French art. For more than three hours Suzanne passed from picture to picture and back again, squinting from behind her large horn-rimmed glasses at brushwork, draftsmanship, the arrangement of light, the treatment of form and shadow—now in excited delight over a composition, the line of an arm, the pearly tone of an expanse of skin, or the color of a bowl; now clicking her tongue loudly in anger as she spotted a "trick," a "lie," or an uncertain perspective. Leaving the show, she was strangely subdued and pensive; and that evening she said to the friend who had gone with her: "You know, *chérie*, I often boasted about my art because I thought that was what people expected—for an artist to boast. I'm very humble after what we have seen this afternoon. The women of France can paint too, *hein?*" Suddenly tears welled in her eyes. "But do you know, *chérie*," she spoke quietly, "I think maybe God has made *me* France's greatest woman painter."

She spoke of God frequently now; the eternal aspects of her earthly mission had begun to trouble her. Still she was unprepared to wrestle with them. By temperament unmystical and from lack of training agnostic, she was loath to fly to the bosom of the Church. Instead, it seemed both reasonable and simple to establish herself on a friendly and respectful basis with the Supreme Being whom she dutifully acknowledged to be the source of her life and powers. Since all her life she had maintained that such powers were hers alone, this transformation had a sacrificial aura about it: it was proof of her humility. God became for her an old and very dear friend whom she had deserted but who would never desert her. Thus her faith was that of a savage child, unadorned, uncomplicated, and forthright. It required neither churchgoing nor acceptance of the sacraments, no meditation, and only short improvised prayer. But it was quite enough from which to draw intermittent peace in this dimming world, and perhaps ensure everlasting excitement in the next. For as time dragged on, it was the turmoil and the bustle of the old days that she really missed most of all. On the increasingly rare occasions when she made her way to the top of the Butte, she relived it all in her mind's eye against the settings which Maurice had captured long ago in his beautiful pictures —the battered and flaked walls, the grimy façades of tumbledown houses, the warped roofs and twisted rusty gates, the stillness of the violet air over the great oyster shell of Paris, the Place du Tertre with its hollow-trunked old chestnuts and the friendly golden glow of café interiors, and the glistening magnet of the Sacré-Coeur, drawing to its white turret the faithful and those who enjoyed heights. But for her these were scenes that had to have people in them—beautiful, odd, and rapturous souls who sold wine and bread and souvenir post cards, who delivered packages and painted pictures, who sang in the streets at night until someone threw a bucket of water on them from a window above, and made the cafés resound with gossip, artistic theories and inspirations, chatter and laughter. The entire fabric of her life belonged to these few acres of tattered and worm-eaten hillside. Here the great ghosts of the past were flesh and blood: Lautrec sitting under a black umbrella painting "Berthe, the Deaf One," in M. Forest's garden; Renoir at the Nouvelle-Athènes doodling with burnt match sticks on the tablecloth; the rough red hands of Vincent Van Gogh greedily shoveling food into his mouth in Mme. Bataille's restaurant; Puvis de Chavannes, looking like Michaelangelo's Moses, stamping up the rue de l'Abreuvoir in a snowstorm; Modigliani, frenzied by dope and alcohol, kicking frantically on Beatrice Hastings' door in the rue Norvins; and the bitter figure of the one who was the greatest artist of all, in his pepper-and-salt tweeds, his throat swathed in woolen scarves, fumbling up the twisted staircase of the rue Cortot to see *her*. Here, along the rue des Saules, she had climbed the acacia trees and picked off the yellow blossoms to sell to the pastry shops in the rue Custine to be embalmed in sugar for cake decorations; here, Chez Bouscarat, with Modigliani, Soutine, and Kisling, she had dined on a Valadon still life "in order to save a Soutine choirboy from the stewpot"; here, on the long flight of steps of the rue Muller, Erik Satie had told Puvis de Chavannes, "I learn more about music from observing your 'Poor Fishermen' than I shall ever learn from musicians. But, monsieur," he added, "you would improve your work if you boiled your wine and drank it cold mixed with fuchsia juice." In this jumble of moldering timbers, plaster of Paris, and gaping windows she, Suzanne Valadon, had passed, in the arms of ardent lovers, nearly all the rapturous hours which her loving nature craved. In this one little cobbled street, the rue Cortot, had been enacted most of the tempest of her marriage, from its joyous springtide to the agony of its collapse. Maurice was there, his elbow on his knee, his chin in the palm of his hand, gazing into the courtyard; so was the pottering figure of Madeleine.

She spoke of her mother sometimes—of the lonely life she had led. Both Maurice and Madeleine had long been in her care; but though she had loved the one and could have loved the other if she had been permitted to do so, she had failed to communicate with either of them. Her sense of responsibility had not always conformed to conventional patterns. Independence of spirit had been the mainspring of her character both as artist and as human being, so that frequently her erratic temperament belied her deep loyalties. Now Madeleine was dead, and Maurice had deserted her. In a painful flash she saw him in the entrance hall of the Avenue Junot, scrawny and shivering, caught up against Lucie's ample bosom, heard her own voice in a careless way ask the fatal question, "What have you decided?" and then his reply, given in the quick, nervous way he spoke, "I'm going with her." As though it were not enough, a few moments later he cried, "And now, long live liberty!" and was gone.

Still, Madeleine's death and Maurice's leaving might not have mattered so much had there been someone else on hand to accept her ministrations. It was only a matter of time before the one she loved most would be gone too.

Shortly after Maurice left the Avenue Junot she had indeed thought that she had found someone to take his place, someone to care for. There had been another row with Utter, and somehow the notion had struck her that in his drunkenness he intended to harm her physically. Carried away by this fantasy, she soon had it firmly in her mind and much on the tip of her tongue that Utter beat her. It made a pathetic and dramatic story, which for a while restored some of her zest. There was not a word of truth in it, of course, but while she was dramatizing its possibilities she asked a young artist she knew to come and live with her.

The situation was one to delight the gossips of the Butte. Shades of the Montmartre of old! The amorous wasp, Suzanne Valadon, had found another young lover at the age of seventy!

Who was this dashing, intense young man with blazing dark eyes and taut, swarthy skin who called himself Gazi–I.G.? A painter of gloomy Montmartre streets lit by reckless explosions of green light—a good painter. It was said that he was a Mongol prince: people called him "Gazi the Tartar." They spoke knowingly of countless amours.

His own story was considerably tamer. He came from Provence. He had first known Suzanne Valadon when he was eight years old. She had been a friend of his aunt's and had wanted to adopt him as her son. He called her "Mémere," and referred to her as his "mother by adoption." "She said I was the son she had been waiting for all her life. She adored me like a god." But the real love of his life was the Blessed Virgin, toward whom he had been drawn by a long series of moving mystical revelations since early childhood. The Holy Mother had instructed him to cherish and care for Suzanne.

Tender though his ministrations were, they were hardly an answer to Suzanne's yearnings. She wanted someone to care for, someone to receive the abundant love and compassion in her heart. Instead, it was Gazi who took charge of her and fairly smothered her in his devotion. He cooked her meals and took charge of the house. He waited on her as though she were a queen. Her health and her state of mind were his hourly concerns. In the evenings they sat long hours together in the kitchen of the house in the Avenue Junot.

Throughout her life she had always resigned herself to listening to the monologues of men—Renoir in the Louvre, Puvis de Chavannes at a table for two at the Tour d'Argent, Satie in his monastic room in the rue Cortot, Utter everywhere. It was almost a form of coquetry with her, for all her belief in herself, to appear to defer to the intellectual force of a man. Now she sat quietly and listened to young Gazi expounding his adoration of the Blessed Virgin. He was pleading with her to embrace the Church, and, as always when it came to matters of the mind, she was evasive. "When I die," she told him, "you will have my soul in your pocket, and you will take care of it, *hein?*" But for the present she would not go to church, and the prayers she said were her own silent ones.

From time to time she would find energy to interrupt Gazi's monologue with one of her own; its subject was always the past, and, strangely, with Gazi it was the unhappier aspects she remembered. She spoke to him of the black days of the Commune, of her mother's rejection of her, of Adrien Boissy, who had raped her when she was "an innocent child of sixteen." Step by step, over and over again, she traced the tragic pilgrimage of Maurice from asylum to asylum. Always she returned to Utter and the heartbreak which had followed the years of the war.

For three years the flickering twilight lingered. More and more she stayed at home, doing little, painting when she could. Occasionally the massive figure of Derain appeared sprawled in the big chair in her studio, talking about the traditions of classical painting which, he said, she and he alone were preserving. Nora Kars came almost every day to see that there were flowers in the house, and to relive with Suzanne briefly the days of their early friendship. Georges Braque and his wife called occasionally. So did Mme. Coquiot, an old friend from the days when they were models together in the Place Pigalle. Nor did the humble people she loved fail her. An old laundress showed up, a waiter, a taxi driver, a prostitute, the butcher's wife whom she had sent to the Riviera. But between these visits long hours passed without the ringing of a doorbell or the buzzing of the telephone.

To one who had been at the hub of the brilliant artistic flame illuminating the entire world, it was heartbreaking to feel cut off from the creative life of the day. Across the city, with its thrashing birth pains of new ideas and concepts, Montparnasse might as well have been at the other end of the earth. Echoes of its discussions reached her. The new movement was Surrealism, completely beyond her powers of understanding, as had been the long line of other movements—even perhaps Impressionism. She did not believe in "movements and schools," she reiterated. But a new movement brought new names, and these in turn were attached to people; and people she always wanted to know. What were they like—these Man Rays and Max Ernsts and Salvatore Dalis? Who were Chagall, Tchelitchev, Chirico, Ives Tanguy, and Miro? Where were they taking the light that had been fired by her old friends of the Nouvelle-Athènes, of the Chat Noir, of Lautrec's studio in the rue Tourlaque? What did they think of the art of a little Montmartre *gamine* who had taught herself to draw and paint, and who just painted what she saw with all the savage intensity of her being?

Fittingly, she was at her easel, painting a bowl of flowers, when the end approached. She had a stroke. Her neighbor, Mme. Poulbot, passing the studio window opened to the air of an April morning, heard her cry out. She summoned her friend Mme. Kvapil, and the two women broke into the house to find Suzanne crumpled on the studio floor. They carried her to bed and called a doctor. Suzanne lay unconscious, breathing faintly, the fine mesh of wrinkles slowly dissolving until her face was a calm and lovely waxen mask. The ghost of a smile trembled about her dry lips. So did the pain of old age and suffering leave at last.

At three o'clock it was decided to remove her to a hospital. Somehow the decision managed to penetrate her unconsciousness. Her last opportunity to do the unexpected arrived, and she did not let it slip by.

"Send for—Lucie," she said weakly.

In the ambulance Mme. Kvapil and Gazi were with her. As the car swung into the broad circle of the Étoile, the early April sunset swept its tawny light dramatically over the massive Arc de Triomphe into the Champs-Élysées. Gazi, the artist, turned to catch a glimpse of it. Beside him the tiny frame of another artist sighed wearily and lay still.

Three days later, on April 9th, 1938, her body lay before the altar of Montmartre's ancient parish church, St. Pierre, "where every true Montmartrois goes in the end." Maurice was in a state of collapse at Le Vésinet, and Lucie had taken capable charge of the arrangements. In the church, crowded with the renowned, the humble, and the ragtag and bobtail company of Bohemia, Edouard Herriot, senior statesman and twice Premier of France, delivered the eulogy. Haggard and trembling, André Utter was sunk in grief. For the rest it was hard to know who mourned a tired, little woman, who a passionate artist, or who wept for an era which had seen the glory of French art.

Bibliography

ADEMA, Marcel. *Appolinaire, le Mal-Aimé.* Paris, 1952.

BAROTTE, René. "Suzanne Valadon," *L'Art et les Artistes.* Paris, 1937.

BASIN, G. *L'Epoque Impressioniste.* Paris, 1947.

BASLER, Adolphe. *Suzanne Valadon.* Paris, 1929.

BEACHBOARD, Robert. *La Trinité Maudite.* Paris, 1952.

BERENSON, Bernard. *Aesthetics and History.* London, 1950.

BOECK, Wilhelm, and SABARTES, Jaime. *Pablo Picasso.* London, 1955.

BOURET, Jean. *Suzanne Valadon.* Paris, 1947.

CARCO, Francis. *Utrillo.* Paris, 1956.

———. *La Legende et la Vie d'Utrillo.* Paris, 1928.

———. *De Montmartre au Quartier Latin.* Paris, 1927.

———. *Souvenirs de Montmartre et d'Ailleurs.* Paris, 1938.

———. *Montmartre à Vingt Ans.* Paris, 1938.

CASSOU, Jean. (Preface). *Hommage à Suzanne Valadon.* Paris, 1948.

COIGNIAT, R. *Au Temps des Impressionistes.* Paris, 1951.

COLOMBIER, Pierre. "Suzanne Valadon," *Amour de l'Art.* Paris, 1926.

COQUIOT, Gustave. *Cubistes, Futuristes, Passéistes.* Paris, 1921.

———. *Maurice Utrillo.* Paris, 1925.

———. *Des Peintres Maudits.* Paris, 1924.

———. *Les Indépendants.* Paris, 1921.

COUGHLAN, Robert. *Wine of Genius.* New York, 1951.

COURTHION, Pierre. *Montmartre.* Geneva, 1956.

———. *Utrillo.* Lausanne, 1948.

CROCE, Benedetto. *The Essence of Aesthetic.* New York, 1935.

DEGAS, Edgar. *Lettres de Degas.* Paris, 1931.

DENIS, Maurice. *Théories du Symbolisme et de Gauguin vers un Nouvel Ordre Classique.* Paris, 1912.

DEROYER, Michelle. *Quelques Souvenirs Autour de Suzanne Valadon.* Paris, 1947.

DOUGLAS, Charles. *Artist Quarter.* London, 1941.

DORGELÈS, Roland. *Le Chateau des Brouillards.* Paris, 1932.

——. *Quand J'étais Montmartrois.* Paris, 1936.

DU MAURIER, Gerald. *Trilby.* London, 1895.

DURET, T. *Les Peintres Impressionistes.* Paris, 1878.

——. *Les Maîtres Impressionistes.* Paris, 1900.

FELS, Robert. "Suzanne Valadon," *L'Information.* Paris, 1921.

FÉNÉON, Félix. *Les Impressionistes.* Paris, 1886.

GALLATIN, A. E. *Georges Braque.* New York, 1953.

GAUNT, William. *March of the Moderns.* London, 1949.

GAZI, I-G. *Notre-Dame de Montmartre.* (Brochures). Paris, 1943, 1946, 1948.

GUENNE, Jacques. "Suzanne Valadon," *Art Vivant.* Paris, 1932.

HARTLAUB, G. F. *Impressionists in France.* Milan, 1956.

HAUSER, Arnold. *The Social History of Art.* New York, 1951.

HERRIOT, Edouard. Preface to catalogue of Suzanne Valadon Exhibition. Paris: Georges Petit Galerie, 1932.

——. Preface to catalog of Suzanne Valadon Exhibition. Paris: "La Portique," 1931.

HUYSMANS, J.-K. *L'art Moderne.* Paris, 1908.

JACOMETTI, Nesto. *Suzanne Valadon.* Geneva, 1947.

JOURDAIN, Francis. *Utrillo.* Paris, 1953.

JOYANT, Maurice. *Henri de Toulouse-Lautrec.* Paris, 1926.

KLEIN, J. *Modern Masters.* New York, 1938.

LAKE, Carlton, and MAILLARD, Robert. *A Dictionary of Modern Painting.* London, 1956.

LE GOAZIOU, Alain. *Le Père Tanguy.* Paris, 1951.

LE PELLETIER, E. *Paul Verlaine.* London, 1902.

LEUDET, S. "Suzanne Valadon chez les Pompiers," *Beaux-Arts.* Paris, 1938.

MACK, Gerstle. *Toulouse-Lautrec.* New York, 1938.

——. *Paul Cézanne.* New York, 1936.

MAC ORLAN, Pierre. *Montmartre Souvenirs.* Brussels, 1946.

MARX, Claude L. *Un Siècle d'Art.* Paris, 1904.

——. *Dixhuit Planches Originales de Suzanne Valadon.* Paris, 1947.

MERMILLON, Marius. *Suzanne Valadon.* Paris, 1950.

MOORE, George. *Confessions of a Young Man.* London, 1888.

——. *Impressions and Opinions.* New York, 1891.

MYERS, Rollo. *Erik Satie*. London, 1948.

NINE, Frank. "André Utter," *Art Vivant*. Paris, 1929.

OSBORNE, Harold. *Aesthetics and Criticism*. London, 1955.

PISSARRO, Camille. *Letters to His Son Lucien*. New York, 1943.

POIRET, Paul. *King of Fashion*. Philadelphia, 1931.

PUVIS DE CHAVANNES, P. *Lettres*. Ed. Conrad de Mandach. Paris, 1910.

RAFOLS, J. F. *Modernismo y Modernistas*. Barcelona, 1954.

RAYNAL, Maurice. *Modern Painting*. Geneva, 1953.

REWALD, John. *Cézanne, Sa Vie, Son Oeuvre, Son Amitié pour Zola.* Paris, 1939.

——. *The History of Impressionism*. New York, 1946.

——. *Post-Impressionism*. New York, 1956.

REY, Robert. Preface to *Dessins et Gravures de Suzanne Valadon.* Paris, 1929.

——. *Suzanne Valadon*. Paris, 1922.

RICTOR, Léon. *Les Arts et les Lettres de Puvis de Chavannes*. Paris, 1901.

RIVIÈRE, Georges. *Le Maître, Paul Cézanne*. Paris, 1923.

——. *Renoir et Ses Amis*. Paris, 1921.

ROSENBERG, Léonce. *Cubisme et Tradition*. Paris, 1920.

ROTHENSTEIN, J. *Nineteenth Century Painting*. London, 1932.

SALMON, André. *Montjoie*. Paris, 1913.

——. *Propos d'Atelier*. Paris, 1922.

——. *La Jeune Peintre Française*. Paris, 1912.

——. *L'Air de la Butte*. Paris, 1945.

SEMBAT, Marcel. *Henri Matisse*. Paris, 1920.

STEIN, Gertrude. *The Autobiography of Alice B. Toklas*. New York, 1933.

——. *Paris, France*. New York, 1940.

STRECKER, P. *Suzanne von Montmartre*. Leipzig, 1938.

TABARANT, Adolphe. "Souvenirs de Modèle de Suzanne Valadon," *Bulletin de la Vie Artistique*. Paris, 1921.

——. *Utrillo*. Paris, 1926.

UHDE, Wilhelm. *Die Impressionisten.* Vienna, 1937.

——. *Henri Rousseau*. Paris, 1911.

UTRILLO, Miguel. *Historia y Anecdota del Cau Ferrat*. Barcelona, 1910.

UTTER, André. "La Carrière de Maurice Utrillo," *Beaux-Arts*. Paris, 1938.

264

VACHON, Marius. *Puvis de Chavannes: Un Maître de ce Temps.* Paris, 1902.

VALADON, Suzanne. "Suzanne Valadon par Elle-Même," Prométhée. Paris, 1939.

VEDRES, Nichole. *Un Siècle d'Élegance.* Paris, 1943.

VOLLARD, Ambroise. *Recollections of a Picture Dealer.* London, 1936.

————. *La Vie et L'Oeuvre de Pierre-Auguste Renoir.* Paris, 1919.

WARNOD, André. *Ceux de la Butte.* Paris, 1947.

————. *Le Vieux Montmartre.* Paris, 1913.

————. "Avec André Utter Nous Perdons un Bon Peintre," *Arts.* Paris, 1948.

WEILL, Berthe. *Pan dans l'Oeil.* Paris, 1933.

WERNER, Alfred. *Maurice Utrillo.* London, 1955.

WHITE, Jack Palmer. *Lucie Valore.* Paris, 1952.

WILENSKI, R. H. *Modern French Painters.* London, 1945.

ZOLA, Emile. *L'Oeuvre.* Paris, 1886.

Index

265